The
Finance of
International
Business

THE FINANCE OF INTERNATIONAL BUSINESS

THE
FINANCE
OF
INTERNATIONAL
BUSINESS

Brian Kettell

Graham & Trotman
Publishers

Published in 1979 by
Graham & Trotman Limited
Bond Street House
14 Clifford Street
London W1X 1RD
United Kingdom

© Brian Kettell, 1979

ISBN: 0 86010 151 7

Printed in England by McCorquodale (Newton) Ltd.,
Newton-le-Willows, Lancashire.

To my wife Alison

CONTENTS

LIST OF TABLES

LIST OF FIGURES

AUTHOR'S NOTE

RELAXATION OF UNITED KINGDOM EXCHANGE CONTROLS

In the United Kingdom Budget Statement of 12 June 1979 the following exchange control relaxations were announced.

Outward direct investment

(i) For new investments, the use of foreign currency purchased at the current market rate in the official exchange market ('official exchange') will be permitted, on application to the Bank of England, up to a total of £5 million per investment project per year. Under the old rules, described in chapter 4, most direct investment abroad had to be financed by foreign currency borrowing or out of profits retained abroad, official exchange being available only in 'super-criterion' cases.

(ii) UK companies will no longer be expected to repatriate annually at least two-thirds of the net taxed earnings of their subsidiaries overseas.

(iii) Existing foreign currency borrowing will be repayable with official exchange in five equal annual instalments; and new authorised borrowing will similarly be repayable over five years to the extent that repayment cannot be met out of the annual entitlement to official exchange in (i) above. In addition it was announced that sterling could again be used by UK resident merchants to finance third country trade.

Outward portfolio investment

(i) Investors will no longer be required to maintain cover in the form of foreign currency securities or investment currency equal to 115 per cent of the value of amounts borrowed to finance portfolio investment.

(ii) Official exchange will be allowed for interest payments on foreign currency borrowing for portfolio investment.

With effect from 19 July 1979, the following additional exchange relaxations were announced:

(i) Currency will be available without limit at the official exchange rate for all outward direct investment, and foreign currency borrowing to finance such investment can be repaid at the official rate;

(ii) UK residents can invest at the official exchange rate in most securities denominated and payable solely in the currencies of other EEC countries, with the exception of unit and investment trusts;

(iii) Foreign currency borrowing by UK residents to finance outward portfolio investment which has been outstanding for at least up to 19 July 1979 will be repayable at the official rate.

Foreword

by Andreas R. Prindl

The literature dealing with the growth of multinational enterprises is itself expanding at an equally rapid pace. Many new studies are appearing which deal with the multinational company's political influence, its inter-relations with host governments and the effects—positive or negative—on labour or on the local markets where it operates or to which it sells. A growing subsection of that literature takes as its focal point the financial management of these companies. Some analysts, for example, have tried to fit the financing/investment decisions of the multinational corporation (MNC) into more general theories of the firm or corporate finance. Others have focused on describing the different environments the MNC faces in various parts of the world. Such analyses have pointed out unique characteristics of multinational enterprises, particularly their fragmentation into disparate segments, isolated by distance, problems of communications, exchange controls and tax differences.

It has been difficult, however, for businessmen or students to find a compact, straightforward account of the financial management problems of the MNC which is not overly theoretical. Mr. Kettell, in this volume, has had filling this gap as his goal, by bringing together three main elements of the multinational finance function. These sectors, treated sequentially, are the market framework in which·the MNC operates, the management of foreign exchange risk, and the international financing decision.

In the chapters on international monetary flows and markets, the author points out the theory of balance of payments accounting and the various mechanisms for dealing with surpluses or deficits in a country's external accounts. This is a clear starting point for understanding the MNC's financial decisions, because any prediction of the movement of currency values or interest rate levels will in part be predicted on analysis of balance of payments positions, how a country's payment flows go awry, and what government authorities may do to bring imbalances back to equilibrium.

Multinationals themselves, of course, can add to disequilibrating forces by their own actions; they are in any case directly affected—more than other economic groups—by balance of payments corrective measures.

From that introduction, the foreign exchange markets—the counter over which international monetary flows pass—are described. The functions of foreign exchange transactions are diverse; the inter-relationships and special functions of the spot and forward exchange markets and deposit markets are brought out with examples. Paralleling a practical description of market mechanics is a chapter on the determination of exchange rate parities.

This area is still controversial, as the author's portrayal of several major theoretical approaches to understanding exchange rate changes points out. There is general agreement that, over the long run, differentials in productivity and inflation rates will directly influence a country's international competitiveness and the value of its currency measured against others. Yet short-term exchange rate movements, often quite dramatic in scope, can be based on expectations, speculative positions or even a sort of panic, none of which may be justified by longer-term economic fundamentals. Indeed, occasionally one feels that a good guide to understanding runs on the exchange markets would to be to study the behaviour and delusions of crowds.

Conversely, a government may delay a corrective movement of its exchange rate, although warranted by economic forces, most commonly these days through 'dirty floating'. Kettell points out how the international monetary system has evolved since World War II to deal with disequilibrium and the conflicting motives of national governments.

The core of the book, mirroring the primary distinguishing characteristic of the MNC, is the function of foreign exchange exposure management in the firm. He follows a stage by stage approach of pointing out firstly the problems of *defining* foreign exchange exposures, then of *measuring* and *identifying* exposed positions. The consolidation rules ordained by each country's accounting profession are the starting point for defining one standard type of exposure: that arising from consolidating the financial statements of a parent multinational and those of its several subsidiaries, when these are carried in a number of currencies. Contrasted with such accounting treatment are two other types of exchange exposure: transaction risk and economic risk. The latter can be particularly critical in a firm's decision making and planning, yet correspondingly difficult to project or quantify.

Kettell's analysis offers managerial guidelines towards controlling and managing these exposures, once defined and identified. Chapter 8 concentrates on *internal* measures open to the MNC to change or protect its positions worldwide, Chapter 9 on the *external* techniques available. It is commonly supposed that buying or selling currencies forward for a future maturity date is the principal hedging method, whereas this may be the last technique utilized by a sophisticated multinational, and then only for residual net positions. Nearly a dozen internal, and an equal number of external hedging applications are described; all of these need to be considered in light of their appropriateness and cost-effectiveness.

The text concludes with two chapters on Euro-currency and international capital markets, combining a run-down of market participants, volumes and constraints with guidelines as to how MNCs tap these markets for funding or investment of their surplus liquidity. Kettell shows how these flexible, wide-spread financial markets complement the needs and the structure of the MNC itself.

The author provides a further service to the reader by summarizing throughout the book a number of theories about the MNC financial function. Recent, sometimes seminal, writings of academics and businessmen are reviewed and their contribution to understanding the decision making process weighed.

Thus, the following text gives a succinct guide to parts of a complex financial function, a guide which can be used by businessmen who have dealt primarily with domestic financial problems or by economics or business students. These days, we are all involved with MNCs—we may manage or be employed by them, lend to or borrow from them, or, if in government, attempt to understand (and often circumscribe) their activities. With certainty, our major firms will be in competition with multinational companies of one kind or another, either for customers, or in a world where resources are finite and being used up at a worrisome pace, for raw materials. The growth of multinationals has also complemented and fostered the mutual interdependence of nations, vastly accelerating a trend which began in the 17th century with exploration voyages and colonizing expeditions. To understand this interdependence is imperative for any thinking person; to study one of its constituent parts—the finance function of the MNC—is one part of the process.

Tokyo
June, 1979

Acknowledgements

The author would like to thank the generous assistance provided on selected chapters by Peter Muller, Assistant Vice President, Morgan Guaranty Trust, New York; John Atkin, Economist at Citibank; B C White, Assistant Manager, Lloyds Bank and Assistant Examiner, Finance and Foreign Trade and Foreign Exchange, Institute of Bankers; Stephen Bell, Senior Economic Assistant, HM Treasury. Responsibility for any error remains with the author.

The publishers are indebted to the following organisations for permission to reproduce previously published material: Amex Bank Limited, The Banker, J F Chown & Company Limited, Continental Illinois Ltd, The Economic Intelligence Dept of the Bank of England, the Economist Intelligence Unit Ltd, Euromoney, The Export Credit Guarantee Dept, The Federal Reserve Board of New York, The Financial Management Association and A C Shapiro and D P Rutenberg, Harper and Row Ltd, Harvard University Press, Her Majesty's Stationery Office, The International Chamber of Commerce, The Institute of Bankers, Macmillan, Morgan Guaranty Trust Company, South Western Publishing Company, Phillips & Drew, John Wiley and Sons Ltd.

1

Introduction

THE IMPORTANCE OF MULTINATIONAL COMPANIES

One of the most remarkable economic phenomena of the post-war period has been the rise of the multinational enterprise. Forecasts indicate that the size and importance of multinational companies, defined as business enterprises which own and control activities in different countries, will increase in the second half of the twentieth century.

The average number of new subsidiaries formed per annum by geographical area for a sample of 187 U.S.-based parent multinational enterprises between 1914 and 1970 can be seen from Figure 1. The 1950s were characterised by a significant increase in the growth of overseas subsidiaries of U.S. multinational enterprises.

In the 1960s there was a significant growth in the average number of new subsidiaries formed per annum by geographical area by certain continental European-based multinational enterprises (Figure 1.2).

The very high levels of U.S. investment in Europe in the early 1960s described by Servan-Schreiber in *'The American Challenge'* have fallen away in the face of a European riposte[1]. However, despite the recent growth of European investment, the U.S.A. remains the principal foreign investor in most countries because of the cumulative effect of its high level of investment throughout the post war period.

The absolute size of multinational business is such that the annual sales of many multinationals is greater than the Gross National Product of many small to medium-sized economies. As can be seen from Figure 1.3, of the 100 largest economic entities in the world in 1973, 43 places were accounted for by multinational companies.

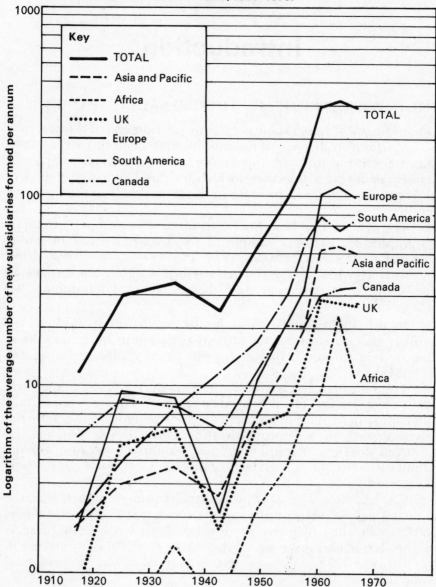

Figure 1.1

AVERAGE NUMBER OF NEW SUBSIDIARIES FORMED PER ANNUM BY GEOGRAPHICAL AREA, FOR A SAMPLE OF 187 US-BASED MULTINATIONAL ENTERPRISES, 1914–1970.

Source : JW Vaupel and JP Curhan. *'The Worlds' Multinational Enterprises'* Geneva, 1974.

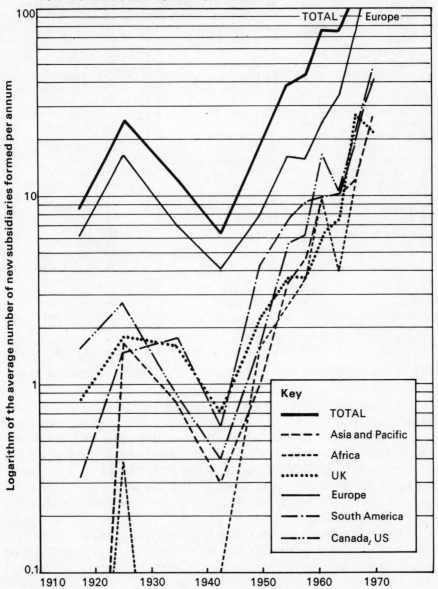

Figure 1.2
AVERAGE NUMBER OF NEW SUBSIDIARIES FORMED PER ANNUM BY GEOGRAPHICAL AREA, FOR A SAMPLE OF CONTINENTAL EUROPEAN-BASED MULTINATIONAL ENTERPRISES AMONG THE 200 LARGEST NON-US INDUSTRIAL FIRMS, 1914–1970

Logarithm of the average number of new subsidiaries formed per annum

TOTAL — Europe

Key

▬▬▬	TOTAL
▬ ▬ ▬	Asia and Pacific
- - - -	Africa
••••••	UK
———	Europe
—·—·—	South America
—··—··—	Canada, US

Source: JW Vaupel and JP Curhan. *'The Worlds' Multinational Enterprises'* Geneva, 1974.

Figure 1.3

Nations and Corporations
(Billions of dollars—1973)

#	Name	Value	#	Name	Value	#	Name	Value
1	United States	1,184.1	35	Greece	16.3	68	Hitachi	6.0
2	USSR	447.5	36	Yugoslavia	13.8	69	Taiwan	5.9
3	Japan	389.6	37	Iran	11.9	70	Westinghouse	5.7
4	Germany	387.6	38	Chrysler	11.8	71	Hoechst	5.6
5	France	256.5	39	General Electric	11.6	72	Daimler-Benz	5.6
6	Britain	172.2	40	Texaco	11.4	73	Toyota	5.5
7	Italy	134.3	41	Mobil	11.4	74	Siemens	5.5
8	China	127.9	42	Unilever	11.0	75	Standard Oil (Ind)	5.4
9	Canada	119.1	43	IBM	11.0	76	BASF	5.4
10	Brazil	76.3	44	Korea	10.8	77	ICI	5.3
11	Netherlands	64.2	45	Indonesia	10.4	78	Dupont	5.3
12	India	59.2	46	Philippines	10.3	79	Mitsubishi	5.2
13	Australia	57.0	47	ITT	10.2	80	Nestle	5.2
14	Poland	47.6	48	Gulf Oil	8.4	81	General Tele-phone	5.1
15	Switzerland	44.6	49	New Zealand	8.1	82	North Korea	5.0
16	Spain	42.2	50	Philips Elec	8.1	83	Shell Oil	4.9
17	East Germany	40.6	51	Thailand	8.0	84	Nissan	4.9
18	Mexico	37.5	52	Standard Oil (California)	7.8	85	Puerto Rico	4.8
19	General Motors	35.8	53	British Pet.	7.7	86	Cuba	4.7
20	Czechoslovakia	33.5	54	Peru	7.6	87	Algeria	4.7
21	Sweden	33.1	55	Nippon Steel	7.6	88	Goodyear	4.7
22	Austria	29.9	56	Chile	7.5	89	Renault	4.7
23	Argentina	29.0	57	Egypt	7.5	90	Bayer	4.7
24	Exxon	28.0	58	Nigeria	7.0	91	Malaysia	4.5
25	Denmark	27.6	59	Western Electric	7.0	92	Montedison	4.5
26	South Africa	26.9	60	U.S. Steel	7.0	93	Hong Kong	4.4
27	Ford	23.0	61	Colombia	6.9	94	Matsushita	4.4
28	Belgium	22.2	62	Bulgaria	6.6	95	British Steel	4.3
29	Turkey	21.0	63	Ireland	6.6	96	ENI	4.3
30	Norway	19.6	64	Portugal	6.5	97	Bangladesh	4.2
31	Romania	19.5	65	Volkswagen	6.4	98	RCA	4.2
32	Royal Dutch Shell	18.7	66	Pakistan	6.3	99	Thyssen-Hutte	4.2
33	Venezuela	16.6	67	Israel	6.1	100	Continental Oil	4.2
34	Hungary	16.6						

Source: D.B. Zenoff, The Future of the Multinational Company, *Euromoney,* September 1975.

According to stockbrokers Phillips and Drew, U.K. companies, based on their published results for the nearest accounting year to calendar year 1978, derived more than half their total pretax profits from overseas operations either through the activities of foreign-based subsidiaries and associates or via U.K. exports (Figure 1.4). As can be seen from Figure 1.4 the proportions were around 52 per cent from industrial operations located overseas and 12 per cent from exports.

Many reasons have been put forward to explain the growth of multinational enterprises. Firstly, a company may wish to improve its access to raw materials e.g. oil producers. Secondly, a company may be looking for lower costs of production e.g. the use of Taiwan as an export platform. Thirdly, multinationals may be anxious to protect their access to supplies of knowledge. The production of knowledge, through research and development, and its implementation in new processes or products, is a lengthy project which

Figure 1.4

Overseas contribution to profits of UK companies (1978)

Oils	87	6	93
Household Goods	46	36	82
Wines and Spirits	5	77	82
Tobacco	70	8	78
Office Equipment	64	12	76
Pharmaceuticals	64	12	76
Engineering Contractors	40	34	74
Food Manufacturing	59	4	63
Motors and Distributors	42	15	57
Contracting and Construction	54	0	54
Textiles	41	12	53
Packaging and Paper	45	6	51
Metals and Metal Forming	36	13	49
Electricals	25	22	47
Mechanical Engineering	19	28	47
Chemicals	30	16	46
Building Materials	40	4	44
Shipping	18	21	39
Light Electronics, Radio, TV	15	9	24
Entertainment and Catering	11	8	19
Breweries	11	5	16
Stores	6	5	11
Food Retailing	5	0	5
Newspapers and Publishing	0	0	0
	—	—	—
Total Industrial including oil	40	12	52
Total Financial	43	3	46

Source: *Phillips and Drew*

requires detailed long-term appraisal. Overseas investment protects this knowledge and enables a company to profit from it. Finally, a company may wish to increase the size of its markets. This, in turn, may be for several reasons. The home market may be saturated due either to the size of the market or due to excessive competition from overseas producers. The distributor of the company's products or its clients may insist on an overseas presence. New opportunities may be lost if the company does not have the flexibility that overseas production gives. Whatever the reason the absolute size and importance of the multinational enterprise is beyond doubt.

THE UNIQUE CHARACTERISTICS OF INTERNATIONAL BUSINESS

What are the characteristics which distinguish the constraints influencing international from national business? These are listed below.

(i) Currency differences and fluctuations.

The national company by and large is only concerned with currency fluctuations if it exports or imports. The multi-national company has to sell, buy, borrow and invest in a wide range of currencies. In a world of 129 national currencies, each independently managed, it is not surprising that currency differences and fluctuations become important.

(ii) Exchange controls.

Many of the operations of a multinational, unlike those of a national company, involve 'cross frontier' transactions. Exchange controls in a number of countries modify, restrict or ban many transactions which the companies, in the interests of profit maximisation, would prefer to undertake.

(iii) Capital and money markets.

A multinational, with its vast capital requirements, can rarely depend on a single capital and money market as a national company can, but rather has to develop the ability to use a number of markets. It has to learn to use the international capital and money markets most suitable to its needs.

(iv) Differing economic conditions.

The continuing debate on inflation accounting illustrates the problems of inflation for national companies. For a multi-national company facing differing degrees of inflation and deflation the problems are even more intractable. Moreover, economic policy changes, involving different tax systems, complicate the problem even more.

(v) Geography

The basic problem of having to operate in a number of different countries simultaneously can create problems. As well as language barriers there is the problem of operating in different time zones.

(vi) Government regulations.

These can take various forms, e.g. price controls, incomes policies, investment regulations, differing social security systems, pollution control measures etc. The sheer variety of these involves multinationals in much time-consuming activity.

(vii) Political risk.

Sovereign governments may interfere with the business operations of multinational firms. At the worst expropriation can occur, although normally it is problems of discriminatory taxation or regulations with which multinationals most concern themselves.

It is the existence of all these risks together which distinguish national from international companies.

SCOPE OF THE BOOK

This book is designed to examine the problems of financing international business. Thus the book is primarily concerned with the first four categories mentioned above although the other three will still have an indirect influence. Broadly speaking, Chapters 2, 3, 4 and 5 outline the environment in which international financial decisions are taken. The remaining chapters examine the choices open to the treasurer or financial officers in deciding on the optimal financing decisions.

Chapter 2 examines the role of the balance of payments with examples of the U.S. and the U.K. balance of payments accounts. Examination is then given of the consequences for multinational companies of differing types of adjustment and financing policies.

Chapter 3 illustrates the major participants in, and role of, the foreign exchange markets. The different markets are identified and examples of how to interpret the financial press in its reporting of the foreign exchange market are given.

Chapter 4 examines the major factors which affect exchange rates. These are explained in a way which would permit businessmen to anticipate, given certain changes in government economic policy, the effect these changes would have on exchange rates. The next section discusses the problems associated with forecasting exchange rates. Some simplistic forecasting systems are then examined.

Chapter 5 summarises the nature of the international monetary system from 1945 to the present. Special emphasis is given to the post 1971 situation. The last section examines the current nature of the international monetary system, including the new European Monetary System.

Chapter 6 outlines the differing ways in which international trade can be financed. The circumstances under which cash on delivery, open account, letters of credit and documentary credits are the most appropriate payment systems are discussed.

Chapter 7 discusses the problem of defining and identifying foreign exchange exposure. Transaction, translation and economic exposure are defined. The differing approaches of the accountant and the economist are summarised. Special emphasis is given to the impact of Financial Accounting Standards Board 8 (FASB8) upon U.S. based multinationals and Exposure Draft (ED21) upon U.K.-based multinationals.

Chapters 8 and 9 are devoted to discussing the alternatives open to companies in controlling foreign exchange exposure in the light of the problems illustrated in Chapter 7. Chapter 8 concentrates on internal, while Chapter 9 concentrates on external, hedging techniques.

Given the need for substantial funds to finance their overseas activities, Chapters 10 and 11 outline the external sources open to multinationals. Chapter 10 concentrates on the Euro-currency markets while Chapter 11 studies the international bond markets. Special emphasis is given to the benefits that multinational companies can derive from appropriate usage of these markets.

References
1. J.J. Servan-Schreiber, *The American Challenge,* (Athenæum House Inc, New York, 1968)

2

International Financial Flows

One of the most important concepts to grasp in international financial management is that of the balance of payments of a country. Information about the balance of payments assists a country in determining its relative strength in the world economy. Data on the balance of payments will give multinational companies an important indicator as to the direction of pressure on a country's exchange rate. A continual deficit is a useful indicator of a likely fall in a country's exchange rate. In addition, the data can be used to forecast changes in macro-economic policy, which may seriously affect future corporate sales, in the economy. A continued deficit is a valuable indicator of likely deflationary policies. Also, balance of payments data may help a multinational to foresee changes in exchange controls which could seriously hinder a company's ability to freely move funds in or out of a country. At a time when multinationals are coming under closer control balance of payments data may also help to show the exact contribution that the company is making to the economy.

In this chapter the structure of the balance of payments is examined with stress being placed on the nature of the balance of payments 'problem'. Special reference is given in the appendices to the U.S. and U.K. balance of payments.

Any discussion of the balance of payments must begin by examining the gains which can occur due to international trade. The fact that different countries have different resources, climates, skills, and so on is a natural reason for trade to take place. When one country can grow bananas but not wheat, it is sensible to exchange. When two countries can make the same product but one is sufficiently more efficient to be able to sell the product in the other country at a cheaper price then trade is likely to take place, particularly when both countries can take advantage of relative efficiences. It is these differences in the structure of costs which lie at the root of the reasons for trade. Specialisation makes for more efficient world use of resources and thus provides general, as well as particular, gains from trade.

9

If there is free trade in goods, then the more efficient industries in the world can expand their output. As the inefficient industries contract they release factors of production which may then be utilised by the efficient industries. Thus prices are kept in line with the costs of the efficient industries and consumers benefit from overall low prices. These gains to producers and consumers are at the basis of the arguments in favour of free trade.

At this stage it is helpful to briefly introduce the foreign exchange market. This is discussed in detail in Chapters 3 and 4. The foreign exchange market is the organisational framework within which individuals, firms, banks and brokers buy and sell foreign currencies. The foreign exchange market for any one currency, e.g. the pound sterling, consists of all the locations such as London, New York, Zurich, and Paris, where the pound sterling is bought and sold for other currencies. One of the main functions of the foreign exchange market is in providing a mechanism for transferring the money of one currency into the money of another currency. Since a U.S. exporter to the U.K. requires payment in his own currency, the dollar, the U.K. importer, whose currency is the pound sterling, may have to convert sterling into dollars. The existence of the foreign exchange market enables him to do this. As long as different currencies exist, in order to facilitate trade a foreign exchange market will be necessary.

A foreign exchange rate is the price of one currency in terms of another currency. When it is said that the exchange rate is £1=$2 the price of one currency is being given in terms of another currency.

The balance of payments summarises the flow of economic transactions between the residents of a given country and the residents of another country during a certain period of time. Transactions that only affect the local residents and which only involve the national currency, in contrast to foreign exchange, are not recorded in the balance of payments. The balance of payments may be divided into three major types of accounts:

(1) The current account
(2) The capital account
(3) The official reserves

The current account records the trade in goods and services. A country increases its exports when it sells more goods abroad; a country increases its imports when it buys more goods from abroad. In order to buy, for example, U.K. goods in the U.S.A. payment will be made either in sterling or in dollars. Since a U.K. company incurs costs denominated in pounds sterling it will need to be able to convert its revenues into sterling. If the U.S. importer pays in sterling he must first sell dollars to obtain the sterling. If the U.S. importer pays in dollars the U.K. exporter will exchange these for sterling. Transactions which earn foreign exchange are recorded in the balance of payments' statistics as a 'credit' or are marked by a plus (+) sign. In Figure 2.1 credits of 1000 are recorded. The converse of exporting is importing. In order that a U.K. importer can pay for U.S. goods, again, he can either pay in sterling or pay in dollars. If he pays in sterling, the U.S. exporter will convert these into dollars. If the U.K. importer pays in dollars he will normally have obtained these by selling sterling. Transactions which expend foreign exchange are recorded as debits and marked with a minus (−) sign. In Figure 2.1 debits of 1200 are recorded. The balance between exports and imports is called the balance of trade. Figure 2.1 shows a net debit of 200.

The other main item of the current account is the balance in invisibles. Some items give rise to payments in foreign currency and yet are not the product of a physical relocation of goods. These items, normally called service products, are included in the invisibles section of the balance of payment. Three main sources of invisible flows are:

(1) Interest, profits and dividends
(2) Expenditures on tourism
(3) Expenditures for shipping, banking, civil aviation etc.

Interest and dividends received measure the services that the country's capital has rendered abroad. Interests and dividend paid measure the payments for foreign borrowing or investment made in the past. Expenditures on tourism are measures of the effect of a country's residents holidaying abroad and vice versa. Financial and shipping charges to foreigners measure the fees that the financial community and shipowners have charged to foreigners because of the special services they rendered. In addition to the items already mentioned the invisible account also includes donations to or from charitable organisations, gifts and legacies, workers' remittances to and from abroad, government grants to overseas countries and certain subscriptions to international organisations.

Again, an export of invisibles is recorded as a credit (+) and imports of invisibles are recorded as a debit (−). The example below is one of invisible exports of 500 and invisible imports of 100. The sum of the balance of trade and the balance on invisibles is the balance on current account. The current account balance shows whether a country has added to or consumed its net external assets in any period. In Figure 2.1 credits of 200 have occurred.

The capital account records international transactions for everything other than what is included in the current account. The capital account is divided into: (i) Direct investment (ii) Portfolio investment (iii) Short-term investment. Direct investment and portfolio investment involve financial assets with a maturity of more than one year. Short-term investment consists of financial assets with a maturity of less than one year. How does overseas investment affect the balance of payments? Consider a U.K. citizen who wishes to invest abroad by lending money to a U.S. industry. It can be said that he is exporting capital from the U.K. to the U.S.A. Suppose he chooses to do this by buying bonds being sold in New York by an expanding U.S. firm. In order to do this he needs to obtain dollars. He is a demander of foreign exchange and a supplier of sterling. This transaction is therefore a debit item in the U.K. balance of payments account.

It sometimes seems confusing that the export of capital is a debit item and the export of goods is a credit item. The situation is, however, really very simple. The export of goods earns foreign exchange, and the export of capital uses foreign exchange, and therefore they have opposite effects on international payments. Another way of looking at it is that the capital transaction involves the purchase of a foreign bond. This has the same effect on the balance of payments as the purchase, and hence the import, of a foreign good. Both transactions use foreign exchange and are thus debit items in the balance of payments.

The sum of the balance on current account and the balance on capital account is what is meant by the balance of payments. In Figure 2.1 there is a balance of payments deficit of 50.

Before examining the balance of payments accounts any further it is important to grasp an essential point. This is that, overall, the balance of payments always balances. What is meant by this? Although it is quite possible for holders of sterling to want to purchase more dollars in exchange for pounds, it is not possible for sterling holders actually to buy more dollars than dollar holders sell. Every dollar that is bought must be sold by someone, and every dollar that is sold must be bought by someone. Since the dollars actually bought must be equal to the dollars actually sold, the payments made between countries must be in balance.

If the simple example is a reflection of the U.K. balance of payments with respect to the U.S.A. one may ask how is a deficit of 50 possible? In other words, the difference between the dollars earned and the dollars spent must have come from somewhere. Somehow actual transactions on the market for foreign exchange have taken place with there being more demand for dollars than there was supply of dollars. The answer to this puzzle is that the extra dollars may have come from two sources: firstly, by the U.K. borrowing dollars and/or secondly, by the dollars coming from the U.K. foreign exchange reserves. In the case of a balance of payments surplus borrowings will be repaid and/or reserves will be built up. The section of the balance of payments which records how a deficit is financed or a surplus allocated is the official financing section. Official financing is sometimes known as the level of accommodating finance. As can be seen from Figure 2.1., the balance of payments must be exactly equal to the amount of official

Figure 2.1.

A simple example of balance of payments accounting

	Credit	Debit	Net Credit (+) or debit (−)
A. Current account			
Exports of goods	1000		
Imports of goods		1200	
BALANCE OF TRADE			−200
Exports of invisibles (e.g. expenditure by foreign tourists in home country, expenditure by foreigners on services such as shipping, banking, etc., property income from abroad)	500		
Imports of invisibles		100	
			+200
B. Capital account			
Direct investment overseas net of direct investment from overseas (e.g.purchase of factories)		−200	
Portfolio investment overseas net of portfolio investment from overseas (e.g. purchase of stocks and shares)		−150	
Short-term lending to foreigners (firms, banks or individuals) net of short-term borrowing (e.g. purchase of Treasury Bills or Commercial Bills)	+100		
BALANCE ON CAPITAL ACCOUNT			−250
BALANCE OF PAYMENTS			−50
C. Official financing			
Official borrowing (drawn +) repaid (−)	+30		
Official reserves (drawings on +) (additions to −)	+20		
TOTAL OFFICIAL FINANCING	+50		

financing. Strictly speaking, all payments inbalances are met by drawings from, or additions to, the reserves. Borrowing merely increases the size of the reserves. The balance of payments deficit (50) is financed by official borrowing (30) and drawing on reserves (20). The simple example given is helpful in understanding the structure of the balance of payments accounts of any one country. The structure of the U.K. and U.S.A. balance of payments can be found in Appendices I and II (pp 26–35). The IMF compiles balance of payments statistics for each of its member countries. These figures are presented in a standard format in its Balance of Payments Yearbook.

At this stage it is useful to mention the balancing item which is sometimes called errors and omissions. Given the many different sources from which balance of payments accounts are compiled and the possibility of timing errors between the recording of transactions and the corresponding payments, it is unrealistic to expect an exact balance for the accounts to be obtained. The balancing item is therefore introduced so that the sum of the identified transactions plus the balancing item add to zero in true accounting fashion. It therefore represents the net total of all the errors and omissions in the accounts.

THE IMPORTANCE OF THE BALANCE OF PAYMENTS

What different types of balance of payments' policies are open to the government? What is the likely corporate impact of these policies? In discussing the balance of payments two terms need to be defined. Autonomous movements are changes induced by economic relationships, e.g. relative prices and incomes. Compensating or accommodating movements are changes that occur mainly because of a need to finance the autonomous movements. Economists normally refer to the autonomous movements as those that determine whether the balance of payments is in surplus or in deficit and accommodating movements as those illustrating how the deficit or surplus is financed.

The balance of payments is in surplus if autonomous receipts exceed autonomous payments. Similarly, the balance of payments is in deficit if autonomous payments exceed autonomous receipts. A surplus in the autonomous accounts is accompanied by an increase in foreign reserves in the compensating accounts. A deficit in the autonomous accounts is associated with a decrease in foreign reserves or an increase in liabilities to foreigners.

It has already been seen that the balance of payments must necessarily balance because of the way it is constructed. A payment deficit on the total of autonomous transactions means of necessity that there exists a sum of accommodating transactions of the same magnitude but of opposite sign. In what sense then can the balance of payments be a 'problem'? The answer to this is bound up with the notion of equilibrium in the balance of payments, or its related concept, the equilibrium exchange rate. The 'problem' of the balance of payments, which is to be discussed in more detail later (pp 19–20), is that accommodating transactions do not fall like manna from heaven. In the longer run they are exhaustible and this means that at some stage drastic measures, potentially damaging to the economy, may need to be taken. The policy aim of equilibrium in the balance of payments is equivalent to a policy aim of avoiding a situation in which such drastic action needs to be taken.

The balance of payments problem of a country will be affected by the sort of exchange rate arrangements that it chooses to operate. Broadly speaking, governments can choose between a fixed rate system and a flexible rate system. Several variants of the flexible rate system exist, such as the adjustable peg system, the wider bands system, the crawling peg system and finally, wholly free exchange rates.

By a fixed rate system is meant an exchange rate which is known to be fixed for the foreseeable future. If there is no band within which the exchange rate can fluctuate, and if the rate is known forever, there is in effect a currency area as between regions of a country. There can be no greater uncertainty in holding one currency than another just as there is no greater currency risk with holdings of dollars in California, instead of in New York.

Under the adjustable peg system which existed from 1946 until 1971 the monetary authorities accepted an obligation to maintain the foreign exchange value of the home currency within very narrow limits of a par value and were committed to intervene in the foreign exchange market whenever these limits threatened to be exceeded. Within the narrow range about the par value, the foreign exchange rate is usually free to vary under the influence of market forces. To take an example, between 1949 and 1967 the sterling dollar exchange rate was fixed at $2.80 = £1. A one per cent variation around this was permitted giving intervention points of $2.82 = £1 and $2.78 = £1. If the sterling exchange rate rose to $2.82 = £1 the U.K. monetary authorities were obliged to sell sterling and buy dollars. This would bring the sterling rate down. If the sterling exchange rate fell to $2.78 = £1 then the U.K. monetary authorities were obliged to buy sterling and sell dollars. This would bring the sterling rate up. In order to continue buying sterling and selling dollars, the authorities must obtain the dollars from somewhere. These dollars can be obtained either by borrowing or by using up the country's foreign exchange reserves.

Another characteristic of the adjustable peg system was that the par value from which the intervention limits were determined was, in the presence of a 'fundamental disequilibrium', changeable.

As is explained in Chapter 5, the Bretton Woods system did not formally define a 'fundamental disequilibrium'. Fundamental disequilibrium can be manifested in a number of ways other than a conventional balance of payments deficit or surplus. An underlying balance of payments disequilibrium can be suppressed by a low level of domestic demand, by import restrictions, by controls over capital flows, or cut-backs in aid, or by an aggressive monetary policy aimed at attracting short-term flows of money from abroad. Where any of the above policies have to be applied in a continuing and substantial manner, a disequilibrium may be said to exist even though there is no severe pressure in the foreign exchange market.

Advocates of the adjustable peg system stress that in order to gain the benefits of international trade and international investment, businessmen need to have the certainty that exchange rate changes will not severely disrupt the profitability of their operations. However, it is important to realise that a one per cent change over one month implies a yearly change of twelve per cent so that exchange rate uncertainty remains important under Bretton-Woods type regimes. Critics of the system stress that it may lead to continually operating the economy at too low a level of economic activity. This occurs since, if the exchange rate is weak and continually having to be defended, the authorities may resort to deflationary policies, which remove the inflationary pressures from the economy, thus taking pressure off the exchange rate at the price of rising unemployment. The deflationary bias of a fixed rate system stems from the asymmetry of response i.e. only weak currency countries are forced to take action. Another serious feature of the adjustable peg system is the incentive it offers to speculators. Once a disequilibrium becomes apparent, speculators are likely to sell the currency of the country in deficit, hoping to profit from a devaluation. The risk involved will be minimal, since there is almost no likelihood that the deficit currency will be revalued. Thus the extent of the loss to which speculators are

Figure 2.2
A FIXED BUT ADJUSTABLE EXCHANGE RATE

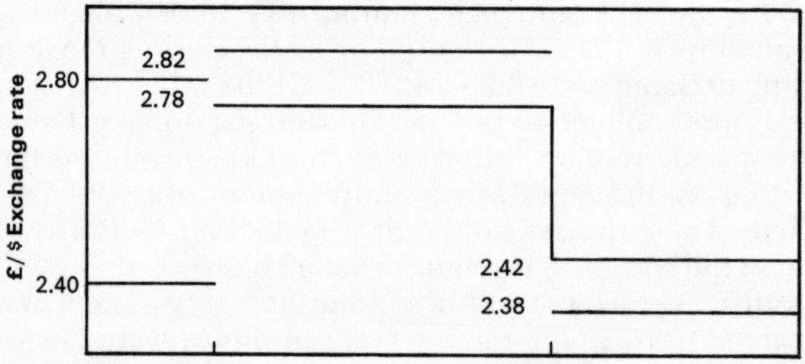

16

exposed is the marginal one of the possible appreciation of the deficit currency within the intervention points. Speculators are in effect being offered one-way options.

Figure 2.2 opposite illustrates the system when, in 1967 the U.K. was defined as having a 'fundamental disequilibrium' and was permitted to change its exchange rate.

The policy of wider bands is one of widening the permissible margin of fluctuation around parity from the one per cent to as much as, say, five per cent. By increasing the scope for movements in a currency's value without a change in parity one could hope that speculation would be deterred. With wider bands, speculative pressure would lead to more downward movement in the rate, and the increased scope that this offered for subsequent upward movement if the parity was successfully defended would, therefore, give rise to counter-speculation of a stabilising character. In addition, a band as wide as, say five per cent, around parity would provide much more scope for exchange rate movements to influence the current account than had been the case when fluctuations were limited to one per cent around par. The principal disadvantage associated with widening the band of fluctuation permitted for currencies lies in the additional uncertainties which such a regime involves for non-speculative transactions. If rate movements are sufficiently great to have an impact on the current account or the long-term capital account, then the uncertainties involved for private traders and investors may be such as to reduce the incentive to engage in international transactions.

Figure 2.3 below illustrates the working of the wider band system with a parity of $2.40 = £1 and intervention points of $2.28 and $2.52.

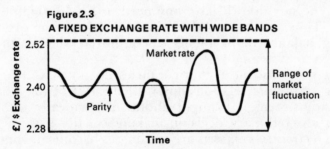

Figure 2.3
A FIXED EXCHANGE RATE WITH WIDE BANDS

The policy of the crawling peg has many variants. In one variant, exchange rates would move weekly or daily according to their moving averages in some past period such as the previous year. This has the advantage of automaticity but the grave disadvantage of complexity. The trigger for a change in par value could be either the position of the market exchange rate over some period within its permitted band or reserve changes or some indicator of the external strength of the currency. Speculation would be controlled by maintaining interest rates in the depreciating countries at a sufficient differential to offset the depreciation.

The essential characteristic of crawling pegs is that exchange rate changes are announced in advance. There is, therefore, the same certainty as under fixed rate systems combined with the ability to adjust the exchange rate. The major problem with crawling peg systems lies in the difficulty of choosing the correct exchange rate path.

Figure 2.4 shows this policy would work well with a maximum annual change in parities of 2-3 per cent monthly. These parity changes could be half-yearly, monthly, weekly or even daily. Intervention margins themselves could be wide or narrow.

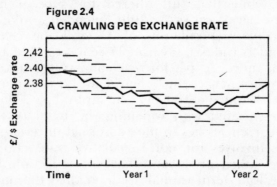

Figure 2.4
A CRAWLING PEG EXCHANGE RATE

The final type of flexible exchange rate policy is one of a wholly free float with no government intervention whatsoever. The principal advantage of this system in which exchange rates are left freely to be determined by the interplay of supply and demand in the foreign exchange market is that the government does not need to intervene nor does it have any need to hold foreign exchange reserves. Thus any system of free floating avoids the problems of financing balance of payments disequilibria inherent in a fixed exchange rate system.

This does not mean that countries do not have to adjust to changing economic relationships with the rest of the world. The needed adjustment is brought about automatically without any need for discretionary decision-making on the part of governments. If a country's exports are tending to become uncompetitive, because, for example, its price level is rising more rapidly than that of its trading partners, then the resulting tendency for its balance of payments to move into deficit will be checked by a downward movement in the country's exchange rate. There will be no need to manipulate the level of domestic demand or place artificial restraints on trade and payments in order to protect the balance of payments.

The disadvantage of freely floating exchange rates lies in the possibility that market mechanisms may not achieve an appropriate exchange rate. The exchange rate which achieves equilibrium in the foreign exchange market at any moment in time may not be the one that is conducive to equilibrium in the medium term. If it is not, then the price mechanism will be giving wrong signals to businessmen seeking to make future contracts or invest now for returns in the future. This in turn may lead to a misallocation of resources. Figure 2.5 illustrates what could happen to a freely floating exchange rate.

Figure 2.5
A FREE FLOATING EXCHANGE RATE

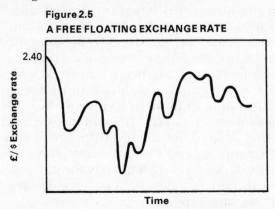

The question of why the balance of payments can be a 'problem' must now be examined. As already explained above, a system of fixed exchange rates necessarily implies that the authorities have access to a buffer stock of reserves of gold or foreign exchange or short-term borrowing facilities so that an excess demand for foreign exchange by its residents can be met. If the excess demand for foreign exchange is not quickly reversed, or reserves are inadequate to act as a buffer, or borrowing is not possible, by definition a disequilibrium situation exists. This disequilibrium becomes a problem, however, only when the authorities are unwilling or unable to satisfy it.

A country can run a persistent deficit on current account only if it has unlimited reserves of gold or foreign exchange to draw upon or if it can borrow persistently from the rest of the world to finance the deficit. No country has unlimited reserves and persistent short-term borrowing would be unwise, even if it were possible, since there is always a danger of cessation or reversal of the short-term capital inflow. In either case the immediate result must be that foreign exchange reserves are liquidated at a speed which may shatter confidence in the country's ability to maintain the external value of its currency and a speculative foreign exchange crisis results. A persistent deficit matched by a long-term capital inflow is both possible and unobjectionable if the capital inflow is associated with policies to raise productive capacity and to stimulate the flow of exports or reduce dependence on imports. In the absence of such long-term loans or grants of aid, the balance of payments may be said to be in disequilibrium if the value of imports persistently threatens to exceed the value of exports. In these circumstances the threatened exhaustion of exchange reserves will induce the authorities to pursue policies to rectify the balance of payments.

What difference, one may ask, does it make if the external value of one's currency declines rapidly? Surely it is the internal value of one's currency that matters to the residents of a country? The answer to the question is based on the benefits of the gains from trading mentioned earlier. Individual countries tend to specialise in producing the goods they produce best and they import the rest. Since, when importing they exchange their own currency for another currency, if their own currency has gone down steeply in value it will require substantially more domestic currency to obtain the same amount of foreign currency as before. This will quickly lead to domestic inflation. If a country's currency depreciates so much that it becomes inconvertible, then this may mean that free trade disappears and that a country which imports much of its food, like the U.K., can no longer pay for it.

Given the existence of a persistent balance of payments deficit, what mechanisms are open to governments to remedy the situation? These can be broken down into three different types: automatic mechanisms, adjustments of the exchange rate and direct government intervention.

AUTOMATIC MECHANISMS

These can be of two types, namely, policies which operate through prices and policies which operate through incomes.

The price mechanism works as follows. In the case of a deficit in the balance of payments money flows from the deficit to the surplus country. This occurs quite simply since more money is being spent on imported goods than foreigners are spending on a country's exports. Unless the central bank acts to counteract these flows, the money supply in the deficit country will contract, putting upward pressure on interest rates. In the surplus country the money supply will increase and dampen interest rates. The new relative yields will encourage capital flows, hopefully of a long-term nature, towards the deficit country and away from the surplus country, helping to bring the payments back into balance. If, as mentioned earlier, the capital inflow is used 'productively', then there will be an emerging balance of payments surplus.

Price changes may also be followed by changes in quantities demanded and supplied. A deficit in the balance of payments caused by an excess of imports over exports implies an increase in demand for the products of the surplus country and a decrease in demand for the products of the deficit country. With flexible prices the surplus country will experience rising prices and the deficit country will experience falling prices. This eventually leads to a falling demand for products of the surplus country and an increasing demand for products of the deficit country.

Whether these price effects are sufficient to correct any original imbalance depends on the response of quantities demanded to prices, i.e. the price elasticity of demand for imports. The Marshall-Lerner conditions have been developed to determine the effect on the trade balance of an exchange rate change[1]. These conditions state that if the sum of the price elasticity of demand for exports and imports is greater than one then a devaluation will be successful. This is, however, only true when certain limiting assumptions are made, viz when the devaluation takes place there is a current account equilibrium and the supply elasticities are high.

The income adjustment works in the following way. For a given value of the exchange rate there will tend to be a positive correlation between the level of expenditure on imports and the level of employment or national income. The precise relationship may change through time as tastes and relative costs, etc. change but some positive correlation is highly probable. This means that if import values exceed export values at a given level of employment and income, a decline in employment and income will tend to restore the balance. Similarly, if export values exceed import values at a given level of employment and income, there will be a rise in incomes, a rise in imports and, again, the balance is restored.

Two major problems with relying on the automatic income mechanism are the existence of time lags and the impact on the local economy. Long time lags may make the automaticity ineffective if, as is likely, other economic policy changes are occurring at the same time. Second, the impact on the domestic economy of a prolonged economic recession with its consequent political repercussions may make this policy infeasible.

Given the problems with automatic mechanisms to correct imbalances, what other alternatives exist?

ADJUSTMENTS OF THE EXCHANGE RATE

Devaluation is defined as a downward alteration in the exchange rate. Revaluation is defined as an upward alteration in the exchange rate. Throughout this section it is intended to examine the consequences of devaluation. Revaluation would have the opposite effect.

The foreign selling price of a commodity is its internal price multiplied by the rate of exchange. Clearly, the lower the rate of

21

exchange, the lower may be the foreign selling price and the greater may be a country's exports. The domestic selling price of an imported good is the foreign selling price multiplied by the exchange rate. A devaluation means that it requires less of the foreign currency to buy the home currency. Similarly, it requires more of the home currency to buy the same amount of foreign currency. Since a devaluation increases the amount of domestic currency needed to obtain the same amount of foreign currency, then the effect is to raise the price of, and consequently reduce the demand for, imports. This will become clearer with a numerical example. It is convenient to illustrate the effect of devaluation by using the exchange rate with the dollar, but the same effects hold for other major currencies.

On 18 November 1967 the U.K. devalued the pound sterling from $2.80 = £1 to $2.40 = £1. A small number of other countries, but none of the major countries, devalued at the same time. What does this devaluation mean in terms of export prices and profitability and of import prices? A U.K. exporter who sold goods for $280 in the U.S.A. before devaluation received £100 for them. After devaluation three options are open to him:

1. Continue to sell the goods in the U.S.A. for $280; then he will receive not £100 but £116.66 and thus have a really big increase in profit per unit.
2. Sell the goods for $240, when he will receive £100 as before but can expect an increase in his total sales because his selling price is now one-seventh (14.3 per cent) less than before. The size of the increase in demand and sales depends on the elasticity of demand, but unless elasticity is zero, there will be some increase in sales.
3. Sell the goods at an intermediate price between $280 and $240, in which case his profit per unit will rise (but not as much as in the first instance) and his sales increase (but not as much as in the second instance). Thus devaluation makes exporting easier and more profitable.

The purpose of a devaluation is to enable a country to earn more foreign currency on exports and spend less foreign currency on imports. Devaluation encourages exports because exports have become cheaper or exporting has become more profitable or a combination of the two; this applies to both visible and invisible exports. It should be stressed that one of the purposes of devaluation is to make exporting more profitable. It does not follow that if a firm retains its pre-devaluation price in terms of foreign currencies (i.e. puts up prices in terms of its own currency), this is necessarily contrary to the purposes of devaluation. For example, the additional profit margin might be more effectively used for a sales campaign than by offering lower prices; if supply or demand is inelastic more foreign currency would be earned by retaining the previous price in terms of foreign currency than by lowering it. Earnings of foreign currencies are only increased from lower export prices if sales expand more than proportionately to the reduction in price (i.e. if the price elasticity of demand is greater than one and supply is elastic).

On the import side the effect of a devaluation is to raise import prices in terms of the domestic currency. An import from the U.S.A. priced at $280 which cost £100 before devaluation costs £116.66 afterwards, a rise of nearly seventeen per cent. This higher price is expected to discourage imports and encourage the substitution of home-produced goods, which are now relatively cheaper, for imports. This reasoning applies also to invisible imports; thus, for example, devaluation not only encourages foreigners to take holidays in the devaluing country because these are cheaper, it also encourages nationals to holiday at home because domestic holidays have become cheaper relative to holidays abroad.

The effectiveness of a devaluation on the import side depends on the elasticity of demand for imports; if demand for imports is elastic, then the rise in price of imports will cause a more than proportionate reduction in purchases, so that less is spent on them than before in terms both of domestic and of foreign currency. But if the elasticity of demand for imports is between one and zero, even though the higher price will lead to a reduction in quantity imported, the total expenditure on imports (measured in domestic currency) will rise.

As already partially indicated, devaluation affects demand and resources in three ways. In the devaluing country, it raises the prices of internationally traded goods relative to the prices of domestic goods and so deflects demand from imports to home-produced import substitutes, from exportables to domestic goods, and it may also deflect resources from goods which are not traded abroad to international goods. In the outside world, devaluation lowers the prices of internationally traded goods in relation to domestic goods' prices, thus deflecting the outside world's demand and resources in the opposite direction and encouraging the devaluing country's exports. Finally, devaluation often adversely affects the devaluing country's terms of trade, raising the prices of its imports more than the prices of its exports, thus further encouraging the outflow and discouraging the inflow of goods.

Devaluation is known as an expenditure switching policy. This is because changes in relative prices causes switching from other countries' exports to one's own and from imports to the consumption of home goods by the population of the devaluing country. To work properly, however, two conditions must be satisfied: (i) resources must be available to be switched from other areas of the economy into industries producing exports or goods which will substitute for imports; (ii) any tendency for wages to rise, following the rise in import prices, must be resisted. In general, price and wage inflation must be controlled to maintain the gain in competitiveness secured by the devaluation.

To ensure the success of a devaluation, therefore, there are two other requirements of domestic economic policy. Firstly, internal demand must be restrained by appropriate fiscal and monetary measures. While probably raising unemployment and therefore being electorally unpopular, such policies will create a situation where firms will be able to switch resources into exports and away from home markets in response to these demand shifts. Policies, like these which seek to create capacity in the economy to augment the effects of devaluation are called expenditure-reducing policies. Secondly, attempts must be made to check any rise in prices and wages. Prices of imported goods and also of goods which use imported raw materials will tend to rise after devaluation. In an open economy like the U.K.'s where twenty per cent of the Gross National Product is exported and a similar amount of expenditure is for imported goods, such considerations are very important. Wages, on the other hand, may tend to rise if workers become aware of the effects of devaluation on prices and seek higher wages in compensation. The success or failure of a devaluation may depend to a large extent on the money illusion of the labour force, or in other words, whether workers are aware that prices have risen because of the devaluation and therefore their real wages have fallen. To combat such pressures on prices and wages, a strong prices and incomes policy may be needed.

It can thus be seen how a company may benefit from a devaluation. Similarly, the above analysis helps a company to perceive what macro-economic policy changes may follow a devaluation.

DIRECT GOVERNMENT INTERVENTION

Other policies open to the authorities include the following. The exchange rate could be pegged and the necessary price and income changes could be induced by means of deflationary monetary and fiscal policy. Restrictions of various kinds such as tariffs, or quotas on imports of goods or services, restrictions on capital outflows and on government overseas expenditure could be introduced. In addition, subsidies on exports of goods or services could be created or inducements could be offered to foreign capital inflows. Convertibility, the ability of being freely able to exchange one currency for another, could be suspended. Exchange controls could be introduced with the objective of rationing the available supply of foreign exchange.

An expenditure-reducing policy such as deflation has as its objective a reduction of incomes with a consequent reduction in the demand for imports. Similarly, it is hoped that since the domestic market is static or falling in size, producers will have more incentive to export. The government can adopt fiscal or monetary measures to achieve this. Fiscal measures take the form of a reduction in government spending relative to tax revenue, i.e. an increased budget surplus (or reduced budget deficit). Monetary measures can take the form of control over the supply of money, credit restrictions and/or the raising of interest rates. Deflation of a sufficient severity will almost certainly improve the balance of payments quickly. However, this will be achieved at a high cost in terms of unemployment and lost output.

Although the other measures mentioned may also achieve the desired objective of reducing the deficit they will mean simultaneously that all the potential gains from trade mentioned earlier will no longer be available.

Any company faced with direct government interference in trade will have to make a careful evaluation of what types of policies are likely to be introduced and then examine the consequences of these for his own company.

Appendix 1

The U.K. Balance of Payments

Table 2.1 gives the official statistics for the U.K. balance of payments. As can be seen this is broken down into current account, investment and other capital flows and official financing. Quite naturally, the breakdown of the actual balance of payments is more complicated than the earlier simplified example. The current balance remains the same as before, i.e. the balance of visible and invisible trade.

The investment and other capital flows account covers the following broad categories of transactions.
(a) Official long-term capital investments. Drawing on or repayment of various inter-government loans and other official long-term capital movements.
(b) Overseas investment in the U.K. and U.K. investment in overseas countries.
(c) Overseas currency borrowing or lending by U.K. banks.
(d) Changes in the sterling exchange reserves of overseas residents held in the U.K.
(e) Changes in the U.K. external banking and money market liabilities in sterling to overseas residents except for central monetary institutions and international organisations
(f) Trade credit for imports and exports.
(g) Other short-term flows.

The balance for official financing is the algebraic sum of the current account balance and the total of investment and other capital flows plus the balancing item. It represents the net balance of official and all private transactions, whether current or capital requiring official accommodating finance. The balance for official financing is similar to the total currency flow (TCF). As Table 2.1 shows the sum of the TCF and total official financing is zero for the years 1973 to 1977 but for 1971 and 1972 the two magnitudes differ. The discrepancy is explained by items which relate to transactions with the International Monetary Fund, allocations of special drawing rights and gold subscriptions. These will be discussed further in Chapter 5.

The total currency flow is important in showing the money the U.K. has available for adding to the reserves or for paying off the country's borrowing. In official financing the '+' and '−' signs may seem rather confusing because '+' is usually taken as favourable and '−' as unfavourable, as is the case in the current account. In fact, the minus sign here means money going 'out' to pay off debts or into the reserves, and is therefore a good indication whereas a plus means added Government borrowing from abroad or 'borrowing' from the U.K. reserves —and that is the kind of money coming 'in' that the U.K. does not want to have to take.

Apart from using up reserves a balance of payments deficit can be financed by borrowing. The foreign currency debt of the U.K. public sector comprises the foreign currency debt incurred by the U.K. central government and the foreign currency loans raised by the nationalised industries, local authorities and other statutory authorities.

Table 2.1
Balance of payments(a)

£ millions

Current account

Seasonally adjusted

| | Visible trade | | | Invisibles | | | | | | | Current balance |
	Exports (f.o.b.)	Imports (f.o.b.)	Visible balance	Services and transfers (net) Government	Other	Interest, profits and dividends (net) Public	Private	Total credits	Total debits	Invisible balance	
1971	9,060	8,799	+ 261	− 520	+ 844	− 204	+ 709	5,573	4,744	+ 829	+ 1,090
1972	9,450	10,172	− 722	− 561	+ 884	− 142	+ 676	6,135	5,278	+ 857	+ 135
1973	12,115	14,498	− 2,383	− 768	+ 932	− 199	+ 1,419	8,240	6,856	+ 1,384	− 999
1974	16,538	21,773	− 5,235	− 858	+ 1,220	− 352	+ 1,634	10,046	8,402	+ 1,644	− 3,591
1975	19,463	22,699	− 3,236	− 999	+ 1,617	− 514	+ 1,277	11,024	9,643	+ 1,381	− 1,855
1976	25,424	29,013	− 3,589	− 1,549	+ 2,686	− 648	+ 1,963	14,354	11,902	+ 2,452	− 1,137
1977	32,182	33,891	− 1,709	− 1,893	+ 3,524	− 685	+ 1,169	16,215	14,100	+ 2,115	+ 406
1976 3rd qtr	6,513	7,645	− 1,132	− 387	+ 742	− 175	+ 535	3,742	3,027	+ 715	− 417
4th „	7,097	8,055	− 958	− 461	+ 750	− 190	+ 533	3,915	3,283	+ 632	− 326
1977 1st qtr	7,512	8,485	− 973	− 451	+ 785	− 204	+ 363	3,935	3,442	+ 493	− 480
2nd „	7,927	8,689	− 762	− 476	+ 872	− 189	+ 275	3,971	3,489	+ 482	− 280
3rd „	8,556	8,525	+ 31	− 501	+ 915	− 152	+ 282	4,103	3,559	+ 544	+ 575
4th „	8,187	8,192	− .5	− 465	+ 952	− 140	+ 249	4,206	3,610	+ 596	+ 591
1978 1st qtr	8,380	9,022	− 642	− 659	+ 766	− 108	+ 230	4,158	3,929	+ 229	− 413
2nd „	8,743	8,925	− 182	− 597	+ 716	− 112	+ 301	4,273	3,965	+ 308	+ 126
3rd „	9,071	9,413	− 342	− 644	+ 774	− 118	+ 304	4,503	4,187	+ 316	− 26

continued overleaf

Table 2.1 continued

Investment and other capital flows

Not seasonally adjusted

	Official long-term capital	Overseas investment in the United Kingdom — Public sector(b)	Overseas investment in the United Kingdom — Private sector	UK private investment overseas	Overseas currency borrowing or lending (net) by UK banks to finance: (c) — UK investment overseas	Overseas currency borrowing or lending (net) by UK banks to finance: (c) — Other transactions	Exchange reserves in sterling — British government stocks	Exchange reserves in sterling — Banking and money-market liabilities	Other external banking and money market liabilities in sterling	Import credit	Export credit	Other short-term flows	Total investment and other capital flows(b)
1971	− 274	+ 107	+ 1,047	− 836	+ 280	+ 191	+ 55	+ 658	+ 709	+ 54	− 287	+ 105	+ 1,809
1972	− 255	+ 120	+ 795	− 1,383	+ 725	+ 254	+ 65	+ 222	− 91	+ 198	− 409	− 402	− 669
1973	− 254	+ 175	+ 1,653	− 1,743	+ 595	+ 70	+ 74	+ 87	− 7	+ 348	− 552	− 141	+ 165
1974	− 276	+ 252	+ 2,287	− 1,118	+ 270	+ 564	− 124	+ 1,534	+ 148	+ 164	− 809	− 67	+ 1,697
1975	− 288	+ 43	+ 1,697	− 1,281	+ 320	+ 85	+ 7	+ 624	+ 550	+ 224	− 570	+ 285	+ 1,278
1976	− 158	+ 203	+ 2,061	− 2,156	+ 165	+ 271	+ 14	− 1,421	+ 255	+ 165	− 1,145	− 608	− 2,896
1977	− 291	+ 2,182	+ 3,019	− 2,276	+ 520	+ 136	+ 5	− 24	+ 1,471	+ 179	− 408	+ 175	+ 4,416
1976 3rd qtr	− 10	+ 58	+ 453	− 509	+ 55	+ 327	− 19	− 330	+ 212	+ 80	− 147	− 160	− 644
4th ,,	− 85	+ 123	+ 461	− 513	− 49	+ 203	+ 56	− 113	+ 49	+ 59	− 359	+ 208	+ 44
1977 1st qtr	− 25	+ 498	+ 929	− 571	+ 85	+ 336	− 165	+ 355	+ 199	+ 35	− 50	+ 97	+ 1,723
2nd ,,	− 20	+ 921	+ 843	− 822	+ 90	+ 796	− 4	+ 394	+ 350	+ 117	− 187	+ 24	+ 1,122
3rd ,,	− 17	+ 289	+ 776	− 442	+ 210	+ 21	+ 31	+ 43	+ 323	+ 31	− 34	+ 65	+ 1,192
4th ,,	− 229	+ 474	+ 471	− 441	+ 135	+ 345	+ 143	+ 28	+ 599	− 4	− 205	+ 119	+ 1,379
1978 1st qtr	− 57	− 3	+ 1,020	− 682	+ 145	− 30	− 34	+ 194	− 59	+ 142	− 318	− 226	+ 92
2nd ,,	− 14	− 15	+ 466	− 513	+ 340	− 1,295	− 20	+ 211	− 156	+ 101	− 345	− 117	− 1,779
3rd ,,	− 17	− 14	+ 415	− 768	+ 160	+ 168	− 38	+ 43	+ 159	− 128	− 18	+ 74	+ 72

28

Table 2.1 continued

Official financing

Not seasonally adjusted

	Current balance	Capital transfers	Investment and other capital flows	Balancing item	Balance for official financial (b)	Allocation of special drawing rights	Official financing				Official reserves (drawings on +/ additions to −)	Total official financing
							Net transactions with overseas monetary authorities		Foreign currency borrowing by:			
							IMF	Other monetary authorities	HM Government	Public sector under the ECS		
1971	+1,090	—	+1,809	+ 247	+3,146	+125	− 554	−1,263	—	+ 82	−1,536	−3,271
1972	+ 135	—	− 669	+ 731	−1,265	+124	− 415	+ 864	—	—	+ 692	+1,141
1973	− 999	−59	+ 165	+ 122	− 771	—	—	—	+ 644	+ 999	+ 228	+ 771
1974	−3,591	−75	+1,697	+ 323	−1,646	—	—	—	+ 423	+1,107	+ 105	+1,646
1975	−1,855	—	+ 278	+ 112	−1,465	—	+1,018	—	—	+ 887	+ 655	+1,465
1976	−1,137	—	−2,896	+ 404	−3,629	—	+1,113	− 34	+ 871	+1,792	+ 853	+3,629
1977	+ 406	—	+4,416	+2,539	+7,361	—	—	—	—	+ 243	−9,588	−7,361
1976 3rd qtr	− 368	—	− 644	+ 150	− 862	—	—	+ 309	—	+ 492	+ 61	+ 862
4th ,,	− 275	—	+ 44	+ 98	− 133	—	—	+ 924	—	+ 441	+ 616	+ 133
1977 1st qtr	− 581	—	+1,723	+ 708	+1,913	—	+ 682	—	+ 584	+ 18	−3,197	−1,913
2nd ,,	− 280	—	+1,122	+1,066	+ 908	—	+ 217	—	—	+ 33	−1,158	− 908
3rd ,,	+ 602	—	+1,192	+ 814	+2,608	—	+ 214	—	+ 287	+ 118	−3,227	−2,608
4th ,,	+ 602	—	+1,379	− 49	+1,932	—	—	—	—	+ 74	−2,006	−1,932
1978 1st qtr	− 554	—	+ 92	+ 635	+ 173	—	− 505	—	—	+ 219	+ 46	+ 173
2nd ,,	+ 213	—	−1,779	+ 72	−1,494	—	− 26	—	+ 191	+ 218	+2,026	+1,494
3rd ,,	+ 3	—	+ 72	+ 141	+ 210	—	—	—	—	+ 130	+ 54	+ 210

(a) Figures as published in the article 'United Kingdom balance of payments in the third quarter of 1978' in *Economic Trends*, December 1978. Definitions of the items in this table are given in *United Kingdom Balance of Payments 1967–77* (HMSO, September 1978) and in a technical note in *Economic Trends*, June 1976. See also additional notes.

(b) This total excludes foreign currency borrowing by the public sector under the exchange cover scheme, which is shown as a financing item.

(c) Includes certain other financial institutions. Excludes foreign currency borrowing under the exchange cover scheme.

Source: *Bank of England Quarterly Bulletin, December 1978*

U.K. foreign currency debt is the foreign currency debt incurred by HMG itself and is of four kinds: direct borrowing by HMG in the international financial markets, drawings on IMF facilities, the recent sales of foreign currency bonds, and long-term loans mainly from the USA and Canada. The totals outstanding at 1st April 1977 are given in Table 2.2

Table 2.2

HMG FOREIGN CURRENCY DEBT
OUTSTANDING AT 1 APRIL 1977

	$ billion
HMG $2.5 billion loan	2.5
HMG $1.5 billion loan	1.0
Drawing on IMF oil facility	1.2
May 1976 drawing on IMF first credit tranche	0.8
January 1977 drawing on IMF $3.9 billion standby	1.2
Foreign currency bonds	0.7
Long-term debts	4.1
TOTAL	11.5

Source. Treasury Progress Report. May 1977[2]

MARKET BORROWING.
This consists of two syndicated credits, which as is explained in Chapter 11, were raised in the Eurodollar market, the first in 1974, and the second in 1977. The first loan was drawn down between October 1974 and February 1975.

IMF DRAWINGS.
These are further explained in Chapter 5. Drawings on the oil facility and on most of the first credit tranche were made in 1976. For the remainder of the credit tranches the agreement recently reached with the IMF provided for a $3.9 billion standby to be available for drawing during 1977 and 1978.

FOREIGN CURRENCY BONDS.
As a contribution to orderly reduction in the level of overseas official balances in sterling toward working levels, the U.K. central government has made a special issue of foreign currency bonds to official holders of sterling. Subscriptions for these bonds closed on 14th April 1977 and some $680 million were sold.

LONG-TERM DEBTS.
These consist mainly of the Lend-Lease settlement and the U.S. and Canadian lines of credit arranged soon after the Second World War. There are, in addition, two smaller loans from the U.S.A. dating from that period and a loan under the German Offset Agreement in 1969.

OTHER PUBLIC SECTOR FOREIGN CURRENCY DEBT.

The nationalised industries, local authorities, and other statutory bodies, such as the National Water Council, have in recent years raised substantial sums in foreign currency. The amounts outstanding are given in Table 2.3. Most of these loans have been raised under the exchange cover scheme, which was in operation from 1969 to 1971 and reintroduced in 1973. This scheme provides borrowers with cover against exchange risk against payment to the Exchange Equalisation Account (EEA) of a charge for cover; the charging arrangement provides that the borrower surrenders most of the interest differential between the rate on the foreign currency loan and the appropriate rate on sterling loans from the National Loan Fund (or in the case of local authorities, the Public Works Loan Board) but keeping an interest 'benefit' of about 1 per cent.

Table 2.3
FOREIGN CURRENCY BORROWING BY
OTHER UK PUBLIC SECTOR BODIES OUT-
STANDING AT 1 APRIL 1977

	Under exchange cover scheme	Not under exchange cover scheme	Total
$ billion			
Nationalised industries	7.3	0.9	8.2
Local authorities	1.2	0.1	1.3
Others	1.2	—	1.2
TOTALS	9.7	1.0	10.7

Source: Treasury Progress Report. May 1977[2]

Appendix 2

The U.S. Balance of Payments

The same principles as were applied in the simple example are also relevant to the U.S. balance of payments. However, an extra complication with the U.S.A. is that the U.S. dollar is, in addition to being the medium of exchange within the U.S.A., an international reserve currency under the present international payments mechanism.

The form in which the balance of payments is presented has been altered, because of major changes in the world economy and in the international monetary system in the past few years, notably the widespread abandonment of par values. A series of meetings between January and November 1975 of the Advisory Committee on the Presentation of Balance of Payments Statistics resulted in a report, which was largely accepted, being presented to the Inter-Agency Committee on Balance of Payments Statistics. It was agreed that the following balances should be retained:

1. Balance of current account

With adjustments for errors and omissions and for valuation changes this balance is the mirror image of changes in the nations' net financial claims on foreigners.

2. Balance of goods and services

This balance is closely related conceptually to an important component in the national income and product accounts, net exports of goods and services. It also represents the net transfer of real resources to or from foreigners.

3. Financing items

There are two components, the net change in U.S. official reserve assets and the net change in U.S. liabilities to foreign official agencies.

It was agreed that the following balances should be discontinued:

1. Official Reserve Transactions balance (ORT)

It was agreed that the ORT balance was no longer justified for three major reasons. First was the advent of generally floating exchange rates and discretionary official intervention to affect currencies' values. Second, much of the increase in U.S. liabilities to foreign official agencies, particularly those of the oil exporting countries, is the result of those agencies' investment decisions rather than a reflection of their exchange rate policies. Thus a surplus or deficit on the ORT basis cannot necessarily be interpreted as indicating relative strength or weakness of the international position of the dollar. Thirdly, it was felt that there was no longer a close connection between the ORT and the U.S. money supply. The Committee reached this conclusion because foreign monetary authorities tend to use the international reserves they acquire to purchase U.S. Treasury obligations and interest-bearing bank deposits, and such transactions do not affect the U.S. monetary base or M1.

2. Net liquidity balance

The net liquidity balance was long viewed as a measure of potential pressure on U.S. primary reserve assets e.g. gold and Special Drawing Rights (SDRs). However, since the dollar is no longer convertible into such assets this rationale for the measure has disappeared.

The Office of Management and Budget has approved the recommendations mentioned above. The new format is set out in Table 2.4.

Table 2.4
U.S. INTERNATIONAL TRANSACTIONS Summary
$ millions, quarterly data are seasonally adjusted except as noted.—

Item credits or debits	1975	1976	1977	1977 Q1	Q2	Q3	Q4	1978 Q1
1 Merchandise exports	107,088	114,694	120,585	29,477	30,638	31,013	29,457	30,664
2 Merchandise imports	98,041	124,047	151,644	36,495	37,259	38,263	39,627	41,865
3 Merchandise trade balance[2]	9,047	−9,353	−31,059	−7,018	−6,621	−7,250	−10,170	−11,201
4 Military transactions, net	−876	312	1,334	568	295	467	5	307
5 Investment income, net[3]	12,796	15,933	17,507	4,399	4,487	4,610	3,812	4,767
6 Other service transactions, net	2,095	2,469	1,705	229	412	583	482	428
7 **Balance on goods and services**[3][4]	**23,060**	**9,361**	**−10,514**	**−1,623**	**−1,427**	**−1,591**	**−5,870**	**−5,700**
8 Remittances, pensions, and other transfers	−1,721	−1,878	−1,932	−490	−480	−490	−473	−502
9 U.S. Govt. grants (excluding military)	−2,894	−3,145	−2,776	−636	−763	−787	−591	−752
10 **Balance on current account**[3]	**18,445**	**4,339**	**−15,221**	**−2,749**	**−2,670**	**−2,868**	**−6,934**	**−6,954**
11 *Not seasonally adjusted*[3]				−2,339	−2,492	−5,179	−5,212	−6,466
12 Change in U.S. Govt. assets, other than official reserve assets, net (increase,−)	−3,470	−4,213	−3,679	−949	−795	−1,098	−838	−900
13 *Change in U.S. official reserve assets (increase,—)*	*−607*	*−2,530*	*−231*	*−388*	*6*	*151*	*−60*	*246*
14 Gold			−118	−58			−60	
15 Special Drawing Rights (SDR's)	−66	−78	−121		−83	−9	−29	−16
16 Reserve position in International Monetary Fund (IMF)	−466	−2,212	−294	−389	−80	133	42	324

continued overleaf/

[1] Seasonal factors are no longer calculated for lines 13 through 50.

[2] Data are on an international accounts (IA) basis. Differs from the Census basis primarily because the IA basis includes imports into the U.S. Virgin Islands, and it excludes military exports, which are part of Line 4.

[3] Includes reinvested earnings of incorporated affiliates.

Table 2.4 continued

17 Foreign currencies	−75	−240	302	59	169	27	47	−62
18 **Change in U.S. private assets abroad (increase,—)[3]**	**−35,368**	**−43,865**	**−30,740**	**3**	**−11,214**	**−5,668**	**−13,862**	**−13,632**
19 *Bank-reported claims*	−13,532	−21,368	−11,427	3,684	−4,582	−1,779	−8,750	−6,270
20 Long-term	−2,357	−2,362	−751	−306	18	−447	−16	−311
21 Short-term	−11,175	−19,006	−10,676	3,990	−4,600	−1,332	−8,734	−5,959
22 *Nonbank-reported claims*	−1,357	−2,030	−1,700	−768	−1,137	1,389	−1,184	−2,015
23 Long-term	−366	5	25	33	66	205	−279	−60
24 Short-term	−991	−2,035	−1,725	−801	−1,203	1,184	−905	−1,955
25 U.S. purchase of foreign securities, net	−6,235	−8,852	−5,398	−736	−1,766	−2,165	−731	−934
26 U.S. direct investments abroad, net[3]	−14,244	−11,614	−12,215	−2,177	−3,729	−3,113	−3,197	−4,413
27 *Change in foreign official assets in the United States (increase, +)*	6,907	18,073	37,124	5,451	7,884	8,246	15,543	15,691
28 U.S. Treasury securities	4,408	9,333	30,294	5,323	5,123	6,948	12,900	12,965
29 Other U.S. Govt. obligations	905	573	2,308	98	610	627	973	117
30 Other U.S. Govt. liabilities[5]	1,647	4,993	1,644	505	417	332	390	785
31 Other U.S. liabilities reported by U.S. banks	−2,158	969	773	−725	752	−163	909	1,456
32 Other foreign official assets[6]	2,104	2,205	2,105	250	982	502	371	368
33 **Change in foreign private assets in the United States (increase, +)[3]**	**8,643**	**18,897**	**13,746**	**−2,962**	**6,180**	**6,005**	**4,522**	**2,125**
34 *U.S. bank-reported liabilities*	628	10,990	6,719	−5,304	6,240	2,640	3,143	−314
35 Long-term	−280	231	373	42	104	194	33	250
36 Short-term	908	10,759	6,346	−5,346	6,136	2,446	3,110	−564
37 *U.S. nonbank-reported liabilities*	319	−507	257	−346	−412	590	425	418
38 Long-term	406	−958	−620	−220	−176	18	−242	45
39 Short-term	−87	451	877	−126	−236	572	667	373
40 Foreign private purchases of U.S. Treasury securities, net	2,590	2,783	563	981	−1,370	1,251	−299	881
41 Foreign purchases of other U.S. securities, net	2,503	1,284	2,869	828	725	513	803	462

34

42	Foreign direct investments in the United States, net[3]	2,603	4,347	3,338	880	996	1,012	450	679
43	Allocation of SDR's								
44	*Discrepancy*	*5,449*	*9,300*	*−998*	*1,593*	*609*	*−4,769*	*1,569*	*3,423*
45	Owing to seasonal adjustments				130	−177	−2,230	2,276	176
46	Statistical discrepancy in recorded data before seasonal adjustment	5,449	9,300	−998	1,463	786	−2,539	−707	3,247

MEMO ITEMS:

Changes in official assets:

47	U.S. official reserve assets (increase, −)	−607	−2,530	−231	−388	6	151		246
48	Foreign official assets in the United States (increase, +)	5,259	13,080	35,480	4,946	7,467	7,914	15,153	14,906
49	Changes in Organization of Petroleum Exporting Countries (OPEC) official assets in the United States (part of line 27 above)	7,092	9,581	6,733	2,927	1,344	1,438	1,024	1,810
50	Transfers under military grant programs (excluded from lines 1, 4, and 9 above)	2,207	373	194	39	53	31	71	77

[4] Differs from the definition of "net exports of goods and services" in the national income and product (GNP) account. The GNP definition excludes certain military sales to Israel from exports and excludes U.S. Govt. interest payments from imports.

[5] Primarily associated with military sales contracts and other transactions arranged with or through foreign official agencies.

[6] Consists of investments in U.S. corporate stocks and in debt securities of private corporations and state and local governments.

Source.—Data are from Bureau of Economic Analysis, *Survey of Current Business* (U.S. Department of Commerce).

References

[1] The Marshall-Lerner condition states that the sum of the elasticities of demand for a country's exports and of its demand for imports has to be greater than unity for a devaluation to have a positive effect on a country's trade balance. If the sum of these elasticities is smaller than unity a country can instead improve its trade balance by revaluation. The Marshall-Lerner condition is built on some drastic simplifications. It assumes that the supply elasticities are large (approaching infinity) and that the trade balance is in equilibrium when devaluation takes place. For a description of the Marshall-Lerner condition see B. Kettell, *Journal of the Economics Association* Summer 1979.

[2] *Economic Progress Report.* Prepared by the Information Division of the Treasury. No. 86 May 1977.

3

The Foreign Exchange Market

This chapter, which examines the working and significance of the foreign exchange market, is broken down into the following sections: definition and function, quotation and interpretation of spot and forward rates, corporate usage of the forward exchange market, forward options, foreign exchange controls, the effective exchange rate and foreign exchange models.

Appendix 1 gives a diagrammatic explanation of interest arbitrage and the determination of forward exchange rates. Appendix 2 gives a Bank of England series of effective exchange rates.

DEFINITION AND FUNCTION

The foreign exchange market is the organisational framework within which individuals, firms, banks and brokers buy and sell foreign currencies. The foreign exchange market for any one currency, e.g. the pound sterling, consists of all the locations such as London, New York, Zurich and Paris where the pound sterling is bought and sold for other currencies.

The foreign exchange market provides three major functions. Firstly, it provides a mechanism for transferring the money of one country into the money of another country. Since an American exporter to the United Kingdom requires payment in his own currency, the dollar, the United Kingdom importer, whose currency is the pound sterling, will have to convert sterling into dollars. The existence of the foreign exchange market enables him to do this. As long as different currencies exist, in order to facilitate trade a foreign exchange market will be necessary. This is only true for countries with freely convertible currencies. Comecon countries trade without foreign exchange markets. Secondly, the foreign exchange market helps in the obtaining of short-term credits to finance trade. In this case, if a British exporter is willing to be paid at the end of a three-month period, an arrangement made possible by the forward exchange market, he is effectively granting credit to the American importer. Thirdly, the market provides facilities for firms to avoid foreign exchange risks. Again the existence of the forward market enables a firm with a future foreign currency asset or liability to sell it forward or buy it forward in order to minimise the exchange risks the firm is faced with. These three functions will become clearer as the workings of the market are examined.

Foreign exchange markets tend to be located in national financial centres near the related financial markets. The more important exchange markets are found in London, New York, Paris, Frankfurt, Amsterdam, Milan, Zurich, Toronto, Brussels, Bahrain and Tokyo. Formerly, there were two main types of foreign exchange markets, the type adopted by the U.K. and the U.S.A., and the European style, although this distinction is rapidly becoming blurred. The U.K. and U.S.market is a market only in the abstract sense since it does not exist in one physical place like, for example, the Stock Exchange, but only in the sense that it is a communications system through which participants transact business. The communication system consists of a network of telephones and telexes that connect exchange markets all over the world. Thus the participants can remain in continuous contact with one another. Indeed, the communications system is so continuous that, despite time and space differences, there exists a single world market. As the market in London is closing the market in the U.S.A. is becoming active and as the market in the U.S.A. closes so the market in Tokyo is becoming active. More recently, active markets in Singapore and the Middle East, particularly Bahrain, have developed. Thus a London based foreign exchange dealer who leaves home may well find that when he arrives back at work the following morning there have have been wide changes in the exchange rates. The European type of market used to lay stress on the physical meeting of the participants in a specific place, usually the Bourse. This type of market has been largely replaced by a communication system like the British-American type. However, daily meetings still take place in some European centres such as Brussels and Frankfurt at what is called the 'fixing'. Here the market participants, normally .banks, can deal until a market equilibrium rate is agreed upon and this rate tends then to be used for transactions where a generally agreed market rate for the day has to be used.

Although the term 'the Foreign Exchange Market' is used, there are, in fact, three types of transactions undertaken. These are transactions in the spot, forward and deposit markets. In the spot market currencies are bought or sold for immediate delivery although in practice, settlement is made after two working days, e.g. Thursday's spot deals are for settlement on Monday, to allow for paperwork to be completed. Settlement must be made on the due day, neither earlier or later. In the forward market, currencies are bought or sold now for future delivery. The principal feature of this market is that payment is in the future although the exchange rate is agreed upon in the present. In the deposit market currencies are borrowed or are lent and thus a bank will have to repay or will itself be repaid when the deposit matures (assuming it is not renewed). Deposit market trading can take place within a country with its own currency, e.g. the sterling inter-bank market in London or with banks in other countries in which case normally with 'Euro-currencies'. Euro-currencies, discussed further in Chapter 10, are currencies which are traded outside their country of origin.

There are three participants in the market. Firstly, there are the participants who require foreign currency, i.e. individuals and institutions such as companies. They may desire a currency other than their own in order to travel or to finance trade or investment abroad. Secondly, there are the commercial banks who operate through their foreign exchange dealing room, normally but not necessarily, at head office. When banks deal with each other in large amounts this is called wholesale business. Wholesale business often takes place with a broker who performs the function of putting buyers and sellers together in return for a commission. Under normal circumstances brokers are only used between banks inside a country, and if a bank wishes to obtain foreign exchange quotations from another country it will do so by contacting the foreign bank directly. Apart from clearing banks, merchant banks also are very active in the market. The third major participant in the market is the central bank of the country. Chapter 2 illustrated that under fixed exchange rates the central bank may intervene to keep the rates within agreed central limits. Thus the central bank is a very important participant in the market.

A rate of exchange is the price of one currency in terms of another. The factors which influence exchange rates are discussed in detail in Chapter 4. In this chapter the workings of the market itself are examined. A foreign exchange dealer will normally quote two rates, the first rate is the rate at which he will buy his own currency and the second rate is the rate at which he will sell his own currency. There are, however, two ways of quoting currency rates.

QUOTATION AND INTERPRETATION OF SPOT EXCHANGE RATES

These two ways are: (i) quotation of the number of foreign units to one local unit; (ii) quotation of the number of local units to one or 100 units of the foreign currency. In London, sterling against foreign currencies is quoted as (i) above For example, Deutschemarks are quoted at 4.01 meaning 4.01 Deutschemarks = £1.

In New York, the dollar against foreign currencies used to be quoted as (ii) above although it has now gone over to the European System (i) (*see Table 3.1*). For example, one Deutschemark was quoted as being worth so many U.S. cents. e.g. DM 1.00 =$.4117.

As from mid 1978 the U.S.A. moved to the European system of quoting rates. Before this date only a few currencies, for instance the Mexican peso, were quoted in European terms. Quotes for certain currencies, particularly sterling and the Canadian dollar, will continue to be expressed in U.S. terms.

TABLE 3.1

System (i) London Spot quotation £ based – Currency Units per £		System (ii) New York Spot Quotation $ based – U.S. units per unit of foreign currency	
Market Sells	Market Buys	Market Buys	Market Sells
$ 1.6850	1.6860	$ 1.6850	1.6860
FF 5.0125	5.0135	FF .1994	.1995
SF 2.4450	2.4460	SF .4088	.4089
DM 2.4275	2.4285	DM .4117	.4119

The dealer quotes two prices, the rate at which he is prepared to sell a currency, known as the 'offered rate', and that at which he is prepared to buy, the 'bid rate'.

If U.S. dollars are quoted in terms of pounds as $1.6850 to $1.6860, it means that the market or dealer will sell dollars 1.6850 to the pound, or buy dollars at $1.6860. As this is a two-way quotation, the converse applies. The dealer will buy pounds at the rate of $1.6850, or sell pounds at $1.6860.

It makes no difference as long as it is clear which way the rates are quoted. It is important to note that where the pound is quoted against the dollar, if the unit rises (falls) the value of the pound rises (falls) and the value of the dollar falls (rises). If the value of the dollar is quoted against the foreign currency, e.g. the Deutschemark, as the unit rises (falls) the value of the dollar rises (falls) and the value of the Deutschemark falls (rises). If, for example, a central rate for the pound against the dollar is taken to be 1.7100, then if this rises to 1.7200, the pound is worth more and the dollar worth less, and if the rate falls to 1.7000 then the pound is worth less and the dollar worth more. Similarly, with a central rate of 30 cents against the Deutschemark if this rises to 33, the dollar is worth less and the Deutschemark is worth more.

The difference between the buying and selling rates is the dealer's spread. In the above sterling-dollar example with a quote of $1.6850-1.6860 the spread is $.0010 or ten points. A point (or a 'pip' as it is widely known) is a unit of a decimal, usually the fourth place to the right of the decimal point. In the earlier example $.0001 would be one 'pip'; $.0010 would be ten 'pips'. A part of one 'pip' is expressed as a fraction; hence one could have a quote of $1.6850-1.6850½. Which decimal place is implied by a 'pip' varies from currency to currency.

The spread fluctuates according to the level of stability in the market and the currency at the particular point in time, the location of the market and the volume of transactions in a particular currency. Higher spreads are caused by higher uncertainty, lower volumes of trade and the remoteness of the market in relation to its currency. Conversely, lower spreads occur with stable conditions, a high volume of trade and an actively traded currency.

Since an exchange rate is the price of a foreign currency in terms of the home currency it follows not only that each country has as many foreign exchange rates as there are currencies but that all these exchange rates imply cross rates between the other currencies. A cross rate is the rate for trading one foreign currency against another foreign currency.

e.g. $1=FF 5.0125 $\dfrac{\$1=FF\ 5.0125}{\$1\quad DM\ 2.4475}$ = 2.0480 FF/DM
       $1=DM 2.4475

The cross rate French franc against the Deutschemark is 2.048.

It can be seen that the foreign exchange market is virtually a world market since it is open twenty-four hours a day. This has important implications. Professional foreign exchange dealers, with a great deal of market information at their fingertips, can in reality bring about the equalisation of exchange rates around the world by the process of arbitrage. How would this work? For example, a bank in New York quotes an exchange rate of $2.3500–2.3700 against the pound and a bank in the U.K. quotes an exchange rate for sterling of $2.3900–2.4100. This is an extreme example but it emphasises what happens. Arbitragists would buy pounds (sell dollars) in New York at 2.3700 and would sell the pounds (buy dollars) in the U.K. at 2.3900, thus making a comfortable spread of 200 pips. As the demand for sterling in New York rises so would the price and similarly, as the supply of sterling sold in the U.K. rises, so there would be a fall in the price of sterling. This process stops when the rates are equalised; thus arbitragists can quickly arbitrage away any variations in spot exchange rates.

QUOTATION AND INTERPRETATION OF FORWARD EX-CHANGE RATES

A forward exchange contract is an agreement to deliver a specified amount of one currency for a specified amount of another currency at some future date. The important point here is that the exchange rate is agreed upon *now* while the currencies are exchanged in the future. Forward exchange rates are normally quoted with a buying and a selling rate for periods of one, two, three and six months for the major trading currencies, e.g. the dollar, pound sterling, Deutschemark, Swiss franc, etc. Up to these maturities the market is fairly 'thick', i.e. trading does not lead to wide rate fluctuations. Beyond these maturities the market is fairly 'thin' i.e. trading does lead to wide rate fluctuations. Although specific maturity dates are normally given, if one is not sure when one may need a foreign currency it is possible to arrange forward option contracts which permit delivery at periods within a month. Normally, these are more expensive than normal maturity date contracts.

Before looking at how rates are quoted and how the market can be used it is necessary to examine the forces influencing the forward market. Under normal market conditions the forward market is determined by international interest rate differentials. Interest rate arbitrage is the process of moving funds from one currency to another currency in order to take advantage of higher rates of interest. Uncovered interest arbitrage is where an investor transfers funds from one currency to another and ignores the fact that currencies with high interest rates tend to be prone to devaluation. Covered interest arbitrage is where an investor transfers funds and takes out a corresponding forward contract which, at a cost, guarantees that he has no exchange risk. In this case the investor has, as is seen below, to decide whether the interest differential in his favour outweighs the loss on the forward deal.

Whether or not it is profitable to move short-term funds from one centre to another depends not only on the additional interest that might be gained by so doing, but also on the relation of the two currencies in the spot and forward markets. If, for example, a U.S. investor is considering investing money in U.K. Treasury bills because the interest rates are higher than on U.S. Treasury bills, it is necessary first to convert dollars into pounds. While he holds sterling Treasury bills he runs an exchange risk in that at the end of three months the pound may be worth a lot less than at the beginning of the period and this could wipe out any increased interest he receives. In order to eliminate any exchange risk the U.S. investor could sell pounds forward, i.e. buy dollars forward. Whenever the amount of a currency being sold forward outweighs the amount being bought forward the price of that currency will go down, and whenever the amount of a currency being sold forward is less than the amount being bought forward the price of that currency will go up.

If a currency is at a discount this means that the forward value of that currency is lower than the spot value. If a currency is at a premium this means that the forward value of that currency is higher than the spot value. In the above example, since there are more forward sellers of pounds sterling the pound is at a discount and the dollar is at a premium. By definition, if two currencies are quoted against each other and one currency is at a discount the other currency must be at a premium.

When examining how forward rates are quoted it will be seen that whether one adds or subtracts the premium or discount depends on which of the two possible ways that exchange rates can be quoted is used. The theory of forward exchange holds that under normal conditions the forward discount or premium on one currency in terms of another is directly related to the difference in interest rates prevailing in the two countries. The currency of the higher interest-rate country should be at a discount in terms of the currency of the lower interest-rate country. Similarly, the currency of the lower interest-rate country should be at a premium in terms of the higher interest-rate currency. The forward exchange rate is said to be at interest parity whenever the interest differential and the forward discount or premium (expressed in per cent per annum) are equal. This relationship is explained diagrammatically in Appendix 2.

In practice, forward rates are determined under normal conditions by differences in Euro-rates. Thus, the forward rate of sterling against the dollar depends on the difference between the rate on Euro-sterling and the rate on Euro-dollars. Essentially, the Euro-markets are free markets and can be freely used by non residents. In order to convert pips into percentage differences the following formula is used:

$$\frac{\text{Forward rate-spot rate} \times \text{Number of days in the year} \times 100}{\text{Spot rate} \times \text{lifetime of the operation in days}}$$

		Bid	Offered
1.	Euro-dollar market (six months)	$5\frac{5}{8}$	$5\frac{3}{4}$
2.	Euro-sterling market (six months)	15	$15\frac{1}{8}$
3.	Spot £	1.6860	1.6850
4.	Six months forward cover	1.6080	1.6090
		780	760 discount

$$\text{Percentage per annum} = \frac{1.6080 - 1.6860 \times 360 \times 100}{1.6860 \times 180} = 9.25\%$$

In order to convert percentage differences into 'pips' the formula becomes the following:

$$\frac{\text{Spot rate} \times \text{Percentage difference in Euro-rates} \times \text{lifetime of the operation}}{100 \times \text{Number of days in the year}}$$

$$= \frac{1.6860 \times 9.25 \text{ per cent} \times 180}{100 \times 360} = 0.779 \text{ or } 779 \text{ pips}$$

Note that for most foreign exchange transactions it is assumed that there are 360 days in the year.

Under normal circumstances these formulae show that forward interest rates are determined by Euro-interest rate differentials.

If sterling is at a discount of 9.25 per cent the dollar is at a premium of 9.25 per cent. The significance of this is discussed in more detail in a later section (pp 46–49) but for the moment it can be interpreted as follows: basically, a U.K. importer from the U.S.A. selling sterling forward to pay for his dollars will lose an annualised 9.25 per cent. He must then decide whether he expects the future decline in spot sterling to be greater or less than this in deciding whether to purchase forward cover.

Forward rates are quoted as being at a discount or premium to the spot rate. As already stated, a currency is at a premium where its future value is greater than the spot value against the base currency and, conversely, a discount means that the future value will be lower than the spot value.

The discount or premium is expressed in points and the future rate is calculated by subtracting or adding the points from or to the spot rate. Where the method of quoting the rate is in units of foreign currency to one unit of base currency, the premium is subtracted from the spot rate and the discount is added, e.g. the closing spot exchange rate for the pound against the dollar for the 7 August 1978, taken from the *Financial Times* and reproduced below, was 1.9295–1.9305. The one month premium of the dollar was 0.72–0.62c. This gives the following:

1.9295	—	1.9305	Spot rates
72		62	Premium (to be subtracted)
1.9223		1.9243	Outright Forward rate

Thus the foreign exchange market will buy pounds sterling one month forward i.e. sell dollars at $1.9223 and will sell pounds one month forward i.e. buy dollars at $1.9243. (*see Figure 3.1*)

Having given an example of a currency at a premium against sterling, it is necessary to give an example of a currency which is at a discount against sterling. Take, for example, the Portuguese Escudo. The Portuguese Escudo is quoted as being at a discount of 50–150c one month forward. This gives the following outrights:

87.70	88.20	Spot rates
50	1.50	Discount (to be added)
88.20	89.70	Outright Forward Rate

Thus the foreign exchange market will buy pounds sterling one month forward for 88.20 escudos and will sell pounds forward for 89.70 escudos.

Figure 3.1

THE POUND SPOT — FORWARD AGAINST £

Aug. 7	Bank rates %	Day's Spread	Close	One month	% p.a.	Three months	% p.a.
U.S. $	$7\frac{1}{4}$	1.9280-1.9325	1.9295-1.9305	0.72-0.62c. pm	4.16	1.47-1.37c.pm	2.94
Canadian $	9	2.1935-2.1975	2.1960-2.1970	0.65-0.55c.pm	3.28	1.35-1.25c.pm	2.37
Guilder	$4\frac{1}{2}$	4.20-4.23$\frac{1}{2}$	4.20$\frac{1}{2}$-4.21$\frac{1}{2}$	$2\frac{3}{4}$-$1\frac{3}{4}$ c.pm	6.41	6-5 c.pm	5.22
Belgian Fr.	6	61.05-61.65	61.10-61.20	15-05 c.pm	1.96	35.25 c.pm	1.96
Danish Kr.	8	10.59$\frac{1}{2}$-10.67	10.60$\frac{1}{2}$-10.61$\frac{1}{2}$	$1\frac{3}{4}$ ore pm-$\frac{1}{4}$ dis	0.85	$2\frac{3}{4}$-$4\frac{3}{4}$ ore dis	—1.41
D-Mark	3	3.87-3.92	3.87$\frac{1}{2}$-3.88$\frac{1}{2}$	$3\frac{1}{2}$-$2\frac{1}{2}$ pf pm	9.28	8-7 pf pm	7.73
Port. Esc.	18	87.30-88.30	87.70-88.20	50-150 c. dis	—13.64	150-430 c. dis	—13.19
Span. Pes.	8	146.65-147.25	146.70-146.80	20c. pm 80c. dis	—2.45	10-110 c. dis	—1.64
Lira	$11\frac{1}{2}$	1618$\frac{1}{2}$-1622$\frac{1}{2}$	1620$\frac{1}{4}$-1621$\frac{1}{4}$	1 lire pm 1 dis	par	6-9 lire dis	—1.85
Nrwgn. Kr.	7	10.20$\frac{1}{2}$-10.27	10.21$\frac{1}{2}$-10.22$\frac{1}{2}$	$4\frac{1}{4}$-$2\frac{1}{4}$ ore pm	3.81	$5\frac{1}{2}$-$3\frac{1}{2}$ ore pm	1.76
French Fr.	$9\frac{1}{2}$	8.42-8.45	8.43-8.44	3.2 c. pm	3.56	5.4 c. pm	2.13
Swedish Kr.	$6\frac{1}{2}$	8.59$\frac{1}{2}$-8.64$\frac{1}{2}$	8.60-8.61	$2\frac{3}{4}$-$\frac{3}{4}$ore pm	2.44	$5\frac{1}{2}$-$3\frac{1}{2}$ ore pm	2.09
Yen	$3\frac{1}{2}$	362-368	364-365	3.85-3.55 ypm	12.18	8.85-8.50 ypm	9.52
Austria Sch	$4\frac{1}{2}$	27.95-28.25	27.95-28.00	15-5 gro pm	4.29	38-28 gro pm	4.72
Swiss Fr.	1	3.26-3.32	3.29$\frac{1}{4}$-3.30$\frac{1}{4}$	$3\frac{7}{8}$-$2\frac{7}{8}$ c.pm	12.28	$9\frac{1}{4}$-$8\frac{1}{4}$ c.pm	10.61

Belgian rate is for convertible francs. Financial franc 63.40-63.50.

Six-month forward dollar 2.42-2.32c pm, 12-month 4.57-4.47c pm.

Source: *Financial Times,* 8 August 1978

The *Financial Times* also quotes spot and forward rates against the dollar (*see Figure 3.2*).

Figure 3.2

THE DOLLAR SPOT — FORWARD AGAINST $

August 7	Day's spread	Close	One month	% p.a.	Three months	% p.a.
Canad'n $*	87.88-87.92	87.89-87.92	0.06-0.04c dis	0.62	0.12-0.09c dis	—0.47
Guilder	2.1782-2.1905	2.1782-2.1792	0.54-0.49c pm	2.76	1.27-1.22c pm	2.58
Belgian Fr	31.66-31.88	31.66-31.67	0.05-0.10c dis	—0.17	0.06-0.10c dis	—0.12
Danish Kr	5.5005-5.5060	5.5005-5.6025	—		—	
D-Mark	2.0085-2.0220	2.0085-2.0095	0.93-0.88pf pm	4.61	2.54-2.49pf pm	4.75
Port. Es	—	45.25-45.40	—		—	
Lira	839.30-839.80	839.60-839.80	3.05-3.45 lire dis	—4.03	9.50-10.25 lire dis	—4.48
Nrwgn. Kr	5.2925-5.3065	5.2925-5.2945	—		—	
French Fr	4.3670-4.3750	4.3670-4.3690	0.20-0.30c dis	—0.69	0.95-1.15c dis	—0.98
Swedish Kr	4.4585-4.4740	4.4585-4.4605	—		—	
Yen	188.35-188.80	188.65-188.80	1.30-1.15y pm	6.79	3.15-3.00y pm	6.38
Austria Sch	—	14.5450-14.5550	—		—	
Swiss Fr	1.6948-1.7065	1.7055-1.7065	1.18-1.12c pm	8.02	3.18-3.12c pm	7.48

*U.S. cents per Canadian $.

Source: *Financial Times,* 8 August 1978.

The same principle as above holds since there is still the system of quoting the rate in units of foreign currency to one unit of base currency, e.g. the dollar.

To take an example of a currency at a premium against the dollar e.g. the Deutschemark, this gives:

Bid	Offered		
2.0085	2.0095	–	Spot rate
.0093	.0088	–	Premium (to be subtracted)
1.9992	2.0007	–	Outright forward rate

In this case the foreign exchange market will buy dollars (sell Deutschemarks) one month forward at D.M. 1.9992 and will sell dollars (buy Deutschemarks) at D.M. 2.0007.

Again, take the example of a currency at a discount against the dollar e.g. the French Franc; this gives:

Bid	Offered		
4.3670	4.3690	–	Spot rate
.0020	.0030	–	Discount (to be added)
4.3690	4.3720	–	Outright forward rate

In this case, the foreign exchange market will buy dollars (sell French Francs) one month forward at F.F. 4.3690 and will sell dollars (buy French Francs) at F.F. 4.3720.

Where the rate is quoted as the value of one unit of foreign currency in terms of the local or base currency the premium is added and the discount subtracted from the spot rate.

Earlier exchange rates were taken from the foreign exchange page of the *Financial Times* (8 August 1978). The front page of the *Financial Times* normally also gives an example of spot and forward rates where the above principle holds.

Figure 3.3

£ in New York

—	Aug. 7	Previous
Spot	$1.9340-9350	$1.9275-9285
1 month	0.70-0.64 dis	0.56-0.50 dis
3 months	1.44-1.38 dis	1.25-1.19 dis
12 months	4.60-4.40 dis	4.20-4.00 dis

Source: *Financial Times,* 8 August 1978.

In this case the one month forward rates would be:

Bid	Offered		
$1.9340	1.9350		
.0070	.0064	–	Discount (to be subtracted)
$1.9270	$1.9286	–	Outright forward rate

In this example the foreign exchange market will buy pounds sterling one month forward i.e. sell dollars at $1.9270 and will sell pounds one month forward i.e. buy dollars at $1.9286

In order to know what the cost is or what is the gain from a forward sale of a currency it is necessary to calculate the discounts and premiums as a percentage. As mentioned earlier, this can be done by using the following formula:

Forward rate–spot rate × time × 100
—————————————————————————————
　　　　　spot rate

which is equivalent to:

Discount/premium in points × time × 100
————————————————————————————————
　　　　　Spot rate

Note that time can be expressed as:—

$$\frac{\text{Number of months in the year}}{\text{Number of months forward}} \quad \text{or as} \quad \frac{\text{Number of days in the year}}{\text{Number of days forward}}$$

Assume a U.K. exporter to the U.S.A. is receiving dollars in one month; he is able, if he wishes, to sell these forward: applying the formula one can calculate what he gains (he gains since the dollar is at a premium against sterling). Take the mid-closing spot rate from Figure 3.1.

$$\frac{.0062 \times 12 \times 100}{1.9300 \times 1} = 3.85 \text{ per cent}$$

The U.K. exporter to the U.S.A. can be said to have gained 3.85 per cent by dealing in the forward market over that which he would have received from dealing in the spot market. A U.K. importer from the U.S.A. will be paying sterling in one month which he can sell forward. In this case he loses, since sterling is at a discount against the dollar:

$$\frac{.0072 \times 12 \times 100}{1.9300 \times 1} = 4.47 \text{ per cent}$$

The U.K. importer can be said to have lost 4.47 per cent by dealing in the forward market over that which he would have received by dealing in the spot market.

The *Financial Times* has recently commenced quoting these annualised costs of cover which saves the tedium of calculation. This is found under the heading: % *p.a.* The rate they give, which is the middle rate, is 4.16 per cent.

Again assume a U.S. company is importing in one month from Holland: in this case the U.S. company loses since the guilder is at a premium against the dollar. Using the mid-closing rate of 2.1787 from Figure 3.2 the calculation is as follows:

$$\frac{.0049 \times 12 \times 100}{2.1787 \times 1} = 2.69 \text{ per cent}$$

In the converse case of a U.S. company exporting in one month to Holland, where it will benefit from the premium, the calculation is:

$$\frac{.0054 \times 12 \times 100}{2.1787 \times 1} = 2.97 \text{ per cent}$$

47

Again the *Financial Times* gives an approximate middle rate of 2.76 per cent.

In these examples the term 'gained' or 'lost' is used in the sense of the difference between dealing forward or dealing spot.

HOW COMPANIES CAN USE THE FORWARD MARKET.

Having seen how the forward market works and how to interpret discounts and premiums it is necessary to examine the benefit to a company of the forward market to see what constraints affect its use and to understand how the company can decide when it is worthwhile to cover forward and when it is not.

By entering into a forward foreign exchange contract a U.K. importer or exporter can:

 (i) fix at the time of the contract a price for the purchase or sale of a fixed amount of foreign currency at a specified future time;

 (ii) eliminate his exchange risk due to future foreign exchange rate fluctuations;

(iii) calculate the exact sterling value of an international commercial contract despite the fact payment is to be made in the future in a foreign currency.

A premium of the foreign currency shows that the currency is 'stronger' than sterling in the forward market. This means that when entering into a forward contract:

 (i) the U.K. exporter will receive more sterling for his currency export proceeds at the future date than at the current spot rate at the time the contract is taken out;

 (ii) the U.K. importer will have to pay more sterling to settle his currency debts at the future date than at the current spot rate at the time the contract is taken out.

A discount of the foreign currency shows that the currency is 'weaker' than for example, sterling, in the forward market. This means that when entering into a forward contract:

 (i) the U.K. exporter will receive less sterling for his currency export proceeds at the future date than at the current spot rate at the time the contract is taken out;

 (ii) the U.K. importer will have to pay less sterling to settle his currency debts at the future date than at the current spot rate at the time the contract is taken out.

In deciding whether to use the forward market a company has to make an assessment of what the future spot rate is likely to be. This can be clarified by the example given earlier (p 44) but with the assumption that the company has a one-month forward payment of dollars to make, i.e. it wants to sell forward pounds sterling. The company has two choices: firstly, it can sell pounds

48

forward now; secondly, it can wait for one month and then sell pounds spot. If it sells pounds spot, the company receives $1.9295 per pound. If it sells pounds forward it receives $1.9223 per pound. It now has to decide whether in the future the pound will be worth more or less than this forward rate. Assume that the future one-month spot value of the pound is 1.9265. This gives a forward discount of .0030, i.e. 1.9295 minus 1.9265 which, substituting into the formula, gives:

$$\frac{.0030 \times 12 \times 100}{1.925 \times 1} = 1.86 \text{ per cent}$$

Alternatively, assume that the future value of the pound is 1.9110. This gives a forward discount of .0185, i.e. 1.9295 minus 1.9110 which, substituting into the formula, gives:

$$\frac{.0185 \times 12 \times 100}{1.9295 \times 1} = 11.5 \text{ per cent}$$

Bearing in mind that the cost of forward cover is 4.47 per cent the company has to decide what action to take. If it expects a future spot of $1.9265, i.e. a loss of only 1.86 per cent, the company would benefit by dealing future spot. However, if the company expects a future spot rate of $1.9110, i.e. a loss of 11.5 per cent the company would benefit by dealing forward. In deciding whether or not to take out forward cover the company needs to take a view as to the likely future spot rate.

Companies operating on high turnover and small profit margins would be strongly advised to take out forward cover. If the company does not take out a forward contract and the 11.5 per cent decline in the future spot rate occurred the company's total profits may be wiped out simply because of an exchange rate movement.

Since the advent of floating exchange rates there has been some controversy about how to calculate the cost of forward cover. This is discussed in more detail in Chapter 9. Robert Ankrom, Treasurer of Chrysler (Europe) contends that while the forward premium or discount is a known, easily calculable number, it is totally misleading as a measure of 'cost'[1]. The true cost is rather the difference between the forward rate and the spot rate at the time the forward contract matures. For a company the important factor in hedging is not the past spot rate but the spot rate which will occur on the day a forward contract matures. Assume that a U.S. manufacturer with a £1 million exposure wants to hedge by selling sterling forward and the current spot rate is $1.77 with a current forward rate of $1.76. The one cent forward discount on £1 million is $10,000. This discount is what was referred to earlier as the cost of cover. Ankrom goes on to ask what happens when the forward contract matures. The hedging company has contracted to deliver £1 million against $1,760,000. If the company does not have sterling, it will be compelled to buy sterling at the spot rate in effect at the time the forward rate matures. The cash outlay the company will have to make or the cash inflow it will enjoy on the closing of the forward contract will depend on that future spot rate.

Assume the future spot rate is $1.75 or less than the forward rate of $1.76: to buy £1 million the company needs $1,750,000. On closing the forward contract, the company will enjoy a cash inflow of $10,000. Assume the spot rate is $1.76 or exactly equal to the forward rate: there will be no cash inflow or outflow on the closing of the contract.

If it is assumed that the.spot rate is $1.77 or exactly equal to the spot rate at the time the forward contract was taken out, the company will have to find $1,770,000 in order to buy the sterling and will have an additional cash outlay of $10,000. It is apparent that the cash outlay equals the forward discount only in the last case, where the spot rate does not change.

Ankrom claims that hedging is analogous to insuring only in that it limits the exposure. A company will receive the forward rate no matter what happens to the spot rate, but the cost of limiting the exposure is not analogous to an insurance premium, for the cost can only be determined after the fact.

FORWARD OPTION CONTRACTS

Not all export receipts or import payments can be predicted with absolute certainty, nor do they fall exactly into the one, three, six, or twelve month framework. For this reason, optional date contracts may be considered, whereby certain currencies to be received can be sold (or those required bought) within a maximum and minimum period in the future. For example, a three-month forward purchase of a foreign currency at a premium can include an option to accept the funds at any time between the beginning and the end of the third month. The word 'option' does not mean the customer has a choice as to whether or not he deals. He actually has dealt and the option is given to him as to when he takes or gives the currency concerned.

The rates for forward foreign exchange option contracts are calculated on the bases that firstly, delivery can be made at any time during the option period, and secondly, that the contract may be completed at the most unfavourable point in time from the bank dealer's point of view. An example may take this clear[2]. Assume that spot dollars against sterling stand at $2.00½–2.00¾ and that one-month dollars are ½–¼ cents premium. This means that the bank sells one-month dollars fixed at $2.00; it sells one-month dollars option at $2.00; it buys one-month dollars fixed at 2.00\frac{1}{2}$, and it buys one-month dollars option at 2.00\frac{3}{4}$.

When the bank is selling a currency which is at a premium, it will always deduct the premium, irrespective of whether the contract is fixed or option, because in the case of an option the customer might not take the option until the last day for which the contract runs. Therefore, the bank is entitled to charge the full premium. Similarly, when buying for a fixed date, the bank must give the customer the benefit of whatever premium rules; but when the bank is buying on an option contract, the customer has the choice of delivering spot and the bank will only pay him the spot price.

A further example will clarify this: assume that the Belgian franc stands at a discount against sterling; assume also that spot Belgian francs against sterling stand at 80.25–80.30, and that one-month Belgian francs stand at a discount of .10–.15. This means that the bank sells one-month Belgian francs fixed at B.Fr.80.35; it sells one-month Belgian francs option at B.Fr.80.25; it buys one-month Belgian francs fixed at B.Fr.80.45, and it buys one-month Belgian francs option at B.Fr.80.45.

When the bank sells at one-month fixed the customer is entitled to whatever discount may be available, but where the bank sells option one-month the customer may decide to take delivery at spot and accordingly will not be entitled to the benefit of discount and, therefore, the bank pays him the spot price. When the bank buys one month fixed there can be no argument; the full discount is payable and the bank will take it. When the bank buys option for one month, the customer has the choice of delivering up to the end of the period; therefore, the bank is again entitled to the full discount for that period.

The technique of using options is useful, but options are rarely used as they can be negotiated in only a few currencies and for strictly limited time periods.

FOREIGN EXCHANGE CONTROLS

In order to prevent currency speculation and to protect their reserves, many countries impose foreign exchange controls. These controls are designed to limit an individual's ability to freely convert one currency into another currency. Normally, there has to be proof of an underlying economic transaction, i.e. exporting or importing, before permission to exchange the currencies is given. Details of different types of foreign exchange controls can be found in the *Annual Reports on Exchange Restrictions,* published by the I.M.F.

In exchange control-free countries, there are no regulations for resident firms concerning forward dealings and they may undertake forward exchange commitments whenever and wherever they desire. Where there are exchange control systems, three types of restrictions generally apply. Firstly, contracts are restricted to legitimate commercial transactions evidenced by appropriate documentation. Secondly, contracts must be concluded with local 'authorised' banks. Thirdly, the final terms of any such contract is also limited, usually to match the existing limits on export or import credit terms. This is to control what is called 'leading' and 'lagging' (*see Chapter 8*)

In the U.S.A. capital controls were introduced in the 1960s and early 1970s, and they took three forms. First, there was the interest equalisation tax, introduced in 1963, which taxed purchases of foreign securities by U.S.A. residents and which was intended to increase the cost to foreigners of raising capital in the U.S.A. markets. Secondly, the Voluntary Foreign Credit Restraint Program introduced in 1965 was designed to check foreign lending by U.S. banks and other financial institutions. Thirdly, there was the Foreign Direct Investment Program, introduced on a voluntary basis in 1965 and made mandatory in January 1969. As the title suggests, the program imposed controls on direct investment overseas by U.S. companies. Debate as to the effectiveness of these controls is still taking place; but it should be borne in mind that, even with these controls, the dollar was devalued in 1971 and again in 1973, and that further deterioration of the balance of payments was not halted.

In Switzerland an inhibition on borrowing Swiss francs has been that the loan has to be converted immediately, usually into dollars. This increases the exchange risk of the debt since an investor may have a depreciating asset and an appreciating liability. In Germany, although it is not immediately necessary for foreigners to convert a Deutschemark loan there have been restrictions on the type of assets which may be held. Tight government control of the Japanese capital market has made it extremely difficult in the past for foreigners to raise money or to hold yen assets; it also enabled the Japanese to maintain an undervalued yen. These exchange controls have an important impact on the euro-currency market and the international bond market outlined in Chapters 10 and 11.

All the U.K. exchange controls stem from the Exchange Control Act 1947. Basically, the following requirements must be observed. Firstly, all British residents must surrender immediately any currency they own, including exporters who are paid in foreign currency. This means that individuals who obtain foreign currency cannot hold on to it in the hope of selling it in the future at a more favourable rate. Secondly, foreign currency payments for exports must be received no more than six months after the goods are shipped. This is to prevent companies 'lagging' their receipts in the hope of obtaining more sterling in the future. This 'lagging' is regulated by the customs authorities. Companies with large foreign currency expenses as well as receipts can apply to the Bank of England to open a retained account, normally called a 'hold account'. This saves the administrative costs of converting currencies and also means that the company does not suffer from a fall in the sterling exchange rate change. However, hold accounts are difficult to obtain. At specified periods any excess foreign currency in the account must be converted into sterling. Thirdly, any businessman wishing to buy foreign currency (to pay for imports) must provide his bank with documentary evidence of the underlying transaction. The objective of this is to prevent the selling of spot sterling with the hope of buying it back later at a reduced rate. If the company can prove it is importing and the goods are already in the country, the bank will provide the currency. If an overseas supplier wants payment in advance, the British importer has to go through a more complicated procedure. Unless the amount involved is less than £5,000 a special form (Form E) has to be completed and sent to the Bank of England to obtain approval.

It has already been seen that companies can, at a cost, eliminate exchange risk by using the forward market. However, the rules for the forward market are also fairly stringent. The bank providing the foreign currency must first be satisfied that its customer has a final and genuine commercial contract. Importers of goods must order their forward currency for delivery not later than six months after the expected date of arrival of the goods in Britain. This, again, is to prevent speculation. Exporters of goods and services may wish to sell their foreign currency forward, especially if they expect the currency they have received to depreciate in value. But they must take delivery of their forward pounds not later than six months after the goods are exported.

In November 1976 restrictions were introduced on the financing by U.K. banks of trade between foreign countries. Formerly, banks had been permitted to finance this trade in sterling. Now they may no longer do so.

Before analysing the foreign exchange rules affecting a company's ability to invest abroad the investment currency market must be examined. In the U.K. there are two recognised foreign currency markets: the official market, through which most payments between residents and non-residents pass, and the investment currency market in which the 'dollar premium' arises. Investment currency is foreign currency which has originated mainly from the sale abroad of foreign currency securities owned by U.K. residents, and which may be used by residents of the Scheduled Territories to acquire foreign assets, for which currency from the official market, due to exchange control, is not made available. The investment currency market is primarily a mechanism to enable portfolio investments in foreign currency securities to be transferred among U.K. residents; other permitted uses include the purchase of properties abroad for private use and, to a very small extent, the financing of direct investments abroad.

For many years transactions in investment currency have taken place at a premium over the exchange rate in the official foreign exchange market. The size of the premium reflects the amount which residents are prepared to pay other residents in order to acquire a part of the limited supply of investment currency. Essentially, it is determined by the attractiveness of investments abroad relative to the U.K., which is influenced, of course, by views on the future of both the sterling exchange rate and of the premium itself. Changes in exchange control rules have, it should be noted, also exerted an influence on the dollar premium.

Calculation of the real additional cost of investment currency to an investor is confused by the fact that the premium is usually expressed as a percentage based on the last fixed official (i.e. not floating) sterling/U.S. dollar exchange rate, which was approximately \$2.60/£1, and not on the current exchange rate. The subsequent decline in the value of sterling has resulted in the published premium rate being far higher than the real premium.

For example, if the nominal premium is quoted as 50 per cent (at \$2.60) and the current spot rate is £1 = \$1.90 the effective premium is found by using the formula:

$$\left(\frac{\text{Nominal premium} + 100}{1} \times \frac{\text{Current spot rate}}{2.60} \right) - 100$$

$$= \left(\frac{50 + 100}{1} \times \frac{1.90}{2.60} \right) - 100 = 10\%$$

Thus the effective premium is well below the nominal premium.

Overseas securities quoted on the London Stock Exchange must include the investment premium in their quoted price. One can find the value of the share without the premium by multiplying the quoted price by the conversion factor provided daily in the *Financial Times*.

The foreign exchange restrictions affecting investment abroad may now be considered. The U.K. authorities do not restrict overseas investment as such, but they do restrict the ways in which it can be financed. The main features of the current rules on direct investment are as follows:

(i) Companies are allowed to finance only a very small proportion of investment with foreign currency out of the official reserves; the only projects which can be so financed to a limited extent are those which meet the 'super-criterion', that is to say, projects which directly promote exports of goods and services and will bring benefits to the balance of payments equal to the cost of the original investment within a period of three years and continuing thereafter.

(ii) Other direct investments must be financed in ways which minimise or eliminate the cost to the reserves. In practice, almost all such investment is financed by borrowing foreign currency (either direct from overseas banks or through U.K. banks) or out of profits retained overseas.

(iii) When companies finance their direct investment by foreign currency borrowing this has to be repaid in due course. To protect the reserves, the regulations require that the amounts repaid out of official exchange do not exceed the inflows of funds resulting from the investment.

(iv) The U.K. controlled subsidiaries and branches overseas are required to remit to the U.K. a large proportion of their profits. The general rule is that at least two-thirds of net taxed earnings must be remitted, although detailed arrangements vary with the type of company and host country regulations.

Undoubtedly, foreign exchange controls play a large part in influencing the foreign exchange market.

EFFECTIVE EXCHANGE RATES

Any discussion of exchange rate movements inevitably includes a mention of effective exchange rates. Effective exchange rate measurements have three broad purposes. Firstly, they provide a convenient measure of the day-to-day behaviour of a currency as other currencies rise and fall against it. Secondly, they supply a quantitative indication of the impact of exchange-rate changes on the competitive position of each country's domestic industry in international markets. This second function has necessitated several revisions to the different effective rate measures. Thirdly, effective rate measurements have been used as a basis for foreign exchange market intervention by the monetary authorities either on a day-to-day basis or on a longer term basis.

As is explained in Chapter 5, in the twenty-five years from 1946 to 1971 exchange rates for most of the major currencies of the world were fairly stable. Usually, only one major currency changed its par value at any one time, and the dollar did not change its parity. While this yielded no adequate measure of change in the dollar's own effective exchange rate, for other currencies the dollar rate provided a fairly accurate standard of measurement. Since 15 August 1971, however, all major currencies have fluctuated by differing amounts. Widespread floating since 1971 has created a situation where changes in the rate against the dollar does not accurately indicate the overall change in the exchange rate for a currency.

An illustration of the problem is evident from the behaviour of the dollar and the 'Snake' currencies, i.e. Belgium, Denmark, West Germany, Luxembourg, Sweden, Norway and the Netherlands, at the beginning of 1975. At this time the dollar was depreciating against the 'Snake', whilst sterling was appreciating against the dollar but depreciating against the 'Snake'. It is clearly impossible in these circumstances to identify the change in the position of sterling by measuring it against other currencies individually.

It is in order to overcome this problem that effective exchange rates have been developed. They use changes in a country's trade balance as a proxy for exchange rate changes. The objective is to calculate an index which expresses the observed change in any currency against several others as the exchange-rate change necessary to achieve the same effect on the trade balance as that of the observed change. Effective exchange rate calculations assume that all other currencies remain unchanged. If there is a 10 per cent effective depreciation, for example, in the pound sterling this means that this is the size of the depreciation which would have been required had all the other currencies remained fixed vis-a-vis one another to produce the same effect on the trade balance of the U.K. as the exchange rate changes that actually did occur.

Whenever central bank intervention on the foreign exchange market takes place the bank must have some form of reference point to decide when it is necessary to intervene. In order to prevent profitable speculation the actual intervention point is kept secret. The U.K. changed its intervention policy in 1977. The Financial Statement described the new policy as follows:

The U.S. dollar was weakening and, in late July, the focus for intervention policy was switched from maintaining a stable pound/dollar rate to maintaining a stable effective rate index[3].

The Bank of England has described the change as follows:

Maintaining a stable rate against the U.S. dollar implied some slight depreciation in effective terms (i.e. on a trade weighted basis) as the dollar weakened. As a result, the authorities decided to switch the focus of their attention to the effective exchange rate and allowed the pound to appreciate so as to restore the effective rate to what it had been earlier in the year[4]

Thus, it can be seen that in the case of the U.K. the concept of the effective exchange rate plays an important role in intervention policy.

The question of how one measures changes in effective exchange rates is best summarised by the Treasury Progress Report as:

Given all the changes in individual rates that have taken place, what uniform and unilateral change in the exchange rate of sterling against all other currencies would have had the same effect on the U.K. trade balance?

Estimates are made of the effects on each country's visible trade balance of the actual changes in the main exchange rates since the base date. The effective change in each case is simply equivalent to an estimate of the unilateral change in the exchange rate which would have produced the same effect[5]

The construction of an index reflecting the change in the value of a currency with respect to a set of currencies depends on what the index is designed to measure; this factor in turn determines the choice of appropriate weights and the choice of the appropriate chronological reference base. Effective exchange rate indices have been developed by the U.K. Treasury, Morgan Guaranty Trust Company, OECD, Reuters, the U.S. Treasury, IMF, Federal Reserve Board and National Westminster Bank, among others. Country coverage ranges from ten industrial countries in the Reuters Currency Index, to the twenty-three members of the OECD in the OECD index, to forty-seven countries in the U.S. Treasury index. The other indices have a country composition in between these two extremes.

The Bank of England has recently introduced a new calculation of effective exchange rates based on an article 'Indices of effective exchange rates' by R. R. Rhomberg in the March 1976 issue of the *International Monetary Funds' Staff Papers*[6].

Appendix II gives the breakdown of effective exchange rates from January 1976 to November 1978 for sterling, U.S. dollars, Belgian francs, Swiss francs, French francs, Italian lire, Dutch guilders, Deutschemarks and Japanese yen.

Crawford has stressed that great care must be taken in interpreting the effective exchange rate movements[7]. A rise or fall of *x* per cent in an effective exchange rate has no effect on the country's trade balance if it merely maintains relative purchasing power parity. As explained earlier, the effective rate measurements show the changes in currency values in terms of their impact on the payments adjustment process. It does not follow that the changes so measured are of any help in the formulation of judgments as to whether a change thus measured has been adequate, or inadequate, to correct any payments imbalance.

In the U.K. the effective exchange rate index has in the past been expressed in the following forms: '*n* per cent below Smithsonian' or an 'effective depreciation of n per cent'. Since March 1977 the value of the index itself is quoted rather than its divergence from Smithsonian. Thus, what would previously have been called an 'effective depreciation of 45 per cent' would now be called an 'effective exchange rate index of 55'.

FOREIGN EXCHANGE MODELS

Given the uncertainty of many of the variables influencing future exchange rates several foreign exchange models have been developed to assist companies in deciding on an appropriate foreign exchange strategy.

The most well-known models are those developed by Shulman, Lietaer, Shapiro and Rutenberg. These models are not widely used as there are significant problems with all of them. Shulman has developed a model to show whether the costs of using the forward market outweigh the benefits[8]. He outlines four variables which, when multiplied together, give the amount a company should be willing to pay to minimise exchange risk. If the costs (benefits) of eliminating the risk outweigh the benefits (costs) the corporate treasurer should not (should) undertake the exchange risk-reduction programme. The first factor is the probability of a devaluation, for example of 20 per cent, i.e. 0.20. Secondly it is necessary to know the probability of the devaluation occurring within the forecast period, say 75 per cent (0.75). Multiplying these two together gives the expected loss from devaluation, i.e. (0.75× 0.20) = 15 per cent. Next, the probable error of the forecast must be introduced into the calculation. If the forecaster has been wrong 10 per cent of the time, 1.0 is added to this error and multiplied by the devaluation loss. Thus, a 10 per cent error factor gives 1.10 and when multiplied by the devaluation loss a figure of 16.5 per cent is obtained. It is then necessary to know the margin of safety the company needs, for example, say 15 per cent, and again this is added to the error factor, 1.0, which gives 1.15. The figure 16.5 is then multiplied by 1.15 which gives 18.98 per cent; this indicates how much the company would be willing to pay to get exchange risk protection. If it costs 15 per cent to cover in the forward market, Shulman's model indicates that the company should cover forward since costs are less than benefits; if it costs 20 per cent to cover in the forward market, his model indicates that forward cover is not worthwhile.

Shulman's model clearly needs accurate forecasts of all his unknown variables for the policy to be effective. He also does not consider any other hedging methods which are available and these need to be taken.into account when one is deciding whether to hedge or not.

Lietaer has developed a sophisticated mathematical quadratic programming model to analyse exchange risk[9]. Lietaer's model is designed to enable a company to minimise its 'net exposure', defined as the difference between a company's exposed assets and its exposed liabilities. The model generates an efficient set of hedging policies, each of which minimises expected costs and maximises protection. In effect, each efficient policy generates the maximum devaluation protection that can be purchased for a given cost; alternatively, the minimum required cost for each possible level of protection. Lietaer seeks to minimise the direct costs of financing and hedging operations, and the loss of profits that a devaluation may cause. Devaluation risk (identified as the likelihood of devaluation and the amount of the devaluation) and an uncertainty risk (which arises when a company has to rely on financing and hedging plans for which costs are uncertain) are the two types of protection that Lietaer is seeking to minimise.

Following the portfolio theory developed by Markowitz, Lietaer sets out an infinite set of optimal solutions which constitute an efficient frontier[10]. Each solution will be optimal if there is no other policy of equal cost which gives greater protection. At one end of the frontier there is a policy emphasising protection irrespective of cost. At the other end of the frontier there is a policy which minimises cost but gives very little protection. Along this efficient frontier the treasurer can choose where he wants to be depending on his assessment of the costs and benefits.

Lietaer's model has been criticised by Goeltz:

> The application of risk preference to determine the composition of currencies in an industrial firm's portfolio and asset structure does not seem appropriate. It is available technique when one of the possible outcomes is 'gamblers ruin' . . . that is a complete loss. It is highly likely that the loss arising from a change of currency values would cause an international firm to become bankrupt or even to suffer a serious inconvenience[11].

Goeltz' criticism may not be true of a bank, as can be seen from the repercussions of recent foreign exchange losses by Herstatt, Lloyds, Credit Suisse and Banque de Bruxelles. An optimisation model similar to that produced by Lietaer optimises losses when the exchange rate moves with the wrong sign.

Lietaer's concept of exchange exposure can also be criticised as being inadequate. An alternative definition of exchange risk based on future cash flows, as outlined in Chapter 7, may well be a more appropriate definition. The problems of defining foreign exchange exposure are also outlined in the same chapter.

Shapiro and Rutenberg analysed the problem of deciding when, if at all, forward cover should be taken as a hedge against devaluation of a specific currency[12]. The model is described for a single devaluation, and losses due to that devaluation accrue only to the period in which it occurs. Their model also describes the handling of successive devaluations and they claim that it can be adapted to deal with floating currencies. They do, however, use a balance sheet approach to defining exposure rather than the cash flow approach. Shapiro and Rutenberg are fully aware of this and state:

> We are well aware, as academics, that exposure should be defined in terms of a devaluation's effects on cash flow.

Carter and Rodriguez have reported the results of conversations of what forty U.S. multinationals thought about foreign exchange exposure models[13]. These firms were in many different industries and had an average sales level in 1976 of $2 billion with a minimum of $400 million. The models employed were very similar to models of working capital management. The behaviour of accounts receivable, accounts payable, inventories, cash, marketable securities, and short-term debt were found at the international level to have basic characteristics amenable to treatment by linear programming. However, at the international level the accounts had to be defined along two dimensions: country of location, and currency of denomination.

The constraints in the international models included the following:
(a) a maximum level of acceptable currency exposure;
(b) a limit on the amount of funds which can be transferred from one subsidiary to another, or to the parent;
(c) a restriction on the size of funds which operations can generate or utilise;
(d) limits on 'leads' and 'lags' in currency payments imposed by government regulations; and
(e) constraints on the level of balance sheet ratios.

Input requirements involved the following:
(a) the amount of funds generated in each currency;
(b) the size of the exposure in various currencies;
(c) current interest rates on different securities in the alternative currencies;
(d) current spot and forward exchange rates;
(e) tax rates in different countries;
(f) transfer costs; and
(g) (the most important of all inputs,) a forecast of currency parities for future periods.

From the characteristics of the companies which actually used exposure management models actively and the comments of other managers Rodriguez and Carter found that the largest advantages were derived under the following conditions:
(i) operations in a large number of currencies;
(ii) sizeable cross-currency flows, both inter-company and with third parties;
(iii) operations which generate highly fluctuating exposure levels;
(iv) large differences in tax rates among the various corporate units;
(v) a sophisticated liquidity management programme; and
(vi) corporate policies which allow for 'creative' financing strategies.

They concluded that the critics of the models had the better case. Given the existence of major problems with these models companies have turned to substituting the services of companies which specialise in providing exchange rate forecasts. These have developed very quickly since 1971 and the well-known services are those provided by Forex, Chemical Bank, Chase Econometrics, and most of the other large banks.

The value of exchange rate forecasting has been severely put to the test by Giddy and Dufey[14]. These writers argue forcefully that, due to the strong and weak version of the 'efficient market' hypothesis, exchange rate forecasts based on past values of exchange rates are unhelpful.

The strong version of the 'efficient market' hypothesis is that a large and competitive group of market participants have access to all information relevant to the formation of expectations about future prices. As a result, at any time, all relevant information is discounted in the present price. A weaker version of the 'efficient market' hypothesis holds that, while not all information is available to a large number of market participants, any information on past price movements is known to a sufficient number of market participants so that profitable speculation based on such information is impossible.

Giddy and Dufey tested whether forecasting exchange rates with techniques based on using past exchange rate values, such as the use of the forward rate as a predictor of future spot rates, the use of the Box–Jenkins Method and the use of exponential smoothing techniques, were better predictors than the 'random walk' hypothesis underlying the efficient market theories. They concluded that the foreign exchange market was an 'efficient market' and accordingly, exchange rate forecasting is not profitable.

Malcolm Crawford, however, finds the arguments of Dufey and Giddy unconvincing[15]. Firstly, he argues, markets have been known to ignore relevant information, e.g. from a rate of $2.35 at the end of 1972 the pound sterling rose to $2.59 on 5 June 1973 at a time when Britain had had an expansionary April budget and when the money supply and public expenditure were rising at record levels. Secondly, exchange rates do rise and fall in the wake of economic events which forecasters can often predict. Thirdly, no intuitive approach to exchange rate forecasts can outwit a systematic approach since the rates themselves and the influences on them may not be consistent.

S.M.Goodman, of the Singer Company also evaluated exchange rate forecasting[16]. In assessing forecasters he divided them into three broad groups: firstly, those that relied on an overall subjective evaluation of economic, political and/or technical factors; secondly, those that relied on econometric models; and thirdly, those that relied heavily on technically-oriented rules, e.g. the use of charts (so-called Chartists).

The services were evaluated on the basis of their predictive accuracy during the January to June 1978 period, using the forecasts actually made at the time for six currencies against the dollar – the Canadian dollar, French franc, Deutschemark, Yen, Swiss franc and sterling.

61

The subjective forecasters were not evaluated, as Goodman felt that these forecasts reflected the subjective judgment of a potentially changing group of individuals. On average, the econometric services did poorly over the relatively short-term horizon considered. These services accurately predicted the direction of trend for the spot exchange rates over the next three months only fifty per cent of the time. With regard to the technically-oriented forecasters Goodman found that they had a very strong predictive performance. This supports the view that speculative runs do occur in the foreign exchange market i.e. a currency that is rising, particularly at an accelerating rate, is likely to continue to rise and a currency that is falling will continue to fall.

This has clear implications for the corporate treasurer trying to manage his company's exposure. It suggests he may wish to use one or more of the technically-oriented foreign exchange rate forecasters. It also suggests that he should hedge outstanding short positions when a currency is rising, particularly if it is rising at an accelerating rate and hedge outstanding long positions when a currency is falling, particularly if it is falling at an accelerating rate. However, one major problem with technically-orientated services is that they do not provide point estimates of future spot exchange rates and would, therefore, be of little use in planning.

REFERENCES

[1] R. Ankrom, 'Among their hedges, treasurers may miss the obvious'. *Euoromoney*, December 1977.

[2] This example is taken from A. Watson, *The Finance of International Trade*. The Institute of Bankers. 1976.

[3] *Financial Statement and Budget Report 1978–79*. Her Majesty's Stationery Office.

[4] *Bank of England Quarterly Bulletin*. September 1977.

[5] *Economic Progress Report*. 'The Effective Exchange Rate for Sterling'. No. 84, March 1977

[6] *Bank of England Quarterly Bulletin*. March 1977.

[7] M. Crawford, 'Currencies in a floating world'. *Economist Intelligence Unit*. 1977.

[8] R.B. Shulman, "Are Foreign Exchange Risks Measurable?" Columbia Journal of World Business. May-June 1970–pages 55–60.

[9] B. Lietaer, *Financial Management of Foreign Exchange. An Operational Technique to Reduce Risk*. M.I.T. Press 1971.

[10] H.M. Markowitz, *Portfolio selection*. Yale University Press 1959.

[11] R.K. Goeltz, "Managing liquid funds on an international scope." *Unpublished paper*, Joseph P. Seagrams , Sons Inc. New York, 1971.

[12] A.C. Shapiro, and D.P. Rutenberg, "When to hedge against devaluation." *Management Science*. Vol. 20. No. 12. (August 1974) pp 1514–1530.

[13] E.E. Carter, and R.M. Rodriguez, "What 40 U.S. multinationals think." *Euromoney* (March 1978) pp. 95–111.

[14] G. Dufey, and I.H. Giddy, "Forecasting exchange rates in a floating world." *Euromoney* (November 1975) pp.28–35.

[15] M. Crawford, ibid.

[16] S.M. Goodman, 'Econometric Exchange Rate Forecasts: No Better than the Toss of a Coin.' *Euromoney*. December 1978, pp. 75–85.

Appendix 1

Interest Arbitrage and the Determination of the Forward Exchange Rate

Plotted on the vertical axis of Figure 3.4 are interest rate differentials, with a plus (+) differential indicating a higher interest rate in the 'foreign' country than in the 'home' country.

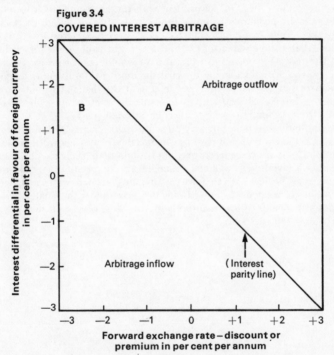

Figure 3.4
COVERED INTEREST ARBITRAGE

Source: Alan Holmes and Francis Schott. *'The New York Foreign Exchange Market'* Federal Reserve Bank of New York, 1965.

Plotted on the horizontal axis are the discounts (minuses) or premiums (pluses) on the forward exchange of the 'foreign' country, expressed in per cent per annum. Any combination of these two variables can be expressed as a point on the chart. The 'interest parity' line joins together those points where the forward exchange rate is in equilibrium with the interest rate differential. Moving along the interest parity line, if interest rates in the foreign country are 2 per cent higher than in the U.S.A., the currency of that country is at a 2 per cent per annum discount in the forward market; if foreign interest rates are 1 per cent below U.S. rates, the foreign currency is at a 1 per cent premium. When the forward exchange rate is at its interest parity, movements of short-term funds between the two centres with exchange risks covered are not profitable, since the gain to be made from the higher interest rate abroad is exactly offset by the cost of covering the exchange risk in the forward market.

When the forward exchange rate gets out 'of line with its interest parity (either because of speculative or other developments in the exchange market or because of

63

changes in interest rates) it becomes profitable for short-term investors to shift funds from one centre to another, i.e. an 'interest arbitrage incentive' emerges.

Point A on the chart indicates a position where interest rates in the foreign country are 1.5 per cent higher than in the home country, while the forward discount on the foreign currency is only 0.5 per cent; a transfer of funds abroad with exchange risks covered would consequently return an additional yield of 1 per cent per annum.

The actual movement of funds abroad tends to restore interest parity by: (a) increasing the forward discount on the foreign currency as a result of the demand for spot exchange and the offering of foreign currency forward by the arbitragers; and (b) lowering the interest rate differential as funds are transferred from one market to another.

Point B also illustrates a position where interest rates abroad are 1.5 per cent above those in the home country, but in this case the forward discount on the foreign currency is 2.5 per cent per annum. Despite the higher interest rates abroad, there would be no incentive to move funds there for investment with the exchange risk covered. On the contrary, it would be profitable to move funds from abroad despite the fact that the investment of these funds would bring a lower yield, since the interest loss of 1.5 per cent would be more than compensated for by the 2.5 per cent gain on the forward exchange transaction. The movement of funds from abroad would again tend to restore interest parity, however, by: (a) reducing the forward discount on the foreign currency as the result of an increased supply of spot exchange and the demand for forward foreign exchange by the arbitrager abroad; and (b) lowering the interest rate differential as funds are transferred from the foreign money market to the home market.

This theory indicates that forward rates fluctuate closely around their interest parities. However, there are several reasons why this theory may not work in practice; the supply of funds able to arbitrage freely may not be unlimited; there may be a shortage of suitable short-term investments in some countries. In the case of potential institutional investors there may be legal restrictions on investing abroad with exchange control limiting the ability of residents to move funds to where they wish. Finally investors may have psychological reasons to fear that funds may become blocked if they are placed in certain currencies.

Appendix 2
Indices of effective exchange rates

21 December 1971=100

		Sterling	US dollars	Belgian francs	Swiss francs	French francs	Italian lire	Nether-lands guilders	Deutsche-mark	Japanese yen
Last working days										
1976	Jan.	73.0	96.2	102.1	140.5	109.0	69.6	111.1	118.5	99.1
	Feb.	72.9	96.0	102.3	142.5	108.9	68.5	110.6	119.7	99.6
	Mar.	69.5	96.9	103.8	145.4	105.4	63.2	111.5	123.0	101.2
	Apr.	66.9	98.2	104.8	147.3	106.8	59.1	112.3	123.8	102.0
	May	64.2	98.1	103.3	151.7	105.7	63.7	110.5	121.6	101.9
	June	64.9	97.4	103.0	150.7	104.8	63.8	111.2	122.2	102.3
	July	65.0	97.4	104.0	150.0	100.6	64.3	112.1	124.2	104.1
	Aug.	64.5	97.0	104.8	149.6	99.9	63.7	114.5	124.6	105.5
	Sept.	60.1	96.5	106.7	150.9	99.0	61.6	116.7	129.1	106.3
	Oct.	57.1	97.2	108.6	152.2	97.6	61.4	118.9	131.5	103.6
	Nov.	60.0	98.9	109.0	152.3	97.9	61.4	118.7	131.4	102.5
	Dec.	61.1	97.2	110.3	150.7	97.5	60.0	119.8	132.8	103.3
1977	Jan.	62.0	97.7	108.2	147.5	98.4	60.0	118.1	130.9	105.5
	Feb.	61.8	97.6	109.0	144.2	97.8	59.7	118.9	131.9	107.7
	Mar.	61.9	97.2	108.8	144.4	97.9	59.3	119.0	131.5	109.7
	Apr.	61.6	96.8	109.9	145.9	97.8	59.1	120.6	133.4	109.4
	May	61.6	96.9	109.8	146.5	98.1	59.2	119.5	133.2	109.7
	June	61.3	96.0	109.2	147.9	98.1	58.9	118.4	133.7	113.6
	July	61.7	95.8	110.5	151.1	98.3	58.9	119.0	136.1	113.8
	Aug.	62.3	96.5	110.2	153.3	98.6	59.2	119.5	135.4	113.9
	Sept.	62.2	96.1	109.6	156.0	98.7	59.0	118.9	135.6	115.5
	Oct.	64.6	94.3	109.3	160.9	98.2	58.2	118.3	136.7	121.4
	Nov.	63.4	93.7	109.0	165.6	97.2	58.1	118.7	138.0	123.4
	Dec.	65.2	90.8	112.5	176.1	97.2	56.5	120.9	142.6	124.1
1978	Jan.	66.5	91.2	113.0	177.1	96.4	56.9	121.5	141.7	123.0
	Feb.	65.2	90.3	114.7	188.1	94.0	57.1	124.09	146.0	123.9
	Mar.	61.7	88.5	113.5	186.0	97.8	56.3	123.6	145.5	133.4
	Apr.	61.4	89.8	112.6	178.8	98.3	56.2	122.7	143.0	132.8
	May	64.4	89.6	111.4	182.5	98.8	56.4	121.2	141.3	134.4
	June	61.5	87.1	109.9	183.5	99.6	56.3	120.2	140.5	145.5
	July	62.5	84.7	109.4	191.0	100.8	56.0	119.2	139.6	155.5
	Aug.	62.4	84.4	110.8	201.0	99.8	55.8	119.9	141.9	153.6
	Sept.	62.7	83.7	111.9	211.3	98.9	55.9	120.8	144.1	153.9
	Oct.	63.1	78.9	116.5	208.7	100.8	54.7	125.5	152.5	158.9
	Nov.	62.7	85.3	113.4	191.0	98.0	54.7	123.1	147.4	146.5

Source: *Bank of England Quarterly Bulletin.*

65

4

Factors Affecting Exchange Rates and the Problems Associated with Forecasting Exchange Rates

Since 1971 the introduction of floating exchange rates has added an extra dimension to business decision making. Managers now have to worry about the effect on their profits of a change in a new variable, the exchange rate, changes in which, prior to 1971, occurred infrequently. Reported losses, due to foreign exchange rate movements, have frequently been large enough to affect total earnings substantially and companies have found the changes hard to explain to stockholders and security analysts. Companies which have made foreign exchange losses since 1971 include the following: Imperial Chemical Industries (U.K.), Rio Tinto Zinc (U.K.), Exxon (U.S.), DuPont (U.S.), Firestone Tire and Rubber (U.S.), Sony Corporation (Japan), Svenska Varx (Sweden), Phillips (Netherlands), Deutsche BP (West Germany). The magnitude of losses involved is both large and geographically widespread.

In Chapter 7 the meaning of foreign exchange gains and losses are discussed. Chapters 8 and 9 discuss respectively internal and external methods open to companies to control their foreign exchange exposure. In this chapter some of the factors affecting exchange rates and some of the problems associated with forecasting exchange rates are discussed. The main emphasis is on spot exchange rate variability i.e. rates of exchange for delivery within two working days. The factors affecting the forward market were discussed in Chapter 3 and are further discussed in Chapter 9.

A foreign exchange rate is the price of one currency in terms of another. Unlike most other prices, however, foreign exchange rates serve as the balancing mechanism for the complete spectrum of internationally traded goods, services and capital movements.

Exchange rate forecasts can be made either on the back of an envelope or with the assistance of a computer model. Both techniques require the isolation of the variables (such as the current account of the balance of payments, the rate of inflation, and the rate of change of the money supply), which are considered to exert the greatest influence on exchange rates. The next step is to estimate the future value of these variables and to weight their relative importance. This information can then be used either to develop a judgmental forecast, or to be fed into a computer model from which the desired result can be obtained.

There are advantages and disadvantages in both approaches. The formal method is capable of treating a lot of data and of yielding a specific value for the exchange rate being forecast. Against this, a model is expensive to construct and tends to be rigid. It is also difficult to alter the relationship between existing variables, and to introduce new variables, especially when they are of a random nature (such as a strike).

The virtue of a judgmental forecast is that the variables covered and the importance attached to them can be altered at a moment's notice. However, two drawbacks are present in this approach; it is impossible for an individual to evaluate the same amount of information as a computer; and it is difficult for an individual to convert a qualitative assessment of a number of variables into a quantitative exchange rate forecast.

Forecasting exchange rates can be a frustrating business. There are many reasons why a forecast can go wrong. A mistake can be made in estimating the value of the variables used, and in the relationship between these variables. Moreover, a new development, such as the resumption of central bank intervention in the exchange markets, can be overlooked. These sort of errors can cause a forecast to be out in timing, level, and even in direction. In spite of these shortcomings, a corporate treasurer is likely to obtain a better indication of a currency's future value from a carefully prepared forecast than from a naive extrapolation of past trends.

Extrapolation is bound to yield poor results because the factors influencing exchange rates are constantly changing. A shift from easy to tight money or from current account deficit to surplus can totally transform a currency's prospects.

Since the exchange rate is a price it is determined by supply, demand and stockbuilding. Stocking or destocking occurs when the official authorities intervene to keep exchange rates higher or lower than they would otherwise have been.

Having already seen the advantages of carefully-prepared exchange rate forecasts over extrapolative forecasts the principal factors which influence sellers of foreign currency, buyers of foreign currency, and government intervention policy need to be enumerated. There are four main factors influencing exchange rates, some of which have already been discussed:

(i) Balance of payments.

(ii) Government economic policy.
(iii) Technical and psychological factors.
(iv) International monetary arrangements.

In discussing these factors account will also be taken of two influential theories of exchange rate determination, purchasing power parity theory and the monetary theory of the balance of payments.

THE BALANCE OF PAYMENTS

The need for foreign-exchange transactions arises because goods, services and capital are traded across national boundaries. As discussed in Chapter 2 these three items form a constituent part of a country's balance of payments.

The exchange of goods is recorded by the visible trade account, the exchange of services by the invisible trade account, and the exchange of capital by the capital account. The first two items are commonly joined together to form the current account, and it is the behaviour of this and of the capital account which can cause an exchange rate to alter.

When a country is in current account deficit, that is, when it buys more goods and services abroad than it sells, there will be an excess supply of its currency on the exchange markets. This excess will have to be absorbed either by inflows on capital account or by central bank intervention. The country's exchange rate will fall unless foreign investors are prepared to buy the excess currency at the prevailing rate, or the central bank is willing and able to finance the current account deficit by running down its foreign currency reserves.

The current account is worth including in the forecasting both for its direct effect on exchange rates and for its indirect effect on exchange market expectations. While a current account surplus causes some operators to buy a currency, the rate at which other operators will be willing to satisfy this demand by selling the currency in question depends, among other things, on their view of the future direction of the current account. If the surplus is expected to rise, existing holders will probably be unwilling to sell unless they are offered a higher rate (since they probably expect the exchange rate to move higher in the future). Conversely, if the surplus is expected to fall, existing holders will probably be willing to sell at the existing, or even at a lower, rate.

It is, therefore, the trend rather than the level of the current account which needs to be captured in an exchange-rate forecast. This influence can be incorporated either through a forecast of the current account itself, or through a forecast of the variables which determine the current account.

There are three variables which largely determine the nature of the trade accounts:

(i) relative prices.
(ii) relative incomes.
(iii) degree of response on the part of the public to changes in the first two variables.

The word 'relative' is used because the absolute level of prices or incomes in a country are meaningless unless they are compared with the levels in the countries with which the country trades. Only those prices of goods traded in each country are relevant for comparison. Changes in prices of non-traded goods, such as service industries, affect prices of traded goods only indirectly.

The prices of goods will depend on the interaction of supply and demand. Costs will determine the prices at which different amounts of goods are offered for sale. Two types of costs are payment for labour and payment for capital. The more capital intensive is the production system then, everything else remaining constant, the higher can money wages be without affecting competivity. The existence of trade unions, or poor labour relations, must be taken into account here. Thus the greater the probablity of a strike, the higher costs will be and, if this is in an industry involved in foreign trade, the less competitive a country's exports become. In assessing the trend of future costs, account needs to be taken of trends in labour relations, wage levels and productivity.

As incomes expand, consumption and investment also tend to expand. Given an economy with full resource utilisation this leads to price increases. The impact on the trade account depends on how the increase in demand is channelled. An increased demand completely channelled into consumption increases the amount of goods imported. On the other hand, an increased demand completely channelled into investment, particularly in the export industries, makes these industries more competitive and increases exports. In analysing demand in an economy the role of the government, discussed in a later section (pp 73–79), must be included.

To understand fully the impact of a change in any of the above-mentioned variables on the trade account it is necessary to study the commodity composition of the trade account. The increase in demand for a country's goods, due to an improvement in its international price competitiveness, is predicted by the price elasticity of demand. The more elastic is the demand for a product the more demand for the product will vary as its price changes. Thus, if a country is exporting a price-elastic product and this product rises in price, the greater is the reduction in demand for it. The more inelastic is the demand for a product, the less demand for

69

the product varies as its price changes. In this case, if the price rises, the less is the reduction in demand for it. These same elasticity considerations can be used in analysing income changes.

It is very important to disaggregate the trade account into the major trading partners of the country of interest. Thus, if one country, say the U.S.A, is a major market and there is a recession there, the impact of this on the trade account is clearly much greater than of a recession in a less important economy.

An historical breakdown of the levels of merchandise trade balances from which the trend can be ascertained for the period 1971–1977 is given in Table 4.1.

Table 4.1
Merchandise Trade Balance (1971–1977)
($ million)

Country	1971	1972	1973	1974	1975	1976	1977
Australia	600	2,104	2,785	101	2,217	2,024	923
Austria	− 897	− 1,178	− 1519	− 1,407	− 1,418	− 2,504	− 3,873
Belgium	831	1,015	1,224	879	548	− 873	n/a
Canada	2,789	2,082	2,992	1,939	− 396	1,387	3,020
Denmark	− 711	− 430	− 1,188	− 1,787	− 1,304	− 2,878	− 2,657
France	1,109	1,299	776	− 3,862	1,507	− 4,671	− 2,703
Germany	6,777	8,360	15,467	22,173	17,677	16,675	19,249
Greece	− 1,099	− 1,326	− 2,357	− 2,352	− 2,363	− 2,692	− 3,163
Italy	581	818	− 3,959	− 8,511	− 1,137	− 4,041	n/a
Japan	7,788	8,971	3,686	1,438	5,030	9,890	17,491
Malaysia	225	130	652	387	441	n/a	n/a
Netherlands	− 613	437	998	595	1,301	1,540	n/a
Norway	− 1,458	− 1,015	− 1,533	− 2,336	− 2,911	− 3,572	− 4,094
Singapore	5,010	− 1,103	− 1335	− 2,264	− 2,386	− 2,212	− 1,829
South Africa	− 680	688	1,054	− 46	− 728	− 237	2,569
Spain	− 1,599	− 2,316	− 3,503	− 7,047	− 7,388	− 7,305	− 6,023
Sweden	893	1,211	2,273	607	695	402	253
Switzerland	− 1,186	− 1,269	− 1,685	− 2,109	98	433	81
United Kingdom	882	− 1,491	− 5,441	− 11,745	− 6,547	− 5,972	− 2,814
United States	− 2,267	− 6,418	916	− 5,363	9,051	− 9,320	− 31,237

Source: *IMF International Financial Statistics 1978*

Table 4.2
Net Balance on Services
($ million)

Country	1971	1972	1973	1974	1975	1976	1977
Australia	− 1,276	1,348	1,994	− 2,292	− 2,474	− 3,012	− 3,104
Austria	796	957	1,107	789	930	912	883
Belgium	180	323	242	410	750	377	n/a
Canada	− 2,631	− 2,756	− 3,230	− 4,055	− 4,703	− 6,147	− 7,386
Denmark	343	457	492	649	742	749	626
France	736	637	574	452	1,086	1,077	2,256
Germany	− 2,606	− 3,227	− 5,094	− 6,028	− 6,522	− 5,643	− 7,663
Greece	271	352	429	467	619	789	966
Italy	1,615	1,666	1,991	988	1,234	1,662	n/a
Japan	− 1,739	− 1,882	− 3,508	− 5,344	− 5,357	− 5,871	− 6,062
Malaysia	− 288	− 323	− 485	− 600	− 575	n/a	n/a
Netherlands	509	978	1,402	1,770	998	1,232	n/a
Norway	934	976	1,215	1,321	556	− 18	539
Singapore	− 5,722	591	764	1,199	1,819	1,556	1,324
South Africa	− 854	− 872	− 1,164	− 1,534	− 1,905	− 1,744	− 1,761
Spain	1,688	2,029	2,679	2,671	2,757	1,874	3,642
Sweden	− 501	− 691	− 746	− 1,121	− 1,665	− 2,119	329
Switzerland	1,643	1,993	2,635	2,985	3,183	3,665	4,542
United Kingdom	− 2,228	2,418	4,286	4,356	3,821	4,989	3,102
United States	4,715	4,476	10,083	13,961	13,551	19,373	22,548

Source: *IMF International Financial Statistics. 1978*

To forecast the trade in services the absolute levels and the trends must be ascertained. The most important items in the service account are tourism, shipping, aviation, interest and dividends. The major factors influencing tourists' expenditures are incomes; the richer the population the more they tend to travel. The volume of insurance and freight clearly depends on the marine tradition of the nation concerned. The amount of investment income depends on past investments made by the nation concerned. Some nations, e.g. U.K. and the U.S.A., derive large returns from overseas investments.

An historical breakdown of the absolute levels (from which the trends can be derived) for the net balance on services for twenty given countries during the period 1971 and 1977 is given in Table 4.2

The OECD have charted the trends of current balances for several major economies and have included forecasts for 1979 (*see Figure 4.1*).

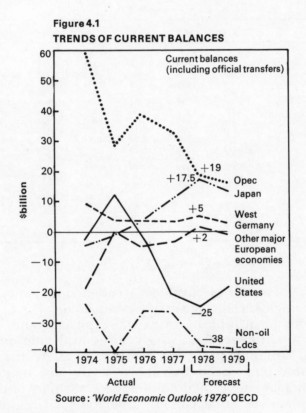

Figure 4.1
TRENDS OF CURRENT BALANCES

Source: '*World Economic Outlook 1978*' OECD

A good current account forecast is no guarantee of a good exchange rate forecast. The reason is fairly obvious. Exchange rates are also influenced by capital movements. When currencies are floating freely, a current account surplus (or deficit) must be offset by a capital account deficit (or surplus). The problem facing the forecaster is that of determining how much, if at all, the exchange rate will have to move to bring forth these off-setting capital flows.

It has already been suggested that the expected trend on current account is one of the factors international money-managers consider when buying or selling a currency. However, the capital account is subject to many other influences. The performance of equity markets both at home and abroad determines the net flow of portfolio investment and comparative business conditions and industrial rates of return determine the net flow of direct investment.

The overall net capital flows in twenty major countries between 1971 and 1977 can be seen in Table 4.3.

Table 4.3.
Net Capital Flows
($ million)

Country	1971	1972	1973	1974	1975	1976	1977
Australia	480	2,174	− 818	974	− 352	− 1,055	− 1,507
Austria	− 265	− 179	156	853	1,537	1,451	2,641
Belgium	− 551	− 798	− 239	−544	− 172	−302	n/a
Canada	352	598	573	1,564	4,322	4,787	2,670
Denmark	602	154	910	543	448	1,849	2,445
France	2,760	1,342	− 1,204	5,589	3,508	3,276	3,386
Germany	3,744	4,200	4,906	10,442	4,871	− 483	881
Greece	523	897	1,187	1,072	904	953	1,403
Italy	− 621	−2,275	2,313	3,427	− 2,123	2,538	n/a
Japan	4,471	3,757	− 6,192	5,934	92	120	− 4,543
Malaysia	171	275	118	469	249	n/a	n/a
Netherlands	319	− 425	− 1,619	− 1,078	− 1,341	− 2,086	n/a
Norway	828	198	608	1,167	2,855	3,760	4,812
Singapore	1,044	847	984	1,400	1,012	1,002	849
South Africa	978	803	62	1,289	1,919	1,141	− 876
Spain	669	867	761	2,526	2,670	3,197	2,725
Sweden	30	165	− 367	169	3,083	1,928	1,337
Switzerland	1,117	366	98	260	− 1,064	−518	− 2,947
United Kingdom	3,548	− 3,913	2,566	5,462	3,675	605	13,780
United States	− 29,046	− 5,095	− 12,248	− 9,989	− 22,396	− 15,176	− 21,422

Source: *IMF International Financial Statistics, 1978.*

The U.K. balance of payments accounts differ from those in International Financial Statistics because in the U.K. there are transfers from the invisible balance to the capital account.

The following section, which deals with the impact of government economic policy on exchange rates, discusses factors affecting the capital account in more detail. One of the major problems in analysing capital flows is the availability of the actual capital account data. Some countries, notably the U.K., the U.S.A. and West Germany publish very detailed historical capital account data while others, notably Switzerland and Italy, produce very scant information. Often, moreover, there is a long time lag before information comes available for analysis.

GOVERNMENT ECONOMIC POLICY

Governments are committed to several objectives. These include increasing the growth rate of the economy, full employment, price stability and improving the balance of payments. The problem is that policies designed to solve one problem may have adverse effects on other problems. Three major policies are available to the goverment to achieve their objectives; these are: (i) monetary policy. (ii) fiscal policy. (iii) other policies such as price controls. All these policies affect the balance of payments and thus the exchange rate. Table 4.4 summarises the effect on other economic objectives of policies designed to solve particular problems; the effect on the exchange rate can be observed from the last column.

Table 4.4

Effect of Government Policies on the Exchange Rate

Problem	Prescription to attack problem	Impact on other economic objectives	Exchange rate
1. High unemployment	Expansionary monetary and fiscal policy	*Price levels:* inflationary trends, *External balance:* deterioration; import increase	Downward pressure
2. High inflation	Contractionary monetary and fiscal policy	*Employment:* tendency to decrease as aggregate demand declines *External balance:* improvement imports decrease,	Upward pressure
3. Balance of payments deficit	Contractionary monetary and fiscal policy	*Employment:* tendency to decrease as aggregate demand declines *Inflation:* tendency to decrease as aggregate demand declines	Upward pressure
4. Balance of payments surplus	Expansionary monetary and fiscal policy	*Employment:* tendency to increase as aggregate demand increases *Inflation:* tendency to increase as aggregate demand increases	Downward pressure

Source: adapted from H. Riehl and R.M. Rodriguez *A Guide to Foreign Currency Operations.* McGraw Hill, 1978

If the government decides that its major problem is unemployment and decides to eliminate this by expansionary economic policy, the effect is to raise prices, stimulate imports and place downward pressure on the exchange rate. High inflation can be counteracted by a contractionary economic policy. This increases unemployment, reduces imports and places upward pressure on the exchange rate. A balance of payments deficit may also be counteracted by a contractionary economic policy. Again, unemployment rises and the rate of inflation falls, placing upward pressure on the exchange rate. Finally, a balance of payments surplus can be counteracted by an expansionary monetary and fiscal policy. This raises employment, imports and inflation and places downward pressure on the exchange rate. It must be stressed that it is via the effect of inflation on traded goods that the exchange rate is affected. Changes in macro-economic policy also tend to have an immediate impact on the exchange rate via the expectation that they will affect the balance of payments.

As is evident from Table 4.4 there may be a dilemma for governments. If high unemployment exists, the solution to this (i.e. reflation) weakens the exchange rate. If at the same time high inflation exists the solution to this (i.e. deflation strengthens the exchange rate. This dilemma has been resolved by directly changing the country's exchange rate. The combination of high unemployment and a balance of payments deficit, with the government placing equal priority on these problems, is resolved by the policy of reflation and devaluation. Similarly, if high inflation corresponds with a balance of payments surplus, the traditional policy solution indicates deflation and revaluation.

Mundell has shown that two expenditure policies, e.g. fiscal and monetary policy, can indeed suffice to maintain both internal equilibrium (full employment without inflation) and external balance, provided only that they do not have identical effects[1]. For any given expenditure reduction, one policy must improve the balance of payments more than the other (or for a given balance of payments improvement, one policy must achieve less expenditure reduction than the other). The particular case considered by Mundell is where (for a given expenditure reduction) monetary and fiscal policy have the same effect on the balance of trade but, in addition, a rise in the interest rate encourages capital inflows and so improves the capital account. He argues specifically that monetary policy ought to be aimed at external objectives and fiscal policy at internal objectives. The practical implications of this theory are that a surplus country experiencing inflationary pressure should ease monetary conditions and raise taxes (or reduce government spending), and that a deficit country suffering from unemployment should tighten interest rates and lower taxes (or increase government spending). His critics would argue that his analysis fails to recognise the importance of 'lags'. Thus the ability of the authorities to change expenditure quickly with fiscal policy is limited. By the time the policy has its effect the nature of the problem may have changed.

Factors affecting the capital account are similar to those affecting investment. Thus direct investment overseas may be for raw materials, cheaper production costs or to increase the size of the available market. Capital flows will depend on expected levels of profit and political stability. Portfolio investment and short-term capital flows depend on the relative returns, a combination of interest yield and exchange risk on these investments, again tied in with political considerations.

Isolating and then estimating all the variables which influence the capital account is virtually impossible. It is for this reason that forecasters often focus their attention on just one variable, namely, the interest rate differential between two currencies. Interest rates can be important in motivating short-term capital movements, and can, by influencing factors such as equity prices, also influence some long-term capital flows.

By appraising the interest rate differential between assets in two major currencies, in conjunction with an expectation about the spot rate, a rational decision can be made as to which currency to hold. If the interest rate on three-month sterling deposits is 11.3 per cent, as it was at the beginning of September 1976, and the interest rate on equivalent euro-dollars is 5.6 per cent an investor who expected the sterling spot rate to decline by 5.7 per cent per annum over the three months (i.e. 1.4 per cent) would have been indifferent between dollars and sterling. If he thought the pound might either rise, or else fall by less than 1.4 per cent, he would hold sterling. It would follow from such behaviour that interest-rate differentials between major centres must exert an influence on spot rates of exchange, and therefore, that governments which are prepared to use domestic money-market rates of interest in a flexible way, in accord with exchange rate objectives, can in this way exert some degree of control over their exchange rates. This means then that a government may raise interest rates (to widen any positive differential over e.g. dollar interest rates) in order to support its exchange rate, or reduce them in order to lower its exchange rate.

A suitable interest-rate differential can sometimes prevent an exchange rate change recommended by other developments. Consider the case of two countries A and B in current account balance, each with the same rate of interest, of for example, 5 per cent. Assuming that the rate of inflation accelerates in country A and that this leads the foreign exchange market to anticipate current account deterioration and, in consequence, a 4 per cent fall in the exchange rate. In this case, funds will be transferred from country A to country B until A's exchange rate has fallen by the anticipated amount. However, country A will be able to prevent this outflow if it offers arbritagists sufficiently high interest rate to compensate them for their anticipated exchange loss. The appropriate interest rate in this example would be 9 per cent.

Relatively high interest rates provide more support to a currency expected to fall gradually over a long period than to one expected to fall sharply over a short period. If country A's currency is expected to fall by 1 per cent per quarter, arbitragists will be willing to maintain a three-month deposit in this country, so long as they are offered an interest rate of 9 per cent per annum (when similar deposits in country B are quoted at 5 per cent per annum). A 4 per cent per annum interest differential is equal to 1 per cent per quarter, which is equal to the expected exchange rate loss. However, if the exchange rate is expected to drop by 4 per cent in a quarter, the three-month interest rate in country A will have to rise to 21 per cent per annum in order to protect depositors (21 per cent per annum less 5 per cent per annum is equal to 16 per cent per annum, which is 4 per cent per quarter). Such a sharp rise, even if it is only for a short period, may be rejected by country A for domestic reasons. If it is, the exchange rate will fall during the three-month period in question.

Where interest rates do not rise sufficiently to encourage arbitragists to finance a country's current-account deficit at the existing exchange rate, one of two consequences ensue; either the exchange rate must fall until the foreign exchange market is prepared to buy the currency in question, or the central bank must finance the deficit by running down its foreign currency reserves. This suggests another variable which needs to be recognised in an exchange rate forecast, namely the level of central bank intervention. This topic is discussed in more detail in a later section (pp 82–83). Central bank intervention can upset the timing, if not the direction, of a forecast. Intervention can prevent a strong currency from rising and a weak one from falling, but not for an indefinite period. This is because the ability of a central bank to resist an exchange rate change warranted by the underlying economic situation is limited for the following reasons. Persistent intervention to prevent a currency from falling eventually depletes a country's exchange reserves; and persistent intervention to stop a currency from rising eventually leads to an unacceptable expansion in domestic money supply. The first reason forced the Bank of England to retreat from the exchange market in 1976 (when there was downward pressure on sterling) and the second reason persuaded it to retreat in 1977 (when there was upward pressure on sterling).

Monetary policy has become an increasingly important economic tool. Monetary policy differs from fiscal policy in that total control over it is not always in the hands of government. The degree of independence possessed by the central banks of the ten major European and the Federal Reserve varies greatly. It depends on:(i) the method of appointment of governors (ii) the length of time for which they serve (iii) whether they have legislated objectives clear enough to be a barrier to government interference and (iv) whether their constitutions provide the bank or the government with the final authority for monetary policy.

In practice, central banks may have rather less, or rather more, freedom than their statutes suggest; but this is likely to depend not only on tradition but also on the personalities involved.

Of the ten major European economies, only two central banks (Switzerland and West Germany) are clearly endowed with final authority for monetary policy, and have governors not directly appointed by the government. Only Holland has a clearly defined economic objective (price stability) built into its constitution. On no other score could it be accounted independent. The others, including the world's two oldest central banks, the Sveriges Riksbank (1668) and the Bank of England (1694) are clearly subservient to their governments in the formation of monetary policy, if not in the day-to-day management of it.

But wherever final monetary authority rests, its ultimate objective is some balance between restraint of inflation and the encouragement of expansion. Fiscal policy aims at this same target by determining the levels of taxation and public expenditure and monetary policy by influencing either the amount of credit available in the economy, or its cost. The central bank cannot fix both the amount of credit and its cost independently. If it wants to restrain the growth in the money supply it must allow interest rates to rise as much as necessary; if it wants to keep interest rates low, it must accept the consequences in terms of monetary growth.

So, in effect, the central bank must choose between two intermediary targets: interest rates or monetary aggregates. Most of the ten major European economies have targets for their monetary aggregates; some of these are outlined in Table 4.5:

Table 4.5
Monetary targets

	Official or semi-official target(%)		
	1978	1977	1976
Britain	8-12	9-13	—
France	12	$12\frac{1}{2}$	14
West Germany	8	8	8
Italy	18-19	—	—
Spain	17	21	17-21
Switzerland	5	5	6

In 1974 the U.S. Federal Reserve announced the setting of interim targets for the growth of selected monetary aggregates. These became more formalised and publicly recognised when the

Federal Reserve promulgated long-run growth targets in 1975. The interim targets, or 'short-run tolerance ranges' (as they are officially called) were determined for the money supply, both narrowly defined as M1 (demand deposits plus currency in the hands of the public) and M2 (broadly defined as M1 plus time and savings deposits of commercial banks excluding certificates of deposit). These targets were in terms of two-month annual rates of change from the month preceding the monthly meeting of the Federal Open Market Committee. The Committee also sets a range for the Federal Funds Rate, i.e. the rate charged on overnight loans of excess reserves within the US banking system during these periods. The long-run growth targets are determined quarterly and

Figure 4.2

OFFICIAL INTERIM TARGETS AND ACTUAL SUPPLY GROWTH RATES AND THE FEDERAL FUNDS RATE

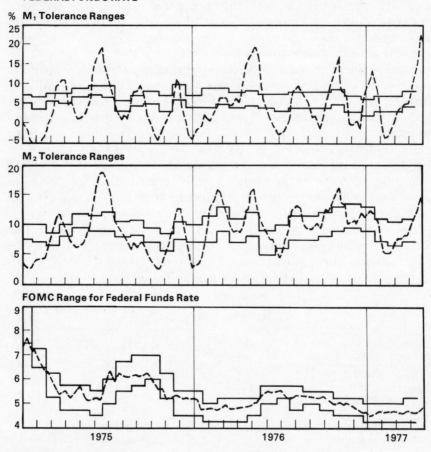

— FOMC interim target ranges.

-- Represents annualized growth rates during latest four-week period for M1 and M2; for Federal funds rate represents weekly average effective Federal funds rate.

Source: 'US Federal Reserve' 1977.

span a yearly period from the most recent quarter to the corresponding quarter in the next year. Official growth paths are now set for M1, M2, M3 (M2 plus savings deposits of thrift institutions) and the credit proxy (deposit liabilities of commercial banks). Figure 4.2 charts official interim targets and actual money supply growth rates and the Federal Funds Rate up to mid-1977.

The introduction of money-supply targets has had a very significant impact on the foreign exchange market. If the money supply is controlled and inflation is reduced, this strengthens the exchange rate. However, as soon as expectations build up that the actual money-supply targets will not be met, this weakens the exchange rate. Thus the central bank must always be willing to raise interest rates when faced with money-supply growth higher than the targeted range. Faced with expectations of future interest rate rises capital inflows may be delayed. In the UK expectations of interest-rate rises reduce the demand for fixed coupon stocks, such as gilt-edged securities, and this in turn weakens the authorities' ability to control the money supply.

The importance of government economic policy in influencing the exchange rate can clearly be discerned. In order to forecast its impact it is necessary to understand two factors: firstly, the likely response of government to changing economic conditions; and secondly, the eventual effect of these policies on the foreign exchange market.

TECHNICAL AND PSYCHOLOGICAL FACTORS

Charles Coombs, former Senior Vice-President of the Federal Reserve Bank, whilst responsible for U.S. Treasury and Federal Reserve operations in the gold and foreign exchange markets, described the foreign exchange market in the following terms:

> By its very nature, the foreign exchange market is a nervous, high risk, ultra-sensitive mechanism primarily geared to short-term developments. Of the tens of billions of dollars in daily transactions cleared through the market, only a fraction derive from such fundamental factors as foreign trade and long-term investment. On a day-to-day basis, the market is instead dominated by short-term capital movements in search of a quick profits or a hedge against exchange rate risks. For months at a time, short-term interest rate differentials between New York and Europe can have a far more decisive effect on exchange rates than do current trade figures.
>
> In such an international market traders are exposed to all the political and economic winds that blow from every quarter of the world. And as exchange rates move in response to the chattering stimulus of news ticker reports, there is an ever present risk that a rate movement in one direction will suddenly become cumulative. The market is characterised by sudden shifts of sentiment that send traders scurrying for cover and violently distort supply and demand relationships[2].

Coombs is arguing that movements in the trade figures and capital account figures determine the behaviour of a currency over

79

a long period of time. However, operators in the markets are very sensitive to short-term psychological and technical reactions which may reverse temporarily the basic longer-term trend of exchange rates. As Keynes once remarked about stock markets (and beauty contests): 'it is not the objective facts but the way the majority of market operators act which shapes the demand and supply in financial markets'.

Expectations have a crucial role to play in exchange rate determination. Whenever there is a discrepancy between the previously held expectation of a given economic event and the actual outcome of that event, exchange rates are usually affected. As already argued, a trade-account surplus causes pressure towards an exchange rate appreciation. However, if the actual reported surplus turns out to be less than the expected outcome this may cause downward pressure on a currency.

Technical factors can also affect exchange rates. Some currencies tend to move together. Examples of this are the Swiss franc with the Deutschemark and the Austrian schilling with the Deutschemark. Thus market operators know that if one currency rises in value, then, in order to maintain the relationship the other currency will follow suit. Thus a rise in the dollar/Swiss franc rate will be followed by a rise in the dollar/Deutschemark rate and vice versa.

Another technical factor is that some currencies are used as world reserve currencies. These currencies are held as a store of value as well as a medium of exchange. Participants in the foreign exchange market who hold, e.g. the dollar, as a store of value may react very nervously to expectations that in the short run the dollar is expected to fall while in the medium term the fundamentals are in the dollar's favour. Since these arbitragists may need to convert their funds at short notice it is not surprising that fears of capital losses worry them. It is not much use to them to be told the market is over-reacting. An example of this took place in July 1978 when there was heavy downward pressure on the dollar and upward pressure on the yen. It was meaningless to explain that the difference between Japan's inflation (retail prices up 3.5 per cent on 1977) and that of the U.S.A. (7–8 per cent) was not enough to justify a dollar worth less than 200 yen.

A related technical influence operates along the following lines. Assume that for various reasons there are numerous market sellers of sterling for Deutschemarks. The market for sterling against Deutschemarks is not so well developed as the markets for pounds sterling against U.S. dollars and for Deutschemarks against U.S. dollars. Therefore, in order to get the most favourable exchange rate the sellers first sell sterling for dollars and then sell dollars for Deutschemarks. The first effect of this is that sterling weakens against the dollar. If the Bank of England then buys sterling in order to stabilise the rate the dollar will strengthen less against sterling than it would have done if the rate had purely reflected supply and demand. At the end of the transaction the sellers of sterling will have obtained their Deutschemarks by using the dollar acting as a vehicle currency.

However, this is not the end of the story. It is unlikely that the German authorities presented with a demand for the Deutschemark will intervene in the market, as this would enable the speculators to buy Deutschemarks at a preferential rate. Instead, the rate will be allowed to adjust to the demand for the Deutschemark, thus weakening the dollar against the Deutschemark. Thus the selling of sterling against Deutschemarks has, due to the intervention of the Bank of England and the absence of support for the dollar, caused the dollar to weaken. If this weakening is noticed and misinterpreted by other market participants, although completely without justification, further pressures may develop against the dollar. The adjustment of the dollar/Deutschemark rate was purely technical and did not indicate a fundamental reason for the dollar to weaken.

Thus technical and psychological factors can have significant effects on exchange rates. These considerations can be in line with underlying fundamentals but can be opposed to them. Participants in the market have to decide whether a movement contrary to the basic trend is of a temporary nature, or whether this movement is the beginning of a change in the basic long-term trend.

THE INTERNATIONAL MONETARY SYSTEM

Having examined alternative exchange rate arrangements in Chapter 2 this section examines the implications of the international monetary system on the forecasting of exchange rates.

Between 1946 and 1971 the international monetary system was one of fixed exchange rates. The monetary authorities pledged, in the form of an agreement with the IMF, to maintain exchange rates within small margins around a target rate, called the 'par value.' This 'par value' might be changed whenever a country's balance of payments moved into fundamental disequilibrium and after it became clear that various alternative policies such as internal deflation and/or controls were ineffective and/or politically not feasible.

Forecasting exchange rates in this environment consisted essentially of a three-step procedure. Firstly, from an examination of a country's balance of payments trends and other fundamentals, such as relative rates of inflation and trade flows, a measure of the pressure on a currency was derived. Secondly, changes in the level of foreign exchange reserves (including borrowing facilities) of the central bank indicated when a situation would become critical. Finally, there was the crucial step of predicting which of the rather limited policy options the economic decision makers of a nation would resort to in the crisis, ie, reinforced attempts at internal deflation, intervention and exchange controls, devaluation or some combination of these policies.

The success or failure of the forecasting game depended on the final step. The difficulty in this was considerably eased by the fact that those who decided on devaluations and revaluations were, unlike private transactors, not guided by profit-maximising objectives. The motives of monetary authorities comprised the full spectrum from national prestige and domestic partisan politics to fears of post-devaluation inflationary pressures or post-revaluation unemployment. One particularly pleasant feature about this era of exchange-rate forecasting for the foreign exchange market was that the downside risk of actions taken on the basis of such forecasts was limited; either the exchange moved in the generally expected direction, or the central bank managed to hold it steady. Thus the risk of making a loss was virtually zero while the possibility of making a gain was quite high.

However, since 1971 the objectives of monetary authorities in their intervention policies have become less clear making the final step very difficult to predict. Kreinin has outlined several objectives of official intervention, namely:

(i) 'Neutral' intervention, designed to smooth out short-run exchange fluctuations, without interfering with long-run trends. Canada pursued such a policy in the 1950s, with the objective of improving the operations of the foreign exchange market. In practical terms such an objective implied that there would be no net change in the countries' reserve position in either direction over a certain given period, such as three months.

(ii) Intervention to offset or moderate the effect of political and economic 'shocks', or non-recurring events, such as the Watergate scandal, a prolonged general strike, or a drought.

(iii) Intervention to offset seasonal and cyclical movements in the trade balance. Many observers believe that such movements are usually well anticipated by the exchange market.

(iv) Extensive intervention to maintain rates consistent with long-run basic balance. In its extreme form such a rule would imply unlimited intervention, and it is based on the supposition that the authorities are a better judge than the market of the long-run equilibrium exchange rate.

82

(v) Intervention to adjust the volume or composition of official reserves. It is usually suggested that such intervention should be limited, and care should be taken that the exchange value of any of the intervention-reserve currencies is not unduly affected in the process.

(vi) Intervention to maintain joint floats or pegged currencies. If such intervention employs only the jointly-floating currencies, its effects on the exchange value of third currencies will be neutral. But if it is undertaken in third currencies, the value of the latter can be affected. For example, if the Belgian franc is supported within the 'snake' by the sale of dollars (rather than Deutschemarks) out of Belgian reserves, the entire joint float would be supported against the dollar. The same consideration applies to the pegging of one currency to another, especially if the pegged currency is a major one[3].

With effect from 1 April 1978, the Second Amendment to the IMF'S Articles of Agreement came into effect. This involves the following significant provisions. Firstly, a member country shall avoid manipulating exchange rates in order to prevent effective balance of payments adjustments, or to gain an unfair competitive advantage over other members. Secondly, a member should intervene in the exchange market, if necessary, to counter disorderly conditions which may be characterised, *intèr alia,* by disruptive short-term movements in the exchange value of its currency. Thirdly, members should take into account, in their intervention policies, the interests of other members, including those of the countries in whose currencies they intervene.

Clearly, forecasting intervention points in the post-1971 situation is a much more complicated procedure than it was in the pre-1971 situation.

Two constraints involving exchange rate intervention have already been mentioned. If an exchange rate is supported at too high a level, eventually the authorities will run out of reserves. Thus, unless these can be replenished by further borrowing there will be pressure for the rate to fall eventually. Similarly, if an exchange rate is fixed at too low a level this will be inflationary. If the foreign exchange market is continually buying, for example, Deutschemarks in exchange for dollars, the Bundesbank in supplying these Deutschemarks is in fact increasing the German money supply and fuelling future inflation. Unless effectively neutralised, the rising money supply will lower the external value of the currency and reduce the demand for it. Clearly, there are automatic forces which may eventually reduce the need for future intervention.

FORECASTING EXCHANGE RATES BY USING ONE SINGLE VARIABLE

Forecasting exchange rates by incorporating the various items already mentioned is a cumbersome process and is also prone to error in view of the number of variables which need to be estimated. It is for this reason that some forecasters prefer to base their predictions on a single variable. Three particular variables have been singled out:

(i) the forward exchange rate.

(ii) the rate of inflation via the concept of purchasing power parity.

(iii) the relative money supply via the international monetary theory of the balance of payments.

Use of the forward rate as a forecaster of future spot rates is discussed further in Chapters 3 and 9. The other two variables will be discussed in this chapter.

PURCHASING POWER PARITY

The theory of purchasing power parity was put forward by Gustav Cassel at the end of the First World War[4]. The purchasing power parity theory states that the exchange rate between two countries will reflect the relative buying power of the respective currencies. An example will clarify this. Assume a motorcycle costs £500 in the U.K. and $1,500 in the U.S.A. If the current rate of exchange is $3 = £1, the motorcycle will cost the same in either country, and the exchange rate reflects purchasing power parity. If however, the exchange rate moved until £1 was worth only $2, it would be cheaper for an American to buy a motorcycle in England because he could then buy it for $1,000 (ignoring transport costs). Assuming flexible prices, as the demand for motorcycles increased in the U.K. the price would rise and, as the demand for motorcycles in the U.S.A. declined, their price would fall. With the increase in demand by Americans for U.K. motorcycles there would be an increase in the demand for sterling, which in turn, would raise the value of the pound and reduce the value of the dollar. This whole process would continue until exchange rates again reflected purchasing power parity.

Purchasing power parity theory is, therefore, an hypothesis about the equilibrium relationship between an exchange rate and a corresponding relative price index; it rests on the notion that the exchange rate and relative price index cannot diverge from their proportionate equilibrium relationship without setting in motion corrective forces that will act to restore equilibrium.

Two requirements are necessary to produce an exchange rate forecast under this approach. First, a base period when purchasing power parity existed between two countries, or when domestic price levels were equal when measured in a common currency, has to be established. Secondly, a run of actual and forecast inflation rates for the two countries in question must be obtained. Taking the exchange rate for the base period and adjusting it for any subsequent inflation differential allows a specific value for the exchange rate to be projected over future periods.

Purchasing power parity is, however, subject to several limitations, one of which is that changes in domestic prices need not cause a change in exchange rates because many goods are not traded internationally. Another criticism is that indirect taxes and tariffs make exchange rates deviate from purchasing power parity. Also, transport and other transactions costs, such as high information costs involved in finding the cheapest products, leave room for large purchasing power disparities. A further problem with the theory is that a country's trade balance responds slowly to the over- or under-valuation of its currency.

Considerations other than price can also affect competitiveness. There are two broad aspects of non-price competitiveness. The first is the act of selling the goods, which includes the amount of advertising undertaken, whether to use agents or subsidiaries, the frequency and length of visits by salesmen to markets and their customer contact. The second aspect concerns the product itself, e.g. its design or fashion, ease of maintenance and operation, quality (including reliability and technical specification), delivery time, and after sales service.

Proponents of the theory often leave vague, or disagree over, which ratio of price indices should be compared with the exchange rate. Such vagueness and disagreement reflects the lack of a satisfactory model of the corrective forces that might prevent the exchange rate from diverging persistently from a proportionate relationship with an appropriate ratio of price indices. Another severe drawback with the theory as a forecasting tool is that it assumes causality runs from prices to the exchange rate and not the other way round. For some commodities, e.g. copper, it is clear that movements in the exchange rate determine the domestic price and not vice versa. Thus a movement away from the theory may imply a disequilibrium price level not a disequilibrium spot rate. The monetary theory of exchange rate determination has the advantage that it can handle causality from money to the spot exchange rate and then to prices or, alternatively, from money to the price level and then to the spot exchange rate.

The outcome of these criticisms is that the theory is useful in indicating the long-term trend in a currency rather than in predicting exchange rates over a period as short as a year. As can be seen from Figure 4.3 if the theory had been used to forecast the sterling/dollar exchange rate since 1960 one would have discovered that purchasing power parity predicted the underlying trend far better than its level in any given year. Brillembourg has made a survey of the empirical validity of the theory[5].

Figure 4.3

PURCHASING POWER PARITY AS A FORECASTING TECHNIQUE OF THE STERLING/DOLLAR EXCHANGE RATE

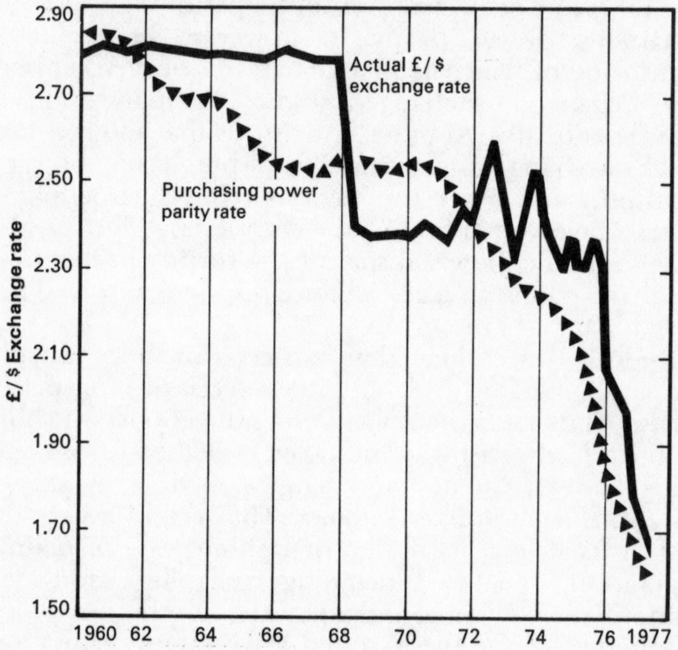

Source: 'The Guardian' 17 July 1978.

THE MONETARY THEORY OF EXCHANGE RATE DETERMINATION

The international monetary theory of exchange rate determination is an old-idea, with Ricardo being an early exponent. The theory, which has seen a resurgence in the 1970s can be applied to either fixed or flexible exchange rates. Suppose that the authorities in some country on fixed exchange rates increase the rate of monetary expansion; assuming that the economy is small and fully employed, individuals now find themselves with excess money balances. They will attempt to exchange them for goods and financial assets, i.e. aggregate demand will increase. Individuals in the country which has increased its rate of monetary expansion will, since the economy is fully employed, eliminate their excess money balances through the balance of payments, that is by exchanging them for foreign goods and securities. Thus as a result of the increase in its rate of monetary expansion the country will develop a balance of payments deficit which in turn will lead to a reduction in its foreign reserves.

In the opposite situation, when the money supply, or its rate of growth, is reduced, individuals and firms find that their real balances are below the desired level. They will, therefore, attempt to accumulate money balances. They can do so by exchanging goods for money balances from abroad, that is, the country will develop a balance of payments surplus.

Thus, under a system of fixed exchange rates, national monetary authorities lose control over the rate of expansion of their nominal money supply. Their freedom is limited to the ability to choose the level of foreign exchange reserves they desire to hold. If they want to increase their holdings of reserves they must reduce the rate of monetary expansion, and vice versa if they find that their foreign exchange reserves are in excess of the desired level.

Assume, in this case, that the economy under consideration is fully employed and that its government abstains from operations in the foreign exchange market, i.e. the country in question operates a system of flexible exchange rates. Now suppose that the rate of monetary expansion increases. This leads to an increase in the amount of real cash balances that individuals and firms hold. They now hold a volume of real cash balances in excess of that which they desire. Their response is to attempt to eliminate their excess cash balances. They will, therefore, try to exchange their excess cash balances for other assets, as well as for goods and services. Thus aggregate demand in the economy will increase. Producers cannot increase their output. Responding to the increase in the demand for their goods and services, they will attempt to hire additional labour to expand their production; but if the economy is already fully employed, all they achieve is to raise wages. Thus the excess demand created by the expansion in the money supply leads to a rise of prices and wages. As prices rise the real value of cash balances held falls. Prices rise until the excess real cash balances are eliminated with individuals now holding the desired level of cash balances. If the rate of monetary expansion is maintained at its new higher level prices will continue to rise, i.e. inflation will emerge.

However, an increase in domestic price inflation will not be the only consequence of the rise in the rate of monetary expansion. When individuals and firms attempt to eliminate their excess money balances they do so partly by offering, say, sterling, in exchange for goods produced abroad and for foreign financial securities. This increase in the supply of sterling in the foreign exchange market leads to a fall in the price of sterling in terms of all other currencies, assuming that the demand for the U.K. currency has not correspondingly increased. If the higher rate of monetary expansion is maintained, the international value of sterling will continuously fall. Thus an increase in the rate of growth of the money supply will lead to inflation and a falling international value for the currency in a fully employed economy on flexible exchange rates.

The outcome is that, if the money supply is higher than the money demand under fixed exchange rates, reserves fall and under flexible exchange rates the exchange rate falls until money supply equals money demand. A falling exchange rate raises domestic prices and increases the demand for cash balances. If the money supply is lower than the money demand under fixed exchange rates, reserves rise and under flexible rates the exchange rate rises. A rising exchange rate lowers domestic prices and reduces the demand for cash balances. Again the process stops when money supply equals money demand.

The encouraging aspect about this approach is the way in which it analyses exchange rate changes within the context of the overall balance of payments. The theory recognises that a country with a large current account surplus can experience downward pressure on its exchange rate when its money supply is growing too fast; and that a country with a large current account deficit can experience upward pressure on its exchange rate, when its money supply is growing too slowly. This follows because excessive or deficient growth in cash balances can be eliminated by a movement on current account or capital account, or by a combination of the two.

The monetary theory has to be used carefully in a world characterised not by full employment but by unemployment. If there are free resources, monetary expansion can stimulate output and increase employment without necessarily producing inflation. The rise in national income might adversely affect the current account as imports are encouraged but the effect is likely to be moderate. An exchange-rate forecaster using the monetary theory must make an assessment, when attempting to predict the exchange rate movements, of whether a monetary expansion will raise output or prices.

In practice the situation is somewhat easier. If the economy is depressed, inflation will be moderating and the exchange rate will be reflecting this. The monetary expansion will reduce the tendency for inflation to drop even if the full impact is on output. Thus a monetary expansion produces downward pressure on the exchange rate even if the economy is depressed.

There are two major problems with the theory. Firstly, it is necessary to obtain accurate estimates of the future demand for money and supply of money. Secondly, given the existence of a world of managed floating exchange rates (*see Chapter 5*) it becomes necessary to estimate the extent to which a monetary imbalance is corrected by a change in the reserves or by a change in the exchange rate or by both.

References

1. R.A. Mundell, 'The appropriate use of monetary and fiscal policy for Internal and External stability.' *I.M.F. Staff Papers* (March 1962).
2. C.A. Coombs, *The Arena of International Finance*. John Wiley and Sons. 1976. pp. 14–15.
3. M.A. Kreinin, 'Living with floating exchange rates. A survey of developments, 1973–1977.' *Journal of World Trade Law*. December 1977.
4. G. Cassel, *Money and foreign exchanges after 1914*. Hartley Withers. London 1922.
5. A. Brillembourg, 'Purchasing power parity and the balance of payments.' *I.M.F. Staff Papers*. March 1977.

5

The International Monetary System from 1945 to the Present

REQUIREMENTS OF AN INTERNATIONAL MONETARY SYSTEM

The international monetary environment within which international companies operate must be designed to achieve three basic objectives. Firstly, it must provide a payment instrument for companies. Secondly, it must provide a mechanism for changing exchange rates when necessary. Thirdly, it must provide a means of providing adequate reserves, so enabling countries to withstand speculative attacks on their exchange rates.

Given the usage of various currencies in different countries a means of enabling an exporter or importer to convert one currency into another currency has to be achieved. The currency needed may be obtained directly or indirectly. Thus it may be easy for an importer in Italy to obtain pounds sterling for lire. However, an Italian importing from Sweden may find it difficult or more expensive to buy Swedish Kroner and may prefer to first buy dollars for lire and then to sell the dollars for Swedish Kroner. The foreign exchange market provides this payment mechanism.

Exchange rate adjustment is necessary, given a world with differing rates of inflation, in order to achieve adjustment in the balance of payments. Various solutions for exchange rate adjustment, many already mentioned in earlier chapters, have been evolved. Firstly, there is the system of adjustment in quantities. Foreign exchange demand comes from importers and for the desire for foreign investment. Foreign exchange supply comes from exporters and from a desire for foreigners to invest in the home country. In order to achieve a balance between supply and demand the central bank intervenes by utilising its foreign exchange reserves or by foreign currency borrowing. This is the fixed exchange rate system. Secondly, there is the system of adjustment in prices. A foreign exchange rate is the price of one currency in terms of another. If, *ceteris paribus,* the amount of domestic currency being supplied for foreign currency by importers exceeds the amount of domestic currency being demanded for foreign currency by exporters, then the domestic exchange rate falls, and vice versa. This is the floating exchange rate system. Thirdly, there are administrative systems of adjustment. Three types of these exist. Firstly, there may be a system of multiple exchange rates. Under this system foreign exchange is allocated by selling it at different prices to importers of different products or to persons making payment abroad for different purposes. It might be sold relatively cheaply, for example, to pay for imports officially considered 'essential' or for goods being imported by agencies of the government. For transactions considered less worthy of encouragement, such as 'luxury' imports, travel, investment abroad, foreign exchange might be sold at a relatively high price. A relative simple multiple rate system, that of the split or dual market, was formerly adopted in Belgium and Luxembourg in 1971. France adopted the system in 1971 and Italy in early 1973, both abolishing it in 1974. In principle, capital transactions, especially short-term capital transactions, were confined to a 'financial market' where supply and demand might establish a different rate than that which prevailed on the 'commercial market'. The rate differential was supposed to discourage officially undesired capital inflows or outflows while allowing trade transactions to take place at a rate acceptable to, or even pegged by, the authorities. The U.K. has the oldest and most successful (as measured by the differences between the exchange rates) dual exchange rate system (the investment currency market).

The second administrative system is that of exchange controls, (see *Chapter 3*). Exchange control may be defined as a system of regulations designed to assure both that foreign exchange coming into the possession of residents of the controlling country is sold in official channels and that this foreign exchange is used only for approved payments. Exchange control is almost always associated with fixed exchange rates since there would otherwise be little need to requisition and ration foreign exchange.

The third administrative system is where there is no foreign exchange market at all. This is the system in the majority of centrally-planned economies. Under this system the state has a monopoly over all foreign trade. Thus the state will allocate foreign exchange for imports in line with the foreign exchange earned by exports.

The third desirable feature of the international monetary system is to provide adequate internationally accepted reserves. In order to prevent countries adopting policies which reduce world trade, such as import quotas or tariffs, there must be a mechanism for allowing countries to finance a balance of payments deficit while allowing adjustment policies to become effective. Reserves are generally used (passively) as a buffer against an adverse movement in the balance of payments and (actively) as a means of managing the exchange rate and domestic money market conditions. The ideal reserve currency should be attractive both as a medium of international exchange and as an international store of value.

THE INTERNATIONAL MONETARY SYSTEM FROM 1945 TO THE PRESENT

By the time peace was restored at the end of the Second World War, the outlines of the international monetary system had already been agreed upon. This was due to the work which was finalised at Bretton Woods, New Hampshire, in July 1944 by John Maynard Keynes, the British representative, and Harry Dexter White, the American representative. Solomon has summarised the agreement, as follows:

(i) A new permanent institution, the International Monetary Fund, was to be established to promote consultation and collaboration on international monetary problems, to administer the Articles, and to lend to member countries in balance-of-payments deficit.

(ii) Each Fund member would establish, with Fund approval, a par value for its currency and would undertake to maintain market exchange rates for its currency within 1 per cent of the declared par value. A related provision was that countries that freely buy and sell gold in settlement of international transactions were 'deemed' to be adhering to the requirement that they maintain exchange rates within the 1 per cent margins. Thus the U.S.A., the only country that met this condition, was not expected to intervene in the foreign exchange markets; rather, other countries would intervene, mainly by buying or selling dollars against their own currencies, to keep their rates within 1 per cent of their parities with the dollar.

(iii) Members would only change their par values after having secured Fund approval. Approval would only be given if there was evidence that the country was suffering from a 'fundamental disequilibrium'. This system reflected the desire to avoid 'competitive depreciation' which had caused a breakdown of international trade during the inter-war years.

(iv)   After a transitional period, currencies would be convertible in the sense that countries would undertake to redeem balances of their currencies acquired by other members; such convertibility would be into either gold or the currency of the member requesting conversion. Restrictions on payments for current transactions and all discriminatory currency practices were to be discouraged, if not eliminated.

(v)   The Fund would be in position to lend to countries in deficit out of its holdings of gold and currencies arising from subscriptions by its members in relation to their 'quotas' (to be determined according to each member's size in the world economy).

(vi)   If a country's currency became 'scarce' in the Fund, the latter could authorise other countries to adopt exchange controls on imports and other current account purchases from the surplus country. This sanction against the countries in large surplus was offered by the Americans at a late stage of the negotiations in response to a charge by Keynes and his colleagues that the proposed system was asymmetrically severe toward countries in deficit. In practice, as Keynes predicted, the scarce currency clause of the Fund Articles has never been invoked[1].

Each member was to pay into the pool a quota, one quarter being in gold and the remainder in its own currency. The member then had an automatic right to 'purchase' in exchange for its own currency the currency of other members of up to 25 per cent of its own quota. This was called the gold 'tranche'. A member then might make up to four further drawings (the credit tranches) at increasing rates of interest, provided that, in the I.M.F.'s opinion the member concerned was likely to implement economic policies suitable for dealing with its balance of payments problem. In effect, therefore, a member country had potential drawing rights on the Fund of up to 125 per cent of its quota. When its balance of payments deficits had been rectified, the country in question would within an agreed time limit, repay its drawing on the Fund.

A system was created in which exchange rates were fixed but, on proof of a 'fundamental disequilibrium', could be altered, and where countries could finance their deficits by borrowing from the I.M.F. This system of exchange rates became known as 'the adjustable peg'.

This system served the world well through the 1950s and 1960s. In the twenty-six years between 1945 and 1971 the world saw a sustained expansion in production and trade on a scale seldom recorded before with, on the whole, low rates of inflation. Recovery from the devastation of war was achieved remarkably swiftly and without the inflation and deflation that had followed all previous wars. Trade was increased almost without interruption and almost everywhere liberalised.

There were three major weaknesses in the Bretton Woods scheme and these have been labelled the 'liquidity problem', the 'adjustment problem' and the 'confidence problem'.

Under a system of fixed exchange rates the extent to which a country can buy its own currency when faced with large market sales depends on the size of the countries reserves and its borrowing facilities. With the value of world trade rising continually any system of fixing exchange rates must provide for an increase in the supply of internationally acceptable money. Only then can exchange rates be fixed. However, the Bretton Woods scheme did not explicitly provide for a systematic means by which world reserves could grow with world trade and the world economy.

The role of creating this internationally acceptable money was undertaken by the U.S.A. Figures 5.1, 5.2 and 5.3 show how the U.S. balance of payments deficit (Figure 5.1) supplied the increase in world reserves (Figure 5.2) which enabled the growth in world exports (Figure 5.3).

Figure 5.1
US BALANCE OF PAYMENTS

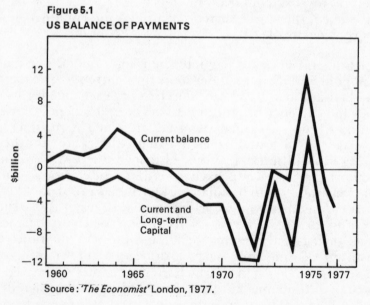

Source : *'The Economist'* London, 1977.

A second weakness of the Bretton Woods system concerned the balance of payments adjustment process. As individual countries encountered balance of payments problems, which invariably meant deficits, they were dealt with on an individual basis, the international community providing both credits and advice, usually through the Fund. Exchange rate adjustment was a rare event among the industrial countries; when it did occur, the

Figure 5.2
COMPOSITION OF WORLD RESERVES

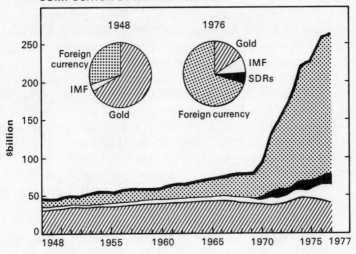

Source: *'The Economist'* London, 1977.

Figure 5.3
WORLD EXPORTS AND WORLD RESERVES (1948-1977)

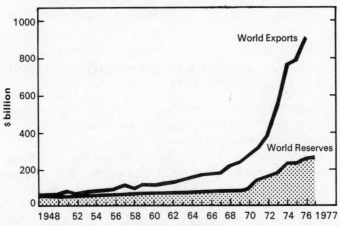

Source: *'The Economist'* London, 1977.

percentage change was normally large. This was called the 'adjustment problem'. The problem basically was that deficit countries and not surplus countries were the ones who were forced to adjust, i.e. devalue their exchange rates.

The third major weakness of the Bretton Woods system was the 'confidence problem'. If there is widespread belief that a currency is going to be devalued, then short-term capital withdrawals may occur, and the more frequently this occurs, the greater is the need, with fixed exchange rates, for international reserves. When the currency in which the foreign exchange market is losing confidence is a reserve currency, such as sterling or the dollar, there will be attempts to convert these currencies into gold and, since the external liabilities of the U.S.A. are much greater than the gold stock, (*see Figure 5.4*) then the whole international monetary system could be put in jeopardy.

The introduction of convertibility for the world's major currencies in 1958 solved the payments problem. The exchange rate adjustment system was based on intervention points with ultimate conversion into gold with exchange rate changes permitted when proof was given of a fundamental disequilibrium. The reserve instruments were those of I.M.F. drawings, gold and foreign exchange. Another reserve instrument, approved by the I.M.F. Board of Governors in May 1968 are Special Drawing Rights (S.D.R.s). These are allocated to individual countries by the I.M.F. They are in effect world paper money created out of thin air through the deliberate decision of I.M.F. members to accept these as a new form of international reserves. They cannot be used in commercial transactions but are used in settlements between central banks and with the I.M.F. However, S.D.R.s have not proved popular. By 1978, the distribution only amounted to 9.3 billion.

THE ROLE OF GOLD IN THE INTERNATIONAL MONETARY SYSTEM FROM 1945 UNTIL 1971

Gold has long existed as a medium of international exchange. However, in its role as a reserve asset gold has significant short-comings. Firstly, it is wasteful to use a commodity with a significant positive cost of production to perform a function which could be equally well performed by a financial instrument with a zero cost of production. Secondly, the use of gold gives benefits to the country where the gold is produced and which may not necessarily benefit the world economy. In this regard there have also been objections to the political nature of the world's largest gold producers, Soviet Russia and South Africa. Thirdly, the increase in the supply of gold may not reflect the world's increasing need for extra international liquidity. Increases in gold supplies may be totally unrelated to the world's needs.

Despite these shortcomings, in 1945 the I.M.F. fixed gold as the *numeraire* of the international monetary system. The price of gold was fixed at $35 an ounce and since other currencies were fixed in relation to the dollar central banks could exchange their currencies for dollars and with their dollars they could obtain gold. The U.S. Federal Reserve was willing to buy and sell gold at this rate. This willingness of the U.S. to back the world monetary system with gold is understandable when it is realised that the U.S.A., at the end of the Second World War, had a gold stock valued at $20 billion which accounted for 60 per cent of the total of official gold reserves. As long as the dollar and its gold backing was considered invulnerable foreign central banks had an incentive to hold currencies, which earned interest, rather than gold, which earned nothing.

In 1954, a gold market was opened in London and the Bank of England occasionally intervened in this to keep prices at the agreed level. This was a market in which private buyers and sellers could operate. This posed problems for the Federal Reserve since they could be exposed to gold sales both to central banks and to the London market if they wished to keep the price down in the face of a heavy demand for gold.

A central bank gold pool of $80 million was set up in 1962. The gold pool was an arrangement among eight countries, including the U.S.A., to sell or buy gold in the free market to keep the price close to the official price of $35 an ounce. France left the gold pool in the summer of 1967.

American officials believed that, if the free market price were to rise sharply, expectation of a rise in the official gold price, and thus a dollar devaluation, would be engendered. The U.S.A. feared several consequences of a rising gold price. Firstly, there would be rising dollar sales by central banks and thus depletion of the gold stock; secondly, central banks could buy gold from the Federal Reserve and sell gold in the private market, thus arbitraging profits. American officials feared that suspension of dollar convertibility would lead to chaos in international financial relations with the danger of spreading restrictions on trade and payments. By the late 1960s there existed a situation whereby the dollar had become convertible into gold not only by foreign central banks but also by private speculators all over the world.

Until 1968, under the so-called 'gold pool', the major central banks clubbed together to hold the gold price at $35 an ounce. As there was no prospect of gold going down, but a good prospect of gold going up, this gave speculators a one-way option. In 1968, central banks were forced to set the gold price free for commercial transactions, but, for settlements between themselves, agreed to stick to the old price and not to sell gold on the free market. The central banks expected that under this two-tier gold system, the free-market gold price would stay within easy reach of the official price. It did not do so for long.

In August 1969 the French franc was devalued and in October 1969 the Deutschemark was revalued. Fixed exchange rates were becoming difficult to defend and this placed extra strain on the roles of the dollar and gold in the international monetary system.

When President Nixon, looking to re-election in 1972, wanted to expand demand to pull the U.S.A. out of the minor world recession in 1970–71, speculation against the dollar mounted. This forced central banks in continental Europe and Japan to buy huge quantities of dollars rather than see their exchange rates rise (which would have adversely affected their exporters and so intensified their recessions). The free-market gold price rose sharply. Seeing this, several countries began to demand conversion of their surplus dollars into gold at the official $35 price. The U.S.A. with $10 billion in gold reserves against liabilities of $50 billion in other countries reserves, decided to suspend convertibility in August 1971. The gold link was broken and the dollar set to float. Figure 5.4 gives details of the U.S. gold reserves and the U.S. external liabilities up to 1974.

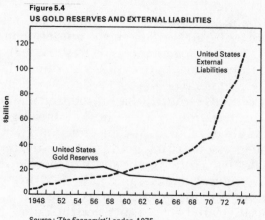

Figure 5.4
US GOLD RESERVES AND EXTERNAL LIABILITIES

Source: 'The Economist' London, 1975.

Finance ministers were still anxious to maintain fixed exchange rates and they arranged a conference at the Smithsonian Institute in December 1971, which resulted in the 'Smithsonian Agreement'. This had two features. First, the maximum spread of a country's fixed exchange rate band was increased from 2 per cent to 4.5 per cent, thus allowing central banks more room for manoeuvre in the use of their reserves to resist speculation. Secondly, a wide ranging set of upward revaluations of currencies against the U.S. dollar took place; at the same time the dollar was formally devalued in terms of gold, the price of which was increased from $35 to $38 an ounce. This was a dollar devaluation in terms of other currencies of approximately 9 per cent.

In early 1972, the members of the E.E.C. were becoming increasingly concerned about the effects of exchange rate changes on the workings of the Common Agricultural Policy and they also had a desire to achieve monetary union inside the E.E.C. whereby a common European currency could be introduced which would replace the national currencies.

THE SNAKE

As a first step the Snake was set up in April 1972, the initial membership consisting of the six original E.E.C. countries; the then candidate countries, the U.K., Denmark and Norway joined shortly afterwards (the last of these, despite not having joined the European Community, remained an associate member of the Snake). Previously, under the Smithsonian Agreement of December 1971, fluctuations of exchange rates of major currencies (including those of E.E.C. currencies) were restricted to 2.25 per cent either side of a central parity rate fixed against the U.S. dollar, which meant that cross-rates of exchange between currencies of E.E.C. member states could fluctuate by a maximum of 4.50 per cent. The graphical representation of this group of currencies within a narrow band of cross-exchange rates, moving within a larger band against the dollar, gave rise to the phrase 'the Snake in the Tunnel'. Subsequently, 'the Tunnel' ceased to exist when central banks stopped supporting the dollar and the latter was floated in March 1973. This is illustrated, using the pound sterling, in Figure 5.5

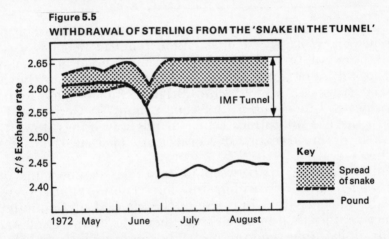

Figure 5.5
WITHDRAWAL OF STERLING FROM THE 'SNAKE IN THE TUNNEL'

For each member state there is, in fact, an individual Snake and this may well be seen mapped out on the wall of the foreign exchange dealing room of banks in the member countries. The Snake is in effect a system of fixing the cross-exchange rates between all the member currencies. Examination of the central rates and intervention points in Table 5.1 between the European countries participating in the joint float as at 16 November 1978 will make this clear. The Central Banks intervene to maintain these cross rates.

In Belgium the lowest point that the Deutschemark can fall is 15.3665 B. Frs. and the highest point that the Deutschemark can rise to is 16.0740 B. Frs. At the lowest intervention point the Belgian Authorities are obliged to buy Deutschemarks and sell

Table 5.1

Central rates and intervention points between the European countries participating in the joint float as at 16 November 1978

Currency	Belgium	Denmark	Netherlands	Norway	West Germany
Belgium	—	17.5585	6.742	16.7808	6.221
Franc 100	—	17.9581	6.89531	17.1626	6.36277
	—	18.3665	7.052	17.5531	6.508
Danish	544.45	—	37.5425	93.4441	34.645
Kroner 100	556.852	—	38.3967	95.5703	35.4313
	569.50	—	39.27	97.7448	36.235
Dutch	1418.00	254.645	—	243.365	90.225
guilders 100	1450.26	260.439	—	248.902	92.2767
	1483.25	266.365	—	254.565	94.375
Norwegian	569.70	102.31	39.2825	—	36.25
Kroner 100	582.662	104.635	40.1764	—	37.0735
	595.90	107.015	41.09	—	37.915
Deutschemark	1536.65	275.96	105.96	263.734	—
100	1571.64	282.237	108.37	269.735	—
	1607.40	288.66	110.835	275.872	—

Belgian Francs. The cross-rates are so calculated that when the Deutschemark is its lowest intervention point in Belgium so the Belgian franc will be at its highest intervention point in Germany. Thus, at the same time as the Belgian Authorities are buying Deutschemarks in Belgium for Belgian francs the German Authorities will be acting in the same manner in Germany. The effect of the two authorities acting in this way brings down the Belgian franc in Germany and brings up the Deutschemark in Belgium.

Intervention occurs between all the Snake members and this keeps their currencies within the intervention limits. It was originally intended that intervention be effected in Community currencies rather than in dollars, but there has been a trend back towards dollar intervention, probably because the number of Snake currencies had declined and transactions in terms of member currencies between Snake participants became less important relative to flows in and out of the dollar. In intervening against the dollar an attempt was being made to smooth, to some extent, any unduly pronounced ('erratic') movement of market rates vis-a-vis the dollar over longer periods.

The settlement of debts resulting from intervention is effected via the European Monetary Co-operation Fund (EMCOF). Credits and debits were made in terms of a common unit of account, in order to provide a uniform measure of members' positions in the Fund. The resulting balances were usually settled between central banks at the end of the month, following the month of intervention, in assets in proportion to the composition of the debtor country's reserves (gold excepted), but could automatically be extended for a period of up to three months. Thus it can be seen that the Snake arrangement did provide facilities for financing intervention (subject to a maximum equal to the debtor's quota under the EEC Short-Term Monetary Support arrangement) to keep exchange rates within the required limits, but these facilities were essentially short-term, and a country with a persistently weak currency would eventually lose reserves if, during the extension period, market conditions for its currency did not improve, so as to enable it to gain reserves with which it could settle its debts to EMCOF.

WITHDRAWALS

The strains imposed on members by the need to keep their currencies within the agreed limits have proved too much on several occasions. Sterling withdrew from the arrangement in June 1972, after a run on the currency had developed.

The Danish authorities also relinquished their commitments to keep their currency within the required limits in the same month, but rejoined in the following October. In February 1973, following a substantial worsening of Italy's current account deficit and inflation rate, the lira was floated, despite credits from the E.E.C. for its support. The next victim of the deteriorating economic conditions, as a consequence of the oil crisis, was the French franc. Against the background of an anticipated worsening in the country's trade deficit, the franc was withdrawn from the Snake in January 1974. However, after having depreciated against its pre-floating partners by up to 13 per cent, high domestic interest rates and heavy borrowing on international capital markets led to a slow improvement in its exchange rate. The appreciation continued into 1974, when, as a result of encouraging trade and inflation figures, the franc emerged as one of the stronger European currencies, and was officially reintegrated in July 1974 into the European joint currency float at its pre-floating central parity rate. In retrospect this decision appears to have been premature, as the French authorities were preparing to embark on a policy of reflation to pull the economy out of recession, leading to a revival in the level of consumer demand and imports and a return to a deficit on foreign trade transactions. Following several weeks of speculative pressure, and despite massive intervention by the French and West German central banks in an effort to keep the franc within the required limits, the currency was again floated independently in March 1976.

In June 1977 following the outcome of protracted wage negotiations in Sweden there was a great deal of discussion of a devaluation of the kroner to offset the impact of rising unit labour costs on competitiveness. Fairly heavy selling of the Swedish kroner and other Scandinavian currencies built up, especially before each weekend (when major currency alignments normally take place). Despite extensive intervention the heavy selling pressure forced the withdrawal of the Swedish kroner from the Snake in September. The Swedish kroner is now pegged against a basket of other currencies.

Movements of spot exchange rates within the joint float of European currencies can be seen from Figure 5.6.

Figure 5.6

MOVEMENTS OF SPOT EXCHANGE RATES WITHIN THE JOINT FLOAT OF EUROPEAN CURRENCIES

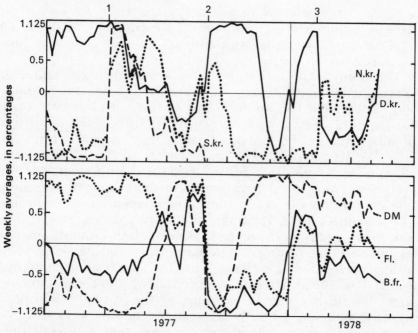

1 Adjustments of central rates on 4th April 1977.
2 Adjustments of central rates on 29th August 1977.
The Swedish krona withdrew from the 'Snake' arrangements on the same day.
3 Adjustments of central rates on 13th February 1978.

Source : 'Bank for International Settlements. Annual Report'
1st April 1977 – 31st March 1978.

In December 1978, following the decision to create the new European Monetary System (EMS) Norway withdrew from the Snake. This withdrawal was based on the fear that Norwegian exports could suffer if the kroner remained tied to the

Deutschemark while important trading partners, such as Sweden and Britain, stayed outside the EMS. As from 12 December 1978 the Norwegian kroner was linked to a trade-weighted basket of foreign currencies.

THE ROLE OF THE DOLLAR

By February 1973, the U.S.A. was again forced to devalue the dollar, raising the 'official' price at which it by now neither bought nor sold gold to $42.22 an ounce. In March, European central banks refused to buy dollars and this heralded a free float for the dollar, so heralding total disintegration of the Bretton Woods Agreement.

The dollar was floating freely from 11 March 1973 to 6 July 1973 and at the end of this time New York banks were refusing to quote rates against the dollar since they were continually having to buy dollars which were going down in value. At a meeting at the Bank for International Settlements on 8 July 1973, it was agreed to maintain orderly foreign exchange markets and, although the dollar was still floating, this was to take place in an orderly fashion. Appendix 1 (p. 118) shows exchange rates movements from July 1972 to November 1978 for the pound sterling, Belgian franc, Swiss franc, French franc, Italian lira, Dutch guilder, the Deutschemark and the Japanese yen; with the exception of sterling, these rates are quoted against the U.S. dollar.

Table 5.2

Distribution of changes in international reserves: 1970–1976

$billion[a]	1970/73[b]	1974	1975	1976	1976[c]
Industrial countries (of which:)	+13.1	+3.6	+4.3	+10.3	131.8
United States	−1.3	+1.4	+0.5	+2.5	18.3
Japan	+2.3	+1.2	−0.6	+3.8	16.6
West Germany	+6.2	−0.9	−1.0	+3.8	34.8
Other developed countries	+3.9	−2.9	−3.1	+0.4	18.3
Oil exporting countries (of which:)	+2.5	+32.4	+9.8	+8.8	65.3
Saudi Arabia	+0.8	+10.4	+9.1	+3.7	27.0
Non-oil developing countries	+4.3	+2.8	−1.2	+10.2	41.2
All countries	+23.8	+35.9	+9.8	+29.8	256.6

Notes: (a) Excludes valuation gains on holdings of gold, SDRs and reserve positions in the IMF due to the devaluations of the dollar in 1971 and 1973, and exclude changes arising from fluctuations in the value of the SDR since mid-1974; (b) annual average; (c) amount outstanding at the end of the period. Source: IMF Deutsche Bundesbank.

The Yom Kippur War in 1973, followed by the oil embargo and the fourfold increase in the price of oil, increased the industrial countries' bill for imported oil by $70 billion a year. This had several serious consequences. Firstly, the oil price rise accelerated cost inflation in industrial countries. Secondly, the price rise acted like an indirect tax, taking money from consumers, thereby reducing incomes without putting it back in the form of expenditure. Naturally, this is deflationary. Thirdly, because the oil producers did not spend more than a fraction of their enhanced export earnings, they moved into substantial balance of payments surpluses in relation to the rest of the world. The extent of these surpluses can be seen from Table 5.2

The increase in reserves for the oil exporting countries alone in 1974 was greater than the total increase in reserves for all countries between 1970 and 1973.

The OPEC balance of payments surplus can be reduced in three ways: firstly, if oil prices are reduced; secondly, if there is a reduction in demand for OPEC oil by importing countries; or thirdly if there is an increase in the imports of goods and services by members of OPEC. In the face of a world-wide recession OPEC has maintained its oil prices, although the fall in real oil prices since 1974 has been very large. The speed of alternative energy supply substitution is occurring, albeit slowly. Finally, the structure of some of the oil exporting economies is such that their capacity to absorb imports is very severely limited. Thus automatic adjustment mechanisms are likely to take place with a long time lag.

The world's reaction to the oil price rises was mixed. Industrial (and non-oil producing, developing) countries were faced with the fact that over $70 billion a year had been added to their price inflations, $70 billion had been added to their balance of payments deficits, $70 billion had been subtracted from world spending and added to Arab saving. The contractionary policies which followed drove the world into the worst economic slump since the 1930s. Countries accustomed to running large trade surpluses found themselves with large trade deficits. Some, such as Japan and the U.S.A., contracted their domestic economies so strongly that trade surpluses were restored in 1975, in which year the volume of world trade fell for the first time in over thirty years. But, on the whole, countries took steps to finance their deficits, a collective necessity with the OPEC countries running such large surpluses.

How were these balance of payments deficits to be financed? In a sense, financing is automatic in that OPEC members have little choice but to invest their surpluses somewhere in OECD. The recycling of oil producers' funds was at first left to the banking system. Most of the money flowed into New York and London and was on-lent in the Euro-dollar market. But there was a limit to which, given OPEC preference for lending short-term, financial institutions could borrow short-term and lend long-term. Thus government assistance was needed. IMF assistance was provided whereby the IMF borrowed directly from the oil producers and on-lent the funds. Similarly, the governments of industrial countries agreed to recycle money among themselves from a $25 billion fund which was set up.

What has been the role of the dollar throughout this time period? As already mentioned, until 1971 the dollar was the world's banking currency. This was for several reasons; firstly, the political and economic strength of the U.S.A.; secondly, the validation of the dollar as the currency against which intervention took place, established at Bretton Woods; and thirdly, due to the depth of the U.S. money markets. Kaufman has outlined other principal developments which have increased the role of the dollar[2]. Suspension of gold convertibility in 1971 removed an important discipline for the dollar. Secondly, there occurred a shift to further reliance on private institutions to finance the payments deficit of foreign nations rather than a dependence upon official institutions. The international capital markets (*see Chapters 10 and 11*) were dominated by the dollar. New instruments, including Euro-dollars and floating rate notes were created to accommodate the enlarged demands of private and official lenders.

The third development, and closely related to the second, was the large increase in the price of oil. This further enhanced the dominance of the dollar because, as already seen, it caused massive balance of payments imbalances around the world, with the dollar being employed to finance the gap between surplus and deficit countries.

Doubts about the ability of the U.S.A. to continue as the principal reserve centre to the international monetary system arise for two fundamental reasons. First, the economic importance of the U.S. has declined in relative terms; the U.S. GNP declined from 39 per cent of world GNP in 1950 to 25 per cent in 1975. Secondly, the openess of the U.S. economy has increased. External U.S. trade roughly doubled over the same period. For both of these reasons the U.S.A. is more vulnerable to changes in the international economy than when it became the principal *de facto* reserve centre after the Second World War. The position of a reserve centre is only basically stable when it is unaffected by external developments. But the increasing vulnerability of the U.S.A. to external developments has not coincided with a diminution of the role of the dollar. On the contrary, the size and the persistence of the U.S. payments deficit (*see Table 5.3*) have ensured that the dollar is as dominant as ever. This is largely due to the fact that there is no other country which comes near the U.S.A. in terms of GNP, or 'closedness'.

Table 5.3

US external liabilities and claims

$b end of period	1970	1971	1972	1973	1974	1975	1976	1977
External liabilities	47.0	67.8	82.9	92.5	119.2	126.6	151.4	174.2
to financial authorities	23.8	50.6	61.5	66.9	76.8	80.7	92.0	110.5
to private institutions	21.8	15.1	19.7	23.6	39.0	40.2	50.9	56.3
to international organisations	1.4	2.1	1.6	2.0	3.3	5.6	8.5	7.4
External claims	13.9	16.9	20.4	26.6	46.1	59.8	80.8	81.1
Net external position	—33.1	—50.9	—62.5	—65.9	—73.1	—66.8	—70.6	—93.1

Notes: 1977 figure is for the end of September. Totals do not always sum, due to rounding.
Source: *IMF*.

THE ROLE OF GOLD SINCE 1971

As the result of decisions taken in December 1971 and February 1973 the official price of gold had increased from $35 to $38, and then to $42.2, an ounce but this was still much below the free market price at which private sector buyers and sellers dealt in the London gold market. No central bank would in these circumstances want to part with its gold at the official price, so official transactions in gold had since the ending of the dollar's official gold convertibility in 1971, effectively ceased.

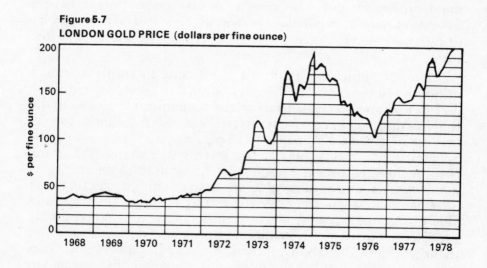

Figure 5.7
LONDON GOLD PRICE (dollars per fine ounce)

In 1974, as can be seen from Figure 5.7, the London gold price rose to a peak, with the prospect of U.S. citizens being allowed to own gold on the last day of the year.

In September 1975, at the IMF annual meeting in Washington, key understandings in principle were reached regarding the role of gold in the monetary system. These were heavily influenced by the criticisms of the role of gold. The official price of gold was abolished and there was no longer an obligation to use gold in transactions with the IMF. In addition, a sixth of the IMF's gold holdings would be returned to members in proportion to their quotas and another one-sixth sold, with the differential between the former official price and the selling price being used to benefit developing countries. Moreover, an agreement not to peg the market price of gold caused the price to fall to about $140 per ounce.

In 1976 the gold price continued to fall with the impact of the IMF's programme of gold auctions. In the autumn, user demand for gold increased and renewed fears of currency unrest helped increase the gold price. The dollar gold price again rose through 1977 mainly due to the weakness of the dollar. Continued IMF auctions did not check the upward trend. In April 1978 the U.S.A. Treasury, in the face of a collapsing dollar, decided to auction 300,000 ounces of gold for at least six months, starting on 23 May. The amount the U.S.A. were proposing to sell was quite small compared with the $277.5 millions held at Fort Knox. Also, in 1978 central banks were freed to buy and sell gold at its market price.

Despite these gold sales lack of confidence in the dollar has led to gold being used as a currency hedge. As can be seen from Figure 5.8, in terms of the Swiss franc, price rises in 1977 and 1978 have been less marked and indeed the Swiss franc price of gold is lower than it was in 1975.

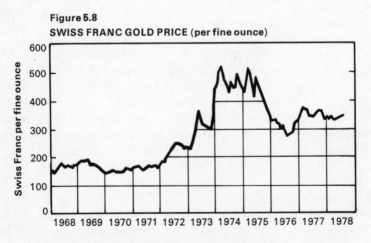

Figure 5.8
SWISS FRANC GOLD PRICE (per fine ounce)

Source : *'IMF International Financial Statistics'* 1978.

Following the ratification of the Second Amendment to the IMF Articles of Agreement in April 1978 the official price of gold has effectively been abolished and gold can therefore be valued at whatever price countries choose. Many countries value their gold holdings at market related rates. In the U.K. gold is valued at the average of the London fixing price over the three months before each 31 March, discounted by 25 per cent. This discount to the gold price takes account of the possibility that, if gold were to be sold or pledged during the course of a year, it might not be possible to realise the market price prevailing in the first three months of the year (when the gold price might have been unusually high.) Most countries adopt a formula which involves no discount; but five countries do adopt a discount, viz Austria (50 per cent), the Netherlands (30 per cent), Italy (15 per cent), South Africa (10 per cent) and Mexico (an unspecified small amount.)

FROM RAMBOUILLET TO THE SECOND AMENDMENT.

After the abandonment of pegged exchange rates in March 1973 floating exchange rates were introduced for many countries. In Europe, the opinion remained widespread that floating should be only temporary, and this point of view was forcibly represented by France. In the U.S.A., however, opinion was moving in favour of a continuance of floating. The Rambouillet Summit on 15 to 17 November 1975 had two aspects. On the one hand, France gave up her insistence on the eventual re-establishment of a system of fixed, but adjustable, rates. Instead, the establishment of such a system would require an 85 per cent affirmative vote in the IMF, which with the IMF's weighted voting, would give the U.S.A. an effective veto. Morever, under the amended Articles pegging could never be at parities expressed in terms of gold. On the other hand, the U.S.A. agreed to a communiqué which committed the six countries at the conference to a statement that they intended to work for greater stability in underlying economic and financial conditions in the world economy with the monetary authorities countering disorderly or erratic fluctuations in exchange rates. However, the U.S. Secretary of the Treasury, William Simon, made it clear that there would be no forceful U.S. intervention in the exchange markets.

In January 1976 work which had been started at Rambouillet was continued in Jamaica on a new IMF Article about exchange rate practices. This was eventually finalised at IMF executive board level and took effect from 1 April 1978. As a result of this second amendment to the Articles of Agreement, the IMF has established three basic principles for the guidance of its 133 members. The first is that 'a member shall avoid manipulating exchange rates or the international monetary system in order to prevent effective balance of payments adjustment or to gain an unfair competitive advantage over other members'.

There is little evidence that individual member countries have deliberately engineered the depreciation of their exchange rates in the period since the onset of managed floating, if only because the experience of exchange depreciation, in periods when it could not be avoided, has tended to increase the rate of inflation in the country concerned, instead of providing its exports with a competitive edge. However, countries in balance of payments deficit have often resorted to foreign currency borrowing to sustain an over-valued exchange rate, for fear of the inflationary conse- quences of depreciation. Similarly, the accumulation of reserves by countries in payments surplus is sometimes construed as a reluctance to allow the exchange rate to appreciate. This has been particularly relevant to Germany and Japan.

The second principle is that 'a member should intervene in the exchange market if necessary to counter disorderly market con- ditions, which may be characterised *inter alia* by disruptive short- term movements in the exchange value of its currency'. The principle of intervention to counter disorderly market conditions has emerged as a result of practical experience in the exchange market in the period since the end of fixed rates, i.e. that exchange rate movements are not necessarily self-correcting, and can become self-fulfilling, without the existence, or at least the threat of, central bank intervention.

The third principle is that 'members should take into account in their intervention policies the interest of other members, including those of the countries in whose currencies they intervene'. This principle has been included because of the disruption in exchange markets caused by the extensive use of the U.S. dollar as a vehicle currency in support operations. The central banks of traditionally weak currencies, such as the French franc and the Italian lira, have often drawn on dollar credits to support their currencies against market pressure, just at the time when other market operators have used borrowed dollars to buy traditionally strong currencies, such as the Swiss franc and the Deutschemark. The effect has been to exaggerate any exchange crisis that has occurred by artificially weakening the dollar.

THE CURRENT NATURE OF THE INTERNATIONAL MONETARY SYSTEM

McMahon, using the jargon of games theorists, has defined three stages of the post-war international monetary system[3]. In the post-war world economy international liquidity was provided by the U.S. running a basic deficit in its balance of payments. This meant that all other countries taken together could be in surplus. Industrialised countries, on balance, prefer a surplus since this eases the achievement of domestic objectives. Thus a balance of payments surplus facilitates expansion of liberal attitudes towards trade. In these circumstances the rest of the world were playing a 'positive sum game'. With the breakdown of the Bretton Woods system and the eventual move to virtually total floating exchange rates the U.S.A. became, as well as the world's banker, one of the participants. Since everybody's surplus was now someone else's deficit the world had moved to a 'zero sum game'. With the advent of OPEC there has been an unrequitable surplus in one part of the world with a corresponding irremovable deficit spread over the rest. The world outside OPEC has been plunged into a 'negative sum game'. Individual nations, with no clearly defined rules for exchange rate policy, or indeed, balance of payments policy generally, have been competing for an overall deficit. Clearly, this gives an *a priori* likelihood that this will lead to cumulative deflation, national recrimination and pressures for protectionism.

What is the current state of the international monetary system? Table 5.4 indicates the *de facto* exchange rate arrangements in existence at the beginning of 1979 for 74 countries.

Category A represents independent floaters. Category B comprises Snake floaters and used to include Sweden and Norway. Category C represents U.S. dollar peggers, and Category D French Franc peggers. Category D comprises countries which have linked the value of their currencies to the SDR unit of the Fund and Category F indicates countries which value their currencies in terms of various baskets of foreign currencies. In the main, Categories A and B are made up of developed industrial countries, while Categories C to F are made up of semi-industrial and less developed countries.

THE NEW EUROPEAN MONETARY SYSTEMS (EMS)

In order to discuss means of reducing exchange rate movements a European summit was held in Brussels in early December 1978 at which agreement was reached on a new European Monetary System (EMS). This was expected to commence on 1 January 1979 but due to a dispute between France and Germany about Monetary Compensation Amounts used in EEC agricultural trade, did not start until 13 March 1979.

The member states participating in the scheme are Germany, Netherlands, France, Belgium, Luxembourg, Italy, Ireland and

Table 5.4
Exchange Rate Systems

A. *Independent Floaters*	C. *U.S.A. Dollar Peggers*	D. *French Franc Peggers*
	Bahrain	Cameroon
	Barbados	Central African Empire
Japan	Bolivia	Gabon
Philippines	Ghana	Ivory Coast
Spain	Guatemala	Madagascar
U.K.	Haiti	Niger
U.S.A.	Indonesia	Togo
Yugoslavia	Pakistan	Upper Volta
Canada	Paraguay	
Greece	Rwanda	E. *SDR Peggers*
Mexico	Ethiopia	Tanzania
Nigeria	Costa Rica	Malawi
Saudi Arabia	El Salvador	Iran
Iceland	Jamaica	Uganda
Portugal	Libya	Zambia
S. Africa	Trinidad	Jordan
	Venezuela	Kenya
B. *'Snake' Floaters*	Dominica	
Belgium	Egypt	F. *'Other' Basket Peggers*
Denmark	Guyana	Tunisia
W. Germany	Honduras	Austria
Netherlands	Iraq	Cyprus
France	Korea	Fiji
Italy	Syria	Finland
Eire	Thailand	Malaysia
		Malta
		Morocco
		Sri Lanka
		Norway
		Sweden

Source: adapted from M.R. Heller, 'Choosing an Exchange Rate System'. *Finance and Development*, June 1977.

Denmark. The U.K. is not participating in the scheme and Norway, as mentioned earlier, has withdrawn from the Snake and is not a member of the EMS.

WHAT ARE THE OBJECTIVES OF EMS

The principal immediate objectives of the EMS proposal is to increase exchange rate stability. There are strong, underlying economic and political motivations for this. Several years after the deep recession, Europe is still experiencing slow economic growth, low capacity utilisation and relatively high unemployment. It is feared that frustration with the economic situation could stimulate protectionism, which would be especially damaging to all the countries in the area because of their close trade ties (*see Table 5.5*).

Table 5.5
Trade patterns of members of the European Communities

	% of total trade with other EC members	total trade* as % of GNP/GDP
Belgium	69	103
Denmark	46	56
France	49	36
Germany	47	43
Ireland	72	106
Italy	45	47
Netherlands	63	85
United Kingdom	38	58

*sum of total exports and total imports, as reported in *Direction of Trade* (IMF) 1978.

The late 1970s saw growing disillusionment with the operation of floating rates. Their contribution to eliminating payments imbalances, though often important, has been slower, smaller and less certain than was hoped. The existence of growing Euromarkets, and the large increase in wealth of OPEC resulted in wide movements in exchange rates. Capital flows rather than economic fundamentals appear to be the dominant force in the foreign exchange market. Coombs described the foreign exchange market in the following manner:

On a day-to-day basis, the market is dominated by short-term capital movements in search of quick profits or a hedge against exchange rate risks. Similarly skilled foreign exchange traders earn their salaries and bonuses by correctly anticipating short-term rate movements. In the jargon of the trade, betting on the long-run fundamentals is an excellent way of losing one's shirt[4].

Exchange rate movements in the latter half of 1978 were so large, especially for the U.S. dollar, that there was a widespread desire to move back towards greater exchange rate stability. This has been reflected in the policies and statements of governments in situations as different as, for example, those of the U.S.A., Japan, Germany, France, the U.K. and other countries of Western Europe. There has been a widespread belief that these large swings in exchange rates have damaged business confidence and deterred private investment.

The second principal reason for desired exchange rate stability is the stiffening European resistance to currency depreciation because of its inflationary consequences. Since foreign trade is so large relative to GNP (*see Table 5.5*) any major currency change has a large impact on export and import prices and on domestic inflation. Accordingly, several European countries prefer to concentrate on restraining domestic costs, rather than devaluing their exchange rates, as a means of improving their international competitiveness.

Thirdly, with some convergence of European economic performance there is a strong desire to promote progress toward monetary unification as a means of ending the slow-down of European Community institutional evolution and giving new thrust to political co-operation.

WHAT ARE THE MECHANICS OF EMS?

Following the Summit in December 1978 a communiqué was issued by Her Majesty's Stationery Office (Cmnd. 7419) as to how the new European Monetary System would work, the broad features of which are outlined below[5].

The heart of the proposed European Monetary System is a scheme to link closely the exchange rates of members, basing the system on the European Currency Unit (ECU). The ECU (discussed further in Chapter 9) is to be composed on the same basis as the present European Unit of Account. This is a basket of the EEC currencies. the amount of each currency included reflecting the distribution of trade between members of the Community. This basket will include all nine EEC members even though some members, as mentioned above, will not participate from the outset.

Cmnd. 7419 sets out the main features as follows:

2.2 The ECU will be used
(a) as the denominator (numéraire) for the exchange rate mechanism
(b) as the basis for a divergence indicator
(c) as the denominator for operations in both the intervention and the credit mechanism
(d) as a means of settlement between monetary authorities of the E.C.

2.3 The weights of currencies in the E.C.U. will be re-examined and if necessary revised within six months of the entry into force of the system and thereafter every five years or, on request, if the weight of any currency has changed by 25 per cent.

Revisions have to be mutually accepted; they will, by themselves, not modify the external value of the E.C.U. They will be made in line with underlying economic criteria.

THE EXCHANGE RATE AND THE INTERVENTION MECHANISM

3.1 Each currency will have an E.C.U.-related central rate. These central rates will be used to establish a grid of bilateral exchange rates.

Around these exchange rates fluctuation margins of ± 2.25 per cent will be established. . .

Italy has negotiated margins of ± 6 per cent, while Ireland has accepted ± 2.25 per cent.

3.2 Adjustments of central rates will be subject to mutual agreement by a common procedure which will comprise all countries participating in the exchange rate mechanism and the Commission. There will be reciprocal consultation in the Community framework about important decisions concerning exchange rate policy between countries participating and any country not participating in the system.

3.3 In principle, interventions will be made in participating currencies.

3.4 Intervention in participating currencies is compulsory when the intervention points defined by the fluctuation margins are reached.

3.5 An E.C.U. basket formula will be used as an indicator to detect divergences between Community currencies. A 'threshold of divergence' will be fixed at 75 per cent of the maximum spread of divergence for each currency. It will be calculated in such a way as to eliminate the influence of weight on the probability to reach the threshold.

3.6 When a currency crosses its 'threshold of divergence', this results in a presumption that the authorities concerned will correct this situation by adequate measures, namely:—

(a) Diversified intervention;
(b) Measures of domestic monetary policy;
(c) Changes in central rates;
(d) Other measures of economic policy.

In case such measures, on account of special circumstances, are not taken, the reasons for this shall be given to the other authorities, especially in the 'concertation between Central Banks'.

Consultations will, if necessary, then take place in the appropriate Community bodies, including the Council of Ministers.

After six months these provisions shall be reviewed in the light of experience. At that date the questions regarding imbalances accumulated by divergent creditor or debtor countries will be studied as well.

In support of this currency mechanism:

3.7 A Very Short Term Facility of an unlimited amount will be established. Settlements will be made 45 days after the end of the month of intervention with the possibility of prolongation for another 3 months for amounts limited to the size of debtor quotas in the Short Term Monetary Support.

3.8 To serve as a means of settlement, an initial supply of E.C.U. will be provided by FECOM against the deposit of 20 per cent of gold and 20 per cent of dollar reserves currently held by Central Banks.

This operation will take the form of specified, revolving swap arrangements. By periodical review and by an appropriate procedure it will be ensured that each Central Bank will maintain a deposit of at least 20 per cent of these reserves with FECOM. A Member State not participating in the exchange rate mechanism may participate in this initial operation on the basis described above.

4.1 The existing credit mechanisms with their present rules of application will be maintained for the initial phase of the E.M.S. They will be consolidated into a single fund in the final phase of the E.M.S.

4.2 The credit mechanisms will be extended to an amount of 25 billion E.C.U. of effectively available credit. The distribution of this amount will be as follows:

Short Term Monetary Support	= 14 bn ECU
Medium Term Financial Assistance	= 11 bn ECU

The Short Term Monetary Support and the Medium Term Financial Assistance will be consolidated into a European Monetary Fund to be established in 1981 when the E.C.U. will also be used as a reserve asset and as a means of settlement.

4.3 The duration of the Short Term Monetary Support will be extended for another 3 months on the same conditions as the first extension.

4.4 The increase of the Medium Term Financial Assistance will be completed by 30 June 1979. In the meantime, countries which still need national legislation are expected to make their extended medium-term quotas available by an interim financing agreement of the Central Banks concerned.

THIRD COUNTRIES AND INTERNATIONAL ORGANIZATIONS

5.1 The durability of E.M.S. and its international implications require co-ordination of exchange rate policies vis-à-vis third countries and, as far as possible, a concertation with the monetary authorities of those countries.

5.2 European countries with particularly close economic and financial ties with the European Community may participate in the exchange rate and intervention mechanism.

Participation will be based upon agreements between Central Banks; these agreements will be communicated to the Council and the Commission of the E.C.

5.3 E.M.S. is and will remain fully compatible with the relevant articles of the I.M.F. agreement.

SIMILARITIES AND DIFFERENCES BETWEEN EMS AND THE CURRENCY SNAKE

The most important similarity between EMS and the old snake is that the same parity grid system for central bank intervention has been established. The first seven columns of Table 5.6 show the upper and lower intervention rates for all currencies within the EMS against all other currencies within the system. Thus the Deutschemark can rise to a maximum level of F.fr 2.3621 while the French Franc can fall to a minimum level against the Deutschemark of DM 4.2335 for 10 francs.

The first major difference between EMS and the old snake, apart from the changing membership, is the role to be played by the European Currency Unit (ECU). The ECU is to be used as a means of settlement between European Community monetary authorities, much as is the present European Unit of account. The ECU will also serve as an indicator of currency divergence. The central rate of each EMS member currency against the ECU is shown in column 8 of Table 5.6. It is against this central rate that the 'ECU divergence indicator' will be calculated. Each currency has been allocated a maximum percentage deviation against its ECU central rate (shown as a percentage figure in column 8). When it has reached this threshold there is a 'presumption' (but not an obligation) that action will be taken to rectify this situation.

The ECU is a basket currency made up of different amounts of national currencies. The weight given to each currency reflects the importance of the different national economies. These weights become distorted over time as currencies appreciate and depreciate against each other. This complication makes it excessively difficult for speculators to perceive whether central bank intervention is likely to take place. As the currency cross rates change so do the weights and so, in turn, do the divergency indicators.

EMS also differs from the snake in that the total amount of credit facilities are substantially enlarged. The total credit facilities of the European Monetary Fund (EMF), discussed earlier, are much larger than those of the European Monetary Co-operation Fund (EMCOF). The credit facilities of EMCOF amount to $7\frac{1}{2}$ billion.

The third element of the new System which distinguishes it from the old snake is the commitment in principle to a substantial increase in intra-regional transfers of resources to bolster the ability of countries in relatively weak economic situations to participate successfully.

Table 5.6

EMS Intervention Rates at 17 March 1979

	D-Mark	French franc	Dutch-guilder	Belgian franc	Italian lira	Danish krone	Irish punt	ECU central rates; % divergence indicator
D-Mark	—	2.2581	1.0596	15.3665	430.698	2.7598	0.25806	2.51064
		2.3621	1.10835	16.0740	485.576	2.8864	0.269937	±1.1325
French franc 10	4.2335	—	4.5880	66.5375	1,864.9	11.9490	1.11739	5.79831
	4.4285		4.7990	69.600	2,102.5	12.4985	1.16881	±1.35
Dutch guilder	0.90225	2.0838	—	14.1800	397.434	2.5464	0.23813	2.72077
	0.94375	2.1796		14.8925	448.074	2.6636	0.249089	±1.5075
Belgian franc 100	6.2210	14.3680	6.7420	—	2,740.44	17.559	1.64198	39.4582
	6.5080	15.0290	7.0520		3,089.61	18.367	1.71755	±1.53
Italian lira 1,000	2.059	4.7560	2.23175	32.365	—	5.8130	0.543545	1,148.15
	2.322	5.3620	2.5160	36.490		6.5530	0.612801	±4.0725
Danish krone 10	3.4645	8.0010	3.75425	54.445	1,526.05	—	0.914343	7.08592
	3.6235	8.3690	3.9270	56.950	1,720.45		0.956424	±1.635
Irish punt	3.7050	8.5555	4.0145	58.2225	1,631.85	10.4555	—	0.662638
	3.8750	8.9495	4.1995	60.9020	1,839.78	10.9365		±1.665

Quantities of each currency in ECU basket + weighting per cent

D-Mark	£ sterling	French franc	Lira	Guilder	Belgian franc	Lux. franc	Danish krone	Irish punt
0.828	0.0885	1.15	109	0.286	3.66	0.14	0.217	0.00759
(33%)	(13.4%)	(19.8%)	(9.5%)	(10.5%)	(9.2%)	(0.35%)	(3.1%)	(1.15%)

Source: *The Financial Times* Monday 19 March 1979

UNANSWERED QUESTIONS ON EMS

The official EEC communiqué still leaves several questions unanswered. First of all there is the problem of which country takes the exchange risk, since the ECU may change in value against the gold and the dollar. The ECUs are still legally owned by the participant countries. They have merely deposited them temporarily as part of the revolving swap arrangements.

A related uncertainty is what form any remuneration of the ECU should take. It is fairly clear that the unit will have to offer some sort of interest rate—as does the SDR unit of the International Monetary Fund. It is not, however, certain how this should be calculated, and what should happen to income from short-term dollar holdings, such as U.S. Treasury Bills, deposited in return for the ECU.

The next problem is what value would be given to gold. The IMF and the U.S. government are in the process of demonetising gold and thus do not want any EEC action which will remonetise it.

A related IMF worry is that expansion of the EEC credit facilities will undermine the role of the IMF.

A further problem is what happens to the ECU divergency indicators if sterling (not a member of EMS but included in the ECU) appreciates as occurred following OPEC price increases in July 1979.

REFERENCES

[1] R. Solomon, *The International Monetary System 1945–1976. An Insiders View.* Harper and Row 1976, pp. 12–13.

[2] H. Kaufman, "The future of the dollar." A talk delivered before the Council on Foreign Relations Inc., New York. April 10th, 1978.

[3] C. W. McMahon, "Is there an international monetary system?" *Bank of England Quarterly Bulletin,* June 1978.

[4] C. A. Coombs, *The Arena of International Finance.* John Wiley & Sons. 1976. pp. 14–15.

[5] Resolution of the European Council on the European Monetary System agreed in Brussels on 5 December on the establishment of the European Monetary System and related matters.

Appendix I
Foreign exchange rates

Quoted against U.S. dollars. (Last working days)[a]

		Pound Sterling (b)	Belgian francs	Swiss francs	French francs	Italian lire	Netherlands guilders	Deutschemark	Japanese yen
1971	Dec.	2.5522	45.24	3.9180	5.2265	594.55	3.2755	3.2785	314.80
1972	July	2.4501	43.82	3.7728	5.0018	580.98	3.1948	3.1746	300.85
	Aug.	2.4485	43.89	3.7814	5.0018	581.13	3.2244	3.1872	300.95
	Sept.	2.4203	44.23	3.8018	5.0120	581.88	3.2370	3.2031	301.03
	Oct.	2.3420	44.12	3.7995	5.0325	584.85	3.2290	3.2048	300.85
	Nov.	2.3527	44.05	3.7762	5.0475	584.43	3.2260	3.1935	301.00
	Dec.	2.3481	44.07	3.7695	5.1180	582.40	3.2270	3.2015	301.43
1973	Jan.	2.3822	43.81	3.6200	5.0225	581.65	3.1800	3.1560	301.05
	Feb.	2.4900	39.39	3.1300	4.5275	566.00	2.8550	2.8360	265.25
	Mar.	2.4777	39.98	3.2390	4.5325	582.00	2.9360	2.8365	266.00
	Apr.	2.4895	40.30	3.2410	4.5680	590.63	2.9595	2.8380	265.33
	May	2.5670	38.44	3.0870	4.3400	582.50	2.8165	2.6995	264.45
	June	2.5820	36.08	2.9250	4.1300	574.00	2.6225	2.4250	262.50
	July	2.5120	35.60	2.8350	4.0950	585.00	2.5865	2.3260	263.05
	Aug.	2.4587	37.58	3.0310	4.3070	565.75	2.6800	2.4587	265.28
	Sept.	2.4139	36.73	3.0290	4.2475	563.50	2.5343	2.4133	265.54
	Oct.	2.4386	36.86	3.0990	4.2125	570.50	2.5385	2.4453	266.81
	Nov.	2.3425	39.48	3.2048	4.4875	604.38	2.7565	2.6223	279.95
	Dec.	2.3235	41.31	3.2480	4.6988	607.50	2.8200	2.7025	279.95
1974	Jan.	2.2750	42.11	3.2550	5.0050	661.50	2.8820	2.7550	298.50
	Feb.	2.3050	40.25	3.1310	4.8363	647.50	2.7935	2.6720	288.00
	Mar.	2.3935	38.98	3.0200	4.7663	624.00	2.6870	2.5180	275.50
	Apr.	2.4218	38.95	2.9300	4.8975	633.25	2.5798	2.4478	279.35
	May	2.3980	37.98	2.9755	4.8900	645.00	2.6445	2.5230	281.70
	June	2.3910	38.00	2.9975	4.8000	647.75	2.6500	2.5445	284.20
	July	2.3869	38.13	2.9670	4.6825	645.45	2.6300	2.5760	298.25
	Aug.	2.3172	39.53	3.0095	4.8230	660.50	2.7120	2.6640	302.80
	Sept.	2.3325	39.23	2.9485	4.7412	660.85	2.7040	2.6530	298.40
	Oct.	2.3362	38.16	2.8685	4.7947	667.20	2.6375	2.5787	300.00
	Nov.	2.3260	37.24	2.7125	4.6875	664.37	2.5665	2.4742	300.25
	Dec.	2.3495	36.05	2.5412	4.4325	649.25	2.5045	2.4070	300.80
1975	Jan.	2.3811	35.01	2.4945	4.3223	639.60	2.4300	2.3380	297.85
	Feb.	2.4292	34.00	2.4025	4.1625	627.50	2.3420	2.2767	286.35
	Mar.	2.4026	34.77	2.5375	4.2250	633.25	2.4017	2.3447	292.10
	Apr.	2.3522	35.08	2.5565	4.1377	631.70	2.4190	2.3790	292.10
	May	2.3167	34.93	2.4990	4.0360	624.85	2.4032	2.3442	291.40
	June	2.1845	35.31	2.5017	4.0400	630.45	2.4400	2.3545	295.47
	July	2.1515	38.34	2.6960	4.3630	665.40	2.6510	2.5682	297.55
	Aug.	2.1102	38.47	2.6850	4.3950	668.50	2.6414	2.5822	297.97
	Sept.	2.0436	39.95	2.7442	4.5100	685.95	2.7290	2.6455	302.70
	Oct.	2.0785	38.56	2.6250	4.3460	673.15	2.6237	2.5567	301.70
	Nov.	2.0202	39.51	2.6780	4.4577	688.75	2.6930	2.6245	303.07
	Dec.	2.0233	39.51	2.6205	4.4662	683.55	2.6835	2.6187	305.07
1976	Jan.	2.0292	39.24	2.6027	4.4767	758.50	2.6652	2.5889	303.67
	Feb.	2.0253	39.19	2.5692	4.4867	771.00	2.6785	2.5695	302.14
	Mar.	1.9158	39.02	2.5398	4.6790	840.50	2.6882	2.5400	299.50
	Apr.	1.8410	38.78	2.5160	4.6610	899.75	2.6833	2.5365	299.00
	May	1.7590	39.70	2.4600	4.7230	843.50	2.7507	2.5912	299.95
	June	1.7847	39.66	2.4680	4.7397	839.25	2.7252	2.5737	298.02
	July	1.7842	39.34	2.4824	4.9145	835.20	2.7067	2.5432	293.25
	Aug.	1.7764	38.85	2.4795	4.9330	840.75	2.6420	2.5291	289.40
	Sept.	1.6680	37.65	2.4457	4.9350	859.50	2.5625	2.4362	286.75
	Oct.	1.5860	36.88	2.4322	5.0010	863.50	2.5090	2.3990	294.32
	Nov.	1.6537	36.76	2.4446	4.9956	865.30	2.5087	2.4061	296.95
	Dec.	1.7020	35.93	2.4450	4.9640	875.12	2.4590	2.3597	293.25
1977	Jan.	1.7150	37.02	2.5097	4.9717	382.05	2.5250	2.4113	288.40
	Feb.	1.7128	36.62	2.5577	4.9820	884.00	2.4967	2.3904	282.82
	Mar.	1.7201	36.61	2.5445	4.9700	887.55	2.4920	2.3907	277.47
	Apr.	1.7193	35.98	2.5135	4.9540	886.70	2.4427	2.3535	277.85
	May	1.7188	36.05	2.5039	4.9420	885.55	2.4659	2.3569	277.25
	June	1.7202	36.05	2.4641	4.9180	884.80	2.4766	2.3394	267.50
	July	1.7375	35.34	2.4090	4.8875	881.75	2.4460	2.2905	266.67
	Aug.	1.7429	35.63	2.3915	4.9025	881.92	2.4470	2.3162	267.45
	Sept.	1.7475	35.71	2.3440	4.8875	882.17	2.4537	2.3062	263.60
	Oct.	1.8396	35.21	2.2350	4.8830	879.27	2.4230	2.2537	249.32
	Nov.	1.8165	35.11	2.1637	4.8555	877.60	2.4048	2.2268	244.92
	Dec.	1.9185	32.70	1.9825	4.6950	871.55	2.2625	2.0925	239.35
1978	Jan.	1.9520	32.65	1.9760	4.7337	867.05	2.2565	2.1062	241.53
	Feb.	1.9364	31.56	1.8445	4.7700	853.05	2.1725	2.0267	238.47
	Mar.	1.8625	31.35	1.8350	4.5550	851.75	2.1485	2.0060	221.25
	Apr.	1.8267	32.21	1.9320	4.6100	866.92	2.2077	2.0687	224.02
	May	1.8284	32.70	1.8932	4.5987	866.00	2.2430	2.0925	221.50
	June	1.8605	32.67	1.8475	4.5000	854.50	2.2305	2.0715	203.65
	July	1.9300	32.17	1.7390	4.3695	842.25	2.2035	2.0410	188.97
	Aug.	1.9420	31.35	1.6410	4.3550	835.15	2.1585	1.9895	190.30
	Sept.	1.9739	30.53	1.7175	4.3300	823.55	2.1057	1.9370	188.80
	Oct.	2.0864	27.27	1.4880	4.0100	791.00	1.8810	1.7935	177.60
	Nov.	1.9443	30.41	1.7320	4.4190	849.05	2.0875	1.9272	199.10

(a) Middle market telegraphic rates taken from the Bank of England Quarterly Bulletin.
(b) Dollars per pound.

118

6

Financing International Trade

As the world economy has expanded, so have the opportunities and the complexities of international trade. Two basic factors dominate the problems of financing international trade: these problems are those of credit risk and foreign exchange risk. Credit risk, i.e. the risk one may never be paid for one's goods, arises since it is difficult to take repossession of your goods, due to non-payment, when they are outside one's own country. Foreign exchange risk, occurs when there is a change in the exchange rate between when a contract is negotiated and when payment is received (*see Chapters 3, 4, 7, 8, and 9*). This Chapter examines the alternative sources of finance open to minimise credit risk for exporters.

For an exporter of goods the banking system provides several methods of receiving payment, and to the importer several ways of making payment. Before any goods are shipped, the importer and exporter should naturally agree upon the terms of the transaction e.g., price, insurance, freight, dates of shipment, etc. In choosing the method of payment the choice lies between the following alternatives:
(1.) Cash with order
(2.) Open account
(3.) Bills of exchange
(4.) Documentary letters of credit
(5.) Government assistance
These alternatives are not mutually exclusive as the use of bills of exchange and letters of credit are often associated with government assistance.

CASH WITH ORDER
There is no doubt that this is the most desirable system from the point of view of the exporter, although in international trade it is the most unusual as some sort of credit to the importer is normally given. If the seller receives cash with the order, this means that he has both the goods and the money.

Cash payment is not attractive to buyers since they bear the entire burden of financing the shipment. The buyer loses the use of

119

funds for a considerable time before the goods are received, incurring a loss in the use of working capital, as well as loss of interest. There may also be resentment of the view that the buyer is unworthy of credit. Furthermore, the buyer is dependent upon the honesty, solvency and promptness of the exporter in the business deal. The buyer has to be sure that the seller's country, for example, for political reasons, will not prohibit the export of the goods after payment, that the exchange control authorities in the buyer's country permit advance payments to be made, and that the buyer has adequate working capital to finance the transaction. From the buyer's point of view it is risky and is only likely to occur if the buyer trusts the seller implicitly and feels that no changes in a country's foreign trade regulations, including exchange control regulations, are likely to occur.

Cash payments are used when the importer is of doubtful credit standing, when the exporter is financially weak, on orders requiring special construction, or when the exporter is not familiar with the competitive situation faced by manufacturers in other countries.

OPEN ACCOUNT

This is the system whereby the importer and the exporter agree that the debt will be settled at a future predetermined date. Meanwhile, the goods and shipping documents are sent direct to the buyer so that the buyer receives the goods and can then do what he wants with them. Thus the open account system is the opposite of the cash method. The open account has serious risks and is subject to the same provisos as cash with order. Since no documentary evidence of ownership or obligation exists, the open account presents difficulties because of differences in the laws and customs of countries, which make it difficult to safeguard the interests of the exporter. The exporter loses control of the goods, and if payment from the buyer is not forthcoming, there is little the exporter can do about it.

Under open account the burden of financing rests upon the exporter. Thus the exporter needs more working capital than under other systems. Trading under 'open account' usually only takes place when there is a strong business relationship between the two parties and the exporter is satisfied as to the credit-worthiness of the importer.

There are four basic ways of paying on open account. Firstly, payment can be by telegraphic transfer. This is an instruction from the importer's bank to the exporter's bank to transfer some of the balance on its account to the exporter. The importer must pay his local bank the local currency equivalent in order to pay the amount of the invoice. This invoice could be expressed in his (the importer's) currency or the currency of the exporter. The importer's bank will sell him the appropriate amount of foreign currency in the latter event and debit him with the local currency equivalent. The importer's bank will cable a correspondent bank in the exporter's country requesting that bank to effect settlement to the exporter. This is the fastest means of payment. Secondly, payment can be by mail transfer. This is the same process as above except that the payment is mailed by the importer's bank to the correspondent bank and thus takes longer. Thirdly, payment can be by bankers' draft. This is a cheque drawn by one bank on another. In this case an importer pays by buying a bankers' draft from his bank drawn on a correspondent bank in the exporter's currency. The exporter, when receiving this draft through the mail from the importer, normally pays it into his bank for collection. Fourthly, payment can be by cheque if exchange controls permit.

In the case of telegraphic transfers or mail transfers cleared funds are released by the exporter. A bankers' draft or a cheque have to be sent for collection upon their receipt and this can take considerable time.

BILLS OF EXCHANGE

Another method of financing trade is by a bill of exchange. This is formally defined in the U.K. Bills of Exchange Act 1882 as:

An unconditional order in writing addressed by one person to another, signed by the person giving it, requiring the person to whom it is addressed to pay on demand or at a fixed or determinable future time a sum certain in money to, or to the order of, a specified person, or to bearer[1].

In examining how bills of exchange can best be utilised, it is important to understand the relevant terminology.

Correct Terminology	Other Terminology
The drawer	Exporter
The remitting bank	Exporter's bank
The collecting bank	Correspondent or agent
The drawee	Importer or buyer

Bills of exchange are drawn by sellers of products, calling upon buyers either to pay, or to accept for payment, a designated sum of money at a determinable future time. Acceptance consists of an acknowledgement to this effect written across the face of the bill and signed by the drawee (buyer), obliging the drawee to provide payment of the amount stated within the period of time designated. When accepted, a draft becomes a trade acceptance. This method of payment provides documentary evidence of obligation. If the acceptor is highly respectable and the country concerned possesses a bill market the trade bill will be readily transferable.

In using the bill of exchange the exporter (the drawer) despatches his goods and can then either send the shipping documents to his bank or send them direct to the drawee (the importer). Exporters who want the proceeds of a sale collected from the overseas buyer will give instructions to their bank to undertake this for them. The exporter requiring collection through his banker will draw a bill of exchange on the buyer, attach the bill of exchange to the documents, and hand 'the collection' to his banker for collection.

Bills of exchange can be of two main types. Firstly, there are clean bills. Where the exporter and the importer know each other well, the exporter may be willing to send the documents of ownership direct to the importer and draw a clean bill (i.e. one without documents attached) which he will then pass to his bank for collection. Only if the exporter has complete trust in the importer will he use this method. This is similar to open account except that the onus of settling lies with the buyer on open account terms and with the seller under a clean collection. Secondly, there are documentary bills. If a bill of exchange is accompanied by documents of title to goods it is called a documentary bill. The exporter sends his documents through his bank for delivery to the importer under acceptance of the accompanying bill of exchange (D/A i.e. documents against acceptance) or upon payment of the bill (D/P i.e. documents against payment).

If the bill is a sight or demand bill, the documents will only be handed over against payment of the bill. If the bill is a usance bill, i.e. some credit is given to the importer, the documents are normally handed over against the drawer's acceptance of the bill.

To illustrate how a bill of exchange operates, Kahler and Kramer have given an example of a US exporter using a 60 day sight draft:

(1) The American exporter makes shipment to a British importer with the billing made out to the name of the exporter.

(2) The exporter delivers the draft and shipping documents to the American bank which sends the draft and shipping documents to the British bank.

(3) The British bank notifies the importer that the documents have arrived and presents the draft to the importer for acceptance, payment in 60 days.

(4) Upon accepting the bill of exchange, the shipping documents are surrendered to the importer and the shipment can now be claimed.

(5) The accepted bill of exchange is returned to the American bank by the British bank.

(6) The exporter discounts the draft and receives advance payment.

(7) The American bank, in turn, disposes of the bill of exchange in the acceptance market.

(8) Upon receiving such funds, the American bank is now in a liquid position again.

(9) When the 60-day maturity approaches, the bill of exchange is sent to the British bank by some financial institution that had purchased it from the American bank.

(10) The British bank receives payment from the British importer in pounds sterling and the conversion of sterling to dollars is made by the British bank.

(11) The funds are transmitted to the present holder of the trade acceptance.

(12) The American exporter settles with the American bank to complete the transaction[2].

122

Figure 6.1 makes this clearer. Stages 5 to 9 will mainly happen for business names of the highest quality. Mostly, the accepted bill would be held by the collecting bank until maturity when it will be presented to the acceptor for payment and in the event of payment the funds are then remitted back to the U.S.A.

Figure 6.1
INTERNATIONAL TRADE FINANCING UNDER A SIXTY-DAY SIGHT-DRAFT TRANSACTION : EXPORTER'S CURRENCY

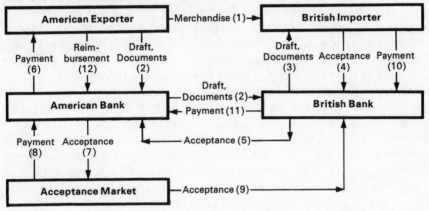

Source : Kahler and Kramer. *'International Marketing'* South Western Publishing, 1977.

Advantages and disadvantages of bills of exchange

The advantages to the exporter of using bills of exchange are the following. In the first place they have the advantage of being cheaper than documentary credits, and secondly, they open the way to several sources of finance. Bills of exchange are discounted by negotiation; this means that a bank buys its customer's outward collection, i.e. the foreign currency proceeds of an export, at the time that the collection is remitted abroad. This provides the exporter with working capital. A further source of finance is provided by bills of exchange in that a bank may give an advance against an outward collection.

The exporter can use a Merchants Bank Acceptance Facility but this is only possible for exporters and importers of fairly substantial turnover and credit-worthiness. Under this scheme documentary drafts drawn by the exporter on the overseas buyer form the security and are handled as documentary collections by the Merchant Bank. These documents are then pledged to the Merchant Bank. The exporter draws a draft on the Merchant Bank and after acceptance by the Merchant Bank (this draft, known as an accommodation bill) is discounted (usually by a discount house) and the proceeds paid to the exporter.

123

A further major benefit bills of exchange may provide is that, where title documents are to be released only against payment, the exporter's position is more secure than on open account terms.

Bills of exchange may, however, give rise to disadvantages to exporters. Firstly, the exporter may not be paid until the money is received by his bank, and if he cannot easily obtain finances from elsewhere it may prove expensive. Secondly, the security of payment is not as good as that offered by cash in advance or a letter of credit. The importer may refuse to pay for various reasons, e.g. he may have no money; there may be a sudden imposition of exchange controls or there may be a political uprising preventing payment. All these events prevent the importer making payment and involve the exporter in costs of storage, legal fees, and perhaps involving the necessity of finding a new buyer.

From the point of view of the importer, bills of exchange have the advantage of providing him with the goods and giving him a period of credit in which to pay for them. Also, the importer can be sure the goods are what he ordered before authorising payment. Finally, it is more convenient and cheaper than using letters of credit. However, there may be disadvantages to the importer. Documents against acceptance collections make the importer legally liable on an accepted bill of exchange. In this case the exporter can sue without the trouble of proving the contract of sale. Also, documents against payment collections may result in the buyer paying for goods which may not be what he ordered.

Bills of exchange are an attempt to increase the degree of certainty of payment in international operations. There is no doubt that, at a higher cost than cash in advance and open account, they do achieve this objective.

DOCUMENTARY LETTERS OF CREDIT

As with bills of exchange documentary letters of credit have a distinctive terminology.

Correct Terminology	Other Terminology
The applicant (or accountee)	Importer
The opening (issuing bank)	Importer's bank
The advising bank	Issuing bank correspondent
The beneficiary	The exporter/seller

A documentary letter of credit is a credit under which drawings are honoured, provided the beneficiary delivers the documents evidencing shipment of the goods ordered. Armed with a documentary letter of credit an exporter is able to receive payment for the goods in his own country, once shipment has taken place, with the buyer secure in the knowledge that payment will not

124

have been made unless the terms and conditions of the credit have been complied with.

With the security of the documentary credit the exporter is able to produce the goods, knowing that he will receive payment promptly; and the importer knows that he will receive the goods when they are required.

The first stage in an export transaction is the sale contract and, if it is agreed between seller and buyer that a documentary credit should be used for payment of the goods, the buyer will make arrangements with his bank for its issue. Thus the onus of drawing up the letter of credit lies with the importer. He will give his bank detailed instructions concerning the description of the goods, their quality and price, the total value of the credit, the documents required, the latest (and sometimes earliest) date on which documents may be presented for payment, the usance, if any, of the draft, and any special provisions which may have been agreed between buyer and seller.

All these terms and conditions will be contained in the advice of issue of the documentary credit sent to the beneficiary (seller, accreditee, exporter). The buyer (accreditor, importer) is also sometimes known as the 'taker'.

As a documentary credit is separate from a sale contract beneficiaries should, on receipt of the credit, check that the terms do not conflict with those agreed in the sale contract. Should they differ the beneficiary must contact the 'taker' and request him to instruct his banker to issue an amendment to the credit to correct the discrepancy

There are three ways in which a bank may advise the beneficiary that a credit has been opened in his favour: (i) they may advise him direct (sometimes indicating a bank in his country where he may obtain payment against the documents); (ii) they may address the advice of opening to the beneficiary, but send it to their branch or correspondent where he is located, for onward transmission; (iii) they may address it to their branch or correspondent there, with a request that he should be notified. The branch or correspondent will then transcribe the details on to their own form of advice, which will be addressed and sent to the beneficiary.

Letters of credit can be of various types e.g. revocable, irrevocable and confirmed irrevocable. The distinction between revocable and irrevocable is best explained by Articles 2 and 3 of *the Uniform Customs and Practice for Documentary Credits*[3].

Article 2

A revocable credit may be amended or cancelled at any moment without prior notice to the beneficiary. However, the issuing bank is bound to reimburse a branch or other bank to which such a credit has been transmitted and made available for payment, acceptance or negotiation, for any payment, acceptance or negotiation complying with the terms and conditions of the credit and any amendments received up to the time of the payment, acceptance or negotiation made by such branch or other bank prior to receipt by it of notice of amendment or of cancellations.

Article 3

a. An irrevocable credit constitutes a definite undertaking of the issuing bank, provided that the terms and conditions of the credit are complied with:

(i) to pay, or that payment will be made, if the credit provides for payment, whether against a draft or not;

(ii) to accept drafts if the credit provides for acceptance by the issuing bank or to be responsible for their acceptance and payment at maturity if the credit provides for the acceptance of drafts drawn on the applicant for the credit or any other drawee specified in the credit;

(iii) to purchase/negotiate, without recourse to drawers and/or bona fide holders, drafts drawn by the beneficiary, at sight or at a tenor, on the applicant for the credit or on any other drawee specified in the credit, or to provide for purchase/negotiation by another bank, if the credit provides for purchase/negotiation.

A revocable credit does not constitute a legally-binding undertaking between the bank or banks concerned and the beneficiary, since it may be modified or cancelled at any time, without the beneficiary being notified, though payment made before receipt of a modification or cancellation remains valid. In other words, it is never 'confirmed'. A bank cannot confirm its own credit but another bank may do so. An irrevocable credit may not be modified or cancelled without the consent of all the parties concerned.

The beneficiary of a credit received from the other end of the world may never have heard of the name of the opening bank, let alone be sure of its standing. If the opening bank becomes bankrupt after the beneficiary's bank has negotiated the credit, but before it has been reimbursed, his bank has recourse to him. As a safeguard, the beneficiary can ask his bank to confirm the credit for a fee provided the bank is satisfied about the standing of the opening bank. Once confirmed, the confirming bank has no recourse to the beneficiary after negotiation of the credit. This results in what is termed a 'confirmed irrevocable documentary letter of credit'.

When the beneficiary has received the documentary credit in the form he requires, and the goods are available for shipment, arrangements are made with a despatching (shipping, forwarding) agent to draw up the documents. The agent is given a copy of the credit enabling him to ensure that they are correctly prepared. After the goods have been shipped, the beneficiary delivers all the documents to his bank, with the credit. The bank compares the documents with the credit, and, if satisfied that they are completely in order, pays the beneficiary. This is known as an availment. Availments may be partial or full, according to the terms of the credit. Tomlinson has set out various procedures that the beneficiary should check carefully. (see p. 135)

126

The advantages and disadvantages of documentary letters of credit

Although the burden of financing is placed upon the buyer under a letter of credit transaction, this method of payment also provides certain advantages. Perhaps the greatest practical benefit derived by the buyer is the protection of a definite date being set by which the seller is required to ship the order. The buyer, accordingly, may expect prompt delivery, as the credit will expire on the date set unless an extension is granted. Secondly, the buyer can receive low prices when a letter of credit is submitted, since contingencies are so fully safeguarded that an exporter finds it unnecessary to cover them in the price. Advance orders, or orders running throughout a period of time, are also well protected by reason of the expiration date of the letter of credit, as well as by the limitation of the sum of money for which it is drawn. Finally, an attractive cash discount may be offered to importers for providing letter of credit payment.

Letters of credit are of greatest benefit when the parties involved are relative strangers or where one of them is in a country where political developments increase the risk of non-payment.

In recent years an ever-rising proportion of world trade has been conducted between multinational companies, subsidiaries and associates of the same company and long-established trading partners. In virtually all these cases the risk of non-payment is so greatly reduced that trading on open account is considered quite satisfactory.

Apart from the changing pattern of international trade, letters of credit themselves have certain drawbacks and increasingly popular alternatives. A small importer wishing to open a letter of credit may be called on by his bank to provide partial (or occasionally, even full) cash cover. The effects on companies' cash flows can be sufficiently serious to encourage them to find other ways of arranging payment. For this they may turn to a confirming house (also known as international trade finance companies) or an international credit union to arrange extended payment terms. Suppliers are invariably content to deal with the confirming house (which makes payment on behalf of the importer) without the superfluous security of a letter of credit. Exporters can likewise improve cash flows by selling their debtors' books to a factoring house. The functions of a factoring house are to give the seller credit insurance by taking over his invoices as the goods are supplied and to provide cash, either immediately or at an agreed future date, for up to 75 per cent of the invoices less the factor's charges.

In conclusion, the credit risk is at a maximum for the exporter when he is dealing on open account. The credit risk is at a minimum if an irrevocable confirmed letter of credit is required from the importer. The exporter will be providing the maximum amount of financing to the importer if it sells the merchandise on open account.

GOVERNMENT ASSISTANCE
Government assistance to U.K. exporters[4]

The Export Credits Guarantee Department (ECGD), which is a department of the U.K. Government, assists exporters both of goods and services in the following ways. First, it insures them against the risk of not being paid, whether through the default of the buyer or through other causes. Secondly, it furnishes unconditional guarantees of 100 per cent repayment to banks. On this security banks provide finance to exporters at favourable interest rates. ECGD insures new investment overseas against the risks of war, expropriation and the restriction of remittances. ECGD now also provides protection against part of the increases in U.K. costs for large capital goods contracts with long manufacturing periods, for major contracts, supports the issue of performance bonds, and for members of a U.K. consortium provides protection from loss by the insolvency of a member of the consortium.

The export trade is classified by ECGD into two broad categories. First, there is trade of a repetitive type, involving standard, or near standard, goods. Cover on these is provided on a 'comprehensive' basis. The exporter must offer for cover all or most of his export business for at least a year in both good and bad markets. Secondly, there are projects and large capital goods business of a non-repetitive nature, usually of high value and involving lengthy credit terms. Such business is not suited to comprehensive treatment and specific policies are negotiated for each contract. Cover for specific insurance is given in one of two ways, according to the manner in which the credit is provided. In the case of 'supplier credit' the manufacturer sells on deferred payment terms, borrowing from a U.K. bank to finance the period from shipment of the goods until payment is received. ECGD insures the exporter and, in many cases, additionally gives a guarantee direct to the bank. In the case of 'buyer credit' the exporter receives prompt payment from his buyer, who draws on a loan from a U.K. bank to provide this payment, the loan being repaid by instalments. ECGD guarantees the bank repayment by the overseas customer.

In understanding the work of the ECGD it is important to distinguish between their role in providing insurance for the provision of supplier credit and in providing guarantees for supplier and buyer credit.

Insurance for supplier credit

The ECGD Comprehensive Short-Term Guarantee has been designed to provide a comprehensive insurance for a volume of sales, on credit terms of up to six months, at a low premium. The policy holder normally undertakes to insure his whole export turnover for a period of not less than twelve months.

Broadly speaking, the risks covered under the Comprehensive Short-Term Guarantee as follows:

(i)   insolvency of the buyer
(ii) the buyer's failure to pay within six months of due date for goods which he has accepted
(iii) the buyer's failure to take up goods which have been despatched to him (where not caused or excused by the policy holder's actions, and where ECGD decides that the institution or continuation of legal proceedings against the buyer would serve no useful purpose)
(iv) a general moratorium on external debt decreed by the government of the buyer's country or of a third country through which payment must be made
(v)   any other action by the government of the buyer's country which prevents performance of the contract in whole or in part
(vi) political events, economic difficulties, legislative or administrative measures arising outside the UK which prevent or delay the transfer of payments or deposits made in respect of the contract
(vii) legal discharge of a debt (not being legal discharge under the proper law of the contract) in a foreign currency, which results in a shortfall at the date of transfer
(viii) war and certain other events preventing performance of the contract provided that the event is not one normally insured with commercial insurers
(ix) cancellation or non-renewal of a UK export licence or the prohibition or restriction on export of goods from the UK by law[5]

ECGD covers 90 per cent of the loss where it arises under the first two risks listed above. Under the third, the exporter bears a 'first loss' of 20 per cent of the full original price, and ECGD bears 90 per cent of the balance. For the other risks ECGD covers 95 per cent of the loss, except where the loss arises before the goods are despatched overseas (pre-credit), where the loss is limited to 90 per cent.

The basis of the comprehensive policies is that an exporter offers for insurance a reasonable spread of business occurring over a future period. Transactions involving capital goods or projects on such a scale that the risk cannot be averaged out are subject to individual negotiation of insurance between the exporter and the ECGD.

Under a Specific Guarantee, cover is available from either the date of contract or the date of shipment, although the lengthy manufacturing periods on purpose-built equipment make the former the more widely used. The risks covered are broadly similar to those covered under the comprehensive policies, except that the top percentage of cover, even after shipment, remains at 90 per cent. No cover is given against the failure of private buyers to take up exported goods. Many sales of capital goods are made to government buyers, and for this type of business ECGD will cover the risk of default by the buyer at any stage in the transaction.

Guarantees for supplier credit financing

Where the credit period is less than two years from the date of export of goods or completion of services and the buyer gives a promissory note or accepts a bill of exchange, ECGD may give an unconditional guarantee to the exporter's bank that it will pay 100 per cent of any sum three months overdue. ECGD agrees a limit for the finance it will guarantee, based on experience during that period and the exporter's general financial standing. To operate the scheme the exporter need only present the bills or notes to his bank after shipment of the goods with the appropriate evidence (shipping documents, etc or buyer's certificate of performance in the case of services) and a standard form of warranty that his ECGD cover for the transaction is in order.

British banks have agreed to finance 100 per cent of the principal value of such transactions charging interest at 0.5 per cent over base rate. The premium for one year is paid by the exporter in advance at 0.125 per cent of the agreed revolving borrowing limit. The exporter signs a recourse undertaking giving ECGD the right to recover from him should the bank claim sums due in advance of, or in excess of, claims payable under the standard ECGD policy. All types of U.K. exports and re-exports qualify for this facility.

For business on terms extending from cash against documents (or cash on completion for services) to six-months credit ECGD will give a guarantee to the financing bank. Thus ECGD is guaranteeing a simple loan from the bank to the exporter in respect of the export transaction and its guarantee is for 100 per cent of the bank loan.

Guarantees for buyer credit financing

In many large contracts for which specific supplier credit insurance is available, exporters may prefer to negotiate on cash terms and arrange a loan to the buyer on repayment terms equivalent to the credit he might expect from the supplier. ECGD Buyer Credit Guarantees are available to banks making such loans in respect of contracts of £1 million or more.

Exporters may prefer this method because, for example, they can more easily arrange for progress payments at intermediate stages of manufacture, or because, being lightly capitalised in relation to their turnover, recourse problems make it difficult for them to arrange for further ECGD guarantees to their bank; or they may find that this form of financing is better suited to the business methods of some buyers.

Under a Buyer Credit Guarantee the overseas purchaser, out of his own resources, is normally required to pay direct to the supplier 15 to 20 per cent of the contract price, including an adequate down payment on signature of the contract. The remainder is paid to the supplier direct from a loan made to the buyer or a bank in his country by a U.K. bank and guaranteed by

ECGD, as to 100 per cent of capital and interest, against non-payment for any reason. The contract may include some foreign goods and services, but the amount of the loan will normally be less than the British goods and services to be supplied.

In consequence, the supplier who has received from the buyer his deposit, the payment on completion, and the whole of the balance guaranteed by ECGD has been paid in full. What remains is a borrowing relationship between the overseas borrower and the U.K. bankers, with ECGD standing as guarantor of repayment by the borrower.

In 1977 ECGD introduced a new Foreign Currency Buyer Credit Facility. Under this scheme the banking system has to finance buyer credits by borrowing foreign currency from the Euromarkets with the risk being guaranteed by ECGD. When submitting a tender, a contractor has, under the new buyer-credit policy imposed by the Government, to quote in foreign currency, although the exporter normally calculates his costs in sterling. The benefit to the exporting company is that, if the foreign currency is at premium in the forward market, he can, if he has invoiced in foreign currency, then sell it forward, so enabling him to reduce his foreign currency price and obtain more business (*see Chapter 9*). However, one problem of the Foreign Currency Buyer Credit scheme was that companies were exposed to a currency risk during the period between submission of a tender for an overseas order and the day when the contract was actually awarded. An example may make this clearer. In November 1976 the premium on one-year forward dollars was 8.5 per cent. In June 1977 the premium on one-year forward dollars was 3.7 per cent. Any exporter to the U.S.A. who reduced his price by 8.5 per cent in November 1976 to reflect this potential gain, but was only given a firm contract in June 1977, would find he was making a substantial loss.

In determining his price the exporter has to estimate the amount of sterling he will receive for a given quantity of foreign currency sold forward during the period of the contract and this will inevitably be based on the forward rates prevailing at the time of tender, although he would not normally enter into a forward commitment at this time. If by the time the contract has been awarded, however, sterling has depreciated on the forward market, the contractor may gain, but conversely, if sterling appreciates, he stands to make a loss. In order to avoid this problem the ECGD has introduced an insurance scheme whereby an exporter wishing to tender for an overseas contract may approach the ECGD and agree appropriate spot and forward rates on which to work out his tender price. ECGD then guarantees those rates for three months in return for a (non-refundable) insurance premium. If and when the overseas contract is concluded the exporter will go into the foreign exchange market and cover himself forward. If forward rates have shifted in the meantime, ECGD will take the profit or suffer the loss.

The Foreign Currency Buyer Credit scheme is primarily for large capital goods contracts and all contracts of £20 million have to be financed in foreign currency. This is also preferred for deals over £5 million. In June 1978 the Government extended this scheme to supplier credits with a maturity of two years or more. Some sectors of U.K. industry, such as the ship and aircraft manufacturers, tend to finance their deals on a supplier credit basis.

Government assistance to non-U.K. exporters[6]

In the U.S.A. a large proportion of official export financing is undertaken by the Export-Import Bank (Eximbank). Eximbank functions in three different financing fields. Firstly, it provides direct loans. These are loans made by the bank directly to buyers outside the U.S.A. for purchases of U.S. goods and services. Secondly, it provides guarantees and insurance. Under its guarantee programme it assures repayment of credits extended by private lenders to purchases of U.S. goods who are outside the U.S.A. Thirdly, it provides discount loans. Under this arrangement Eximbank offers both a medium and short-term discount programme to commercial banks. The Eximbank does not purchase the export obligations but instead lends funds to the commercial banks to assist the banks in financing current exports.

In Belgium, medium and long-term export credits are provided by Creditexport, a non profit-making association set up in 1959. In 1976 this association disposed of 48 billion Belgian francs in a revolving fund, about half of which was provided by public institutions, thus making financing possible at relatively favourable terms. The remainder was provided by the commercial banks. The resources of commercial banks come from the financial market in the form of term deposits or savings certificates and bank bonds. Accordingly, their cost corresponds to the market rate to which must be added collection costs. The rates set by Creditexport which are fixed for the life of the credit are thus based on the cost of this capital, it being understood that in the long run no bank could participate at a loss.

In France, the 'Compagnie Francaise pour l'Assurance du Commerce Exterieur' (COFACE) is a joint stock company of a para-public character. It covers short-term commercial risks for its own account, while operating the credit insurance service on behalf of the Government. On all policies, the proportion covered for supplier credit varies from 80 to 85 per cent for commercial risks, 90 per cent for political risks, and 95 per cent in the case of buyer credit. The cost of financing is derived from the average rate of several sources of finance (the '*taux de sortie*'). This rate is stable and independent of the monetary situation although adjustable periodically and is fixed for the entire term of the credit.

In Germany, under the official export credit insurance scheme the Federal Government carries both the political and the commercial risks, but it has entrusted two private companies, the Hermes Kreditversicherungs AG (Hermes) and the Deutsche Revisions- und Treuhand AG (Treuarbeit), with the business management and they act as the Federal Government's agent.

In addition, the Kreditanstalt für Wiederaufbau Bank (KfW) was set up in 1948 to finance the reconstruction of Germany's post-war economy by means of low-interest investment loans, but since 1955 it has taken part in providing long-term finance for German exports, and since the early 1960s it has been the official executive agency for the German capital aid programme for developing countries.

The KfW provides both supplier credits and buyer credits. In the case of supplier credits (refinancing of supplier credits for German exporters) the KfW normally lends to a commercial bank which, in turn, grants a loan in respect of a specific transaction to the exporter as the final borrower. The funds are usually disbursed when the warranty period expires, but not later than four years after the contract was signed, and are normally 60 per cent of the contract value. In the case of buyer credits, which are the most common type, the borrower is the foreign buyer and the loan covers about 76 per cent of the contract value or 100 per cent of the credit element for contracts worth up to DM 50 million.

In 1934 the Swiss authorities introduced a system of insurance of non-commercial risks involving non-payment for exports. The system is governed by a 1958 Law and a 1969 Order (amended on 1 July 1973 and 12 September 1973 respectively). The SWLSS Office for Guaranteeing Export Risks (GERG), whose headquarters are in Zurich, acts on behalf, and on the directives, of the Federal Administration.

In the case of supplier credits the commercial banks refinance exporters up to their share of the GERG policy, with a maximum of 95 per cent; the amount of refinancing may be lower in the case of large risks or in accordance with government economic policy. The rights of the insured may be transferred to the financing body with the approval of GERG but the right to proceed against the exporter remains. In the case of buyers' credits, the banks, and in the case of transfer credits, the banks and the Government, finance the entire credit system (the amount delivered less advances). In the case of transfer credits, the banks have the right to proceed against exporters in case of damage for the amount of the risk not covered by the export risks guarantee.

The Italian mechanism for financing medium and long-term export credits (short-term credits are left to the banking system and are provided on market terms) is based on the major medium-term credit institutions which finance or refinance export credits, buyer credits and supplier credits, and which have recourse to an official rediscount agency, the Istituto Centrale per il Credito a Medio Termine (Mediocredito Centrale). The Mediocredito Centrale either refinances the export credits extended by the banks or pays an interest rebate, so as to enable exports to be financed at predetermined fixed rates of interest and, at the same time to afford a return on their capital at a rate determined by agreement with the government authorities.

In Canada, the Export Development Corporation (EDC) provides long-term loans, i.e. in excess of five years, directly to foreign borrowers and guarantees private loans to such borrowers to finance Canadian exports of capital equipment and services. The interest rate on funds which EDC borrows from the Consolidated Revenue Fund is the lending rate to Canadian Crown Corporations and is established quarterly by the Minister of Finance on the basis of the Government of Canada's cost of borrowing for like maturities.

In Holland, the Nederlandsche Credietverzekering Maatschappij N.V. (NCM), a privately owned insurance company, has provided export credit insurance since 1925. An agreement with the Dutch Government in 1932, broadened in 1946 and renewed in 1961, provides for reinsurance by the Dutch Government of non-commercial and commercial risks which fall outside the scope of private insurance. The NCM, which insures commercial risks for its own account reinsures with the state non-commercial risks and such medium and long-term commercial risks which it cannot take for its own account. In 1976 NCM insured or guaranteed about 8 per cent of total Dutch exports.

In Japan, the Export Insurance Division (EID) of the Ministry of International Trade and Industry (MITI) began operations in 1930. EID insures combined commercial risks from non-payment of Japanese exports of goods and services from the dates of contract or of delivery. The EID covers, under General Export Insurance, 90 per cent of pre-shipment and post-shipment political risks, and 60 per cent of pre-shipment commercial risks, and 80 per cent of pre-shipment commercial risks under insurance policies established for exports for certain sectors of industry. On the other hand, under Export Proceeds Insurance, the EID covers 90 per cent of post-shipment political risks and 90 per cent of post-shipment commercial risks. Banks can subscribe to a policy covering 80 per cent of loss on commercial paper accepted on post-delivery export credits or on pre-shipment financing. Until recently, cover was provided uniquely on a supplier credit basis. There is now a scheme for buyer credit.

REFERENCES

[1] s.3(i).

[2] R. Kahler, R.L. Kramer, *International Marketing*. South Western Publishing Company, 1977.

[3] *Uniforms Customs and Practice for Documentary Credits*. Copyright 1975 ICC, publication no. 290 of the International Chamber of Commerce available from ICC Services, 38 Cours Alber 1er, 75008 Paris, and from British National Committee of the ICC, 6/14 Dear Farrar St., London, SW1H 0DT.

[4] For exact details of ECGD facilities, see *Insurance Facilities of the British Governments Export Credits Guarantee Department* (published annually).

[5] ibid, 1977, p 10 *et seq.*

[6] See, *'The Export Credit Financing System in O.E.C.D. Member Countries.'* Published by the O.E.C.D., Paris 1976.

[7] G.W. Tomlinson, *Pointers on Export Letters of Credit*. (Philadelphia, Pa: The First Pennsylvania Banking and Trust Company, 1953) p.11.

Appendix 1

Tomlinson has set out various procedures that the beneficiary should check carefully[7].

(1) Has the correct title been used in addressing you as beneficiary?

(2) Has the correct title of the buyer been used?

(3) Is the amount sufficient? Take into consideration the terms of the sale and possible addition of any charges.

(4) Is the tenor of the drafts the same as your quotation to the buyer?

(5) Is the credit available at the banking institution or in the locality requested by you?

(6) Are the documents required in the credit in accordance with your arrangements with the buyer and can such documents be furnished?

(7) Is the description of the merchandise correct? (Check unit price, trade definition, point of shipment, and destination)

(8) Do you agree with any special instructions which may appear in the credit?

(9) Is the expiration date and place of expiration satisfactory?

(10) Is the credit confirmed by a domestic bank, or is an unconfirmed credit satisfactory?[7]

7

Foreign Exchange Risk: The Problems of Definition, Measurement and Identification

The current nature of the international monetary system has markedly increased the frequency and size of exchange rate changes. For companies with overseas operations, whether as exporters or as multinationals, this has added a dimension to business decision making which could be widely ignored prior to 1971[1].

Irrespective of the nature of these overseas activities companies need to control the degree of foreign exchange exposure. In order to do this it is necessary to introduce an organisational framework which generates answers and action to the following key questions:

(1) What is the exact nature of the company's foreign exchange exposure?
(2) How can this be identified?
(3) Given its measurement and identification how can the degree of risk be measured?
(4) What is the corporate attitude to this risk?
(5) What policies are available to control this risk and at what costs?
(6) Given the adoption of policies to control foreign exchange risks, what constraints have to be taken into account?

This chapter concentrates on issues (1) to (4) while issues (5) and (6) are dealt with in Chapters 8 and 9.

Even under fixed exchange rates Robbins and Stobaugh found that the risk most often faced by managers of U.S. multinational enterprises in the past has been that of devaluation of other currencies[2]. Brooke and Remmers found that 'in financial matters it seems to be the exchange risk that pre-occupies management most'[3].

136

THE NATURE OF A COMPANY'S FOREIGN EXCHANGE EXPOSURE

Transaction and translation exposure.

In defining exposure it is traditional to distinguish between transaction exposure and translation exposure. The existence of transaction exposure indicates that the value of a transaction would be affected by an exchange rate change between its initiation and completion, for example, where a U.S. firm exports to Britain and invoices in pound sterling. The U.S. firm is not sure how many dollars the pounds will be worth when it is paid. The amount subject to loss is the transaction exposure, and there are three ways in which these occur:

(i) if a currency has to be converted to make or to receive payment for goods or services

(ii) if a currency has to be coverted to repay a loan plus the interest; and

(iii) if currency conversion is needed to make dividend payments.
Table 7.1 gives an example of where transaction exposure exists.

Table 7.1

AN EXAMPLE OF WHERE TRANSACTION EXPOSURE EXISTS

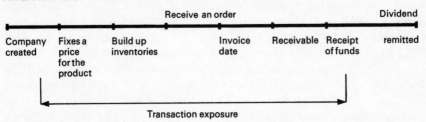

The company sets up in business and decides to export. It fixes product prices, builds up inventories, receives an order, sends an invoice, accepts credit (giving the company a receivable) and is eventually paid. During the whole time period of fixing the product price and actually receiving payment the company is subject to transaction exposure. A very important point to stress about transaction exposure is that it may involve a future cash loss to the company. In other words, it could involve a negative cash flow.

Translation exposure (sometimes called accounting exposure) arises from having assets and liabilities in one or more currencies and consolidating them into a base currency. In this case, it is important to stress that no funds are actually moved and, therefore, translation exposure has no direct effect on cash flow. This is however, only true if there are no tax effects.

Table 7.2 shows where translation exposure occurs.

Table 7.2

WHERE TRANSLATION EXPOSURE OCCURS

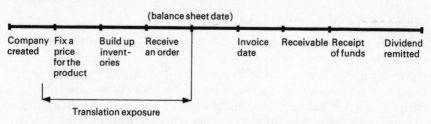

Transaction exposure involves current cash flows, results in realised gains and losses, may have a tax effect in that realised, and in some cases, unrealised gains and losses are taxable or allowable against tax, can affect all parts of the company, and can have important future implications for the company.

Translation exposure is an accounting concept which may affect future cash flow; it is a book value, results in unrealised gains and losses, and usually has no tax effect; it is primarily to do with the past of the company and affects principally the parent company. It is often claimed that transaction exposure affects the income statement while translation exposure affects the balance sheet. This, however, is not strictly accurate. Transaction exposure affects assets and the rules of translation exposure applied will affect profits. The parent company with receivables in a foreign currency will be affected by both translation and transaction exposure. Appendices I, II and III give examples of how transaction and translation gains and losses can occur.

Another type of exposure is off-balance-sheet exposure. How does this arise? To take an example: a U.K. company bids for a contract in Sweden which has been put out to tender in which all bids are to be denominated in Swedish kroner. The contract is for the supply and installation of equipment over a four-year period, with payment spread over the same period. What does the U.K. company do when all its costs are denominated in sterling and it has no future requirement for Swedish kroner? If it bids in sterling and takes no exposure it could lose the contract for non-compliance with the currency of the contract. If it bids in Swedish kroner, what exchange rate does it use for the conversion of the sterling price, in the knowledge that there may only be a six-month forward market in Swedish kroner? In this example, if the U.K. company wins the contract and the Swedish kroner diminishes appreciably against sterling in the future, the U.K. company risks a large foreign exchange loss which is not yet incorporated into the balance sheet.

Another example of off-balance-sheet exposure is lease rental It may be a very substantial legal obligation but it does not appear on the face of the accounts. If it is denominated in foreign currency it represents economic exposure but fluctuations in a lease rental will never be identifiable in annual accounts.

Table 7.3 summarises the possibility of exchange exposure.

Table 7.3

POSSIBILITY OF EXCHANGE EXPOSURE

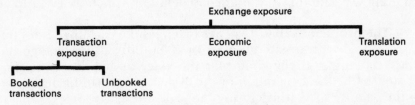

As can be seen from Table 7.3 a new term, economic exposure, has been introduced. Economic exposure consists of transaction exposure plus those items on the balance sheet which will actually be converted at market rates.

How does economic exposure occur? Assume the French subsidiary of a German company imports goods from Germany and sells them exclusively in France. Also, assume that the subsidiaries' annual funds flow in French francs is as follows:

SALES PROCEEDS	1000
TOTAL F.F. DISBURSEMENTS	(350)
	–––––
DISPOSABLE PROFIT	650
D.M. IMPORT PAYMENTS	500 (Equivalent in FF)
TAX RATE	50%

TOTAL F.F. EXPOSURE $= 150 + (\frac{1}{2} \times 500) = 400$

Economic exposure exists only for those French francs which are to be converted into Deutschemarks. In this example, economic exposure is FF 400. If the goods were obtained in France, the FF exposure position would only amount to FF150, which is the disposable profit. There are no Deutschemark import payments but the FF150 still has to be converted into Deutschemarks

THE ACCOUNTING TREATMENT OF EXPOSURE

The accountant is faced with a problem when there has been a change in the exchange rate. He has to decide which exchange rate to use for translation: the old or the new rate. The core of the problem is the translation of the subsidiary's assets and liabilities as stated in its balance sheet. The profit and loss account is essentially subsidiary to the balance sheet. Once the values of a company's assets and liabilities are established, its profit is also established since its profit is, by definition, the increase in the value of the net assets of the company over the year. Thus accountants have tended to focus attention on the problem of establishing the exchange rate to be used for translating the items in the foreign subsidiary's balance sheet. Economists have approached the problem in a different way and this is examined in detail in Appendix IV (p. 168 *et seq*).

The problem is that there are two possible exchange rates that can be used to translate an asset or a liability; the exchange rate that was ruling at the time that the asset or liability came into existence (the 'historic rate'); or the exchange rate ruling at the date of the balance sheet (the 'closing rate').

Accountants have developed three principal different methods of translating the assets and liabilities of foreign subsidiaries. They are:

(i) Current/non-method (also called the working capital method).

(ii). Closing-rate method (also called the current rate method).

(iii). Monetary/non-monetary method.

Walker has summarised these different methods[4]. (*See Table 7.4, p. 142.*)

Current/non-current method

This is based on the conventional accounting distinction between current items (assets or liabilities to be received or paid within one year) and long-term items. Current items are translated at the closing rate; long-term items are translated at their historical rates. The implicit argument is that only short-term items held abroad are subject to exchange-risk. Long-term items are assumed to be fixed in terms of their parent currency values, that is, until they become short-term. The accounting exposure inherent in each foreign subsidiary, as measured by this method, consists, therefore, of its net current assets.

During the last twenty years this method has been the subject of increasing criticism from within the accounting profession, particularly with regard to the inherent assumptions that inventory is exposed to exchange risk while long-term debt is not. There has been a shift away from the current/non-current method, although in this regard the U.S.A. and the U.K. have moved in different directions.

Closing-rate method

According to this method all foreign currency-denominated items are translated at the closing rate of exchange. Therefore, all foreign assets and liabilities are assumed to be equally at risk, and the accounting exposure inherent in each foreign subsidiary is simply its net equity.

Since the parent company's net equity stake in each of its foreign subsidiaries is positive (except in the unusual case of those in a loss carry-forward position) all companies using the closing-rate method are 'long' in the currency of each foreign subsidiary. In other words, in the normal case each foreign subsidiary's exposed assets exceed its exposed liabilities. Clearly, then, if the parent currency depreciates vis-a-vis its subsidiaries' currencies, as has been the case for most UK companies in recent years, the closing-rate method will produce persistent translation gains. Exposure Draft 21, summarises the advantages of the closing rate method[5]

(i) It deals effectively with the situation where fixed assets located overseas have been financed by foreign currency borrowings and a change in the exchange rate results in offsetting gains and losses.
(ii) The relationship existing between balances in accounts as originally prepared in a foreign currency is preserved in the translated accounts whereas this is not the case where historical rates are used for translating certain assets.
(iii) It is not necessary to maintain sterling records of fixed assets and inventories located overseas which would be required if historical rates were to be used.
(iv) It is simple to operate and the results are easily understood by users of accounts.

The arguments against the closing rate method are that it is not universally agreed that the exchange risks of holding cash or short-term investments abroad are the same as holding fixed assets; nor is a short-term debt of a subsidiary payable in the near future comparable to the long-term foreign currency debt which has been used to buy fixed plant.

Monetary/non-monetary method

Monetary items are translated at closing rates; non-monetary assets (both short-term and long-term) are translated at their historical exchange-rate. The accounting exposure inherent in each foreign subsidiary, as measured by this method, is therefore defined as its net financial assets.

The main departures from the current/non-current method are that inventory is treated as a non-exposed items and long-term debt now becomes exposed. The second difference is the most significant, since long-term debt is often the largest single component in a company's accounting exposure. This can produce very large translation (and real) losses if the parent or one of its subsidiary companies holds loans which are denominated in a currency which is appreciating vis-a-vis the parent currency, as was the case in the early 1970s for the U.S.A. and (to a lesser extent) for U.K. companies holding massive Deutschemark and Swiss franc loans.

Table 7.4 summarises the translation rules in the different accounting methods. A cross indicates whether assets and liabilities are translated at the closing or historical rates of exchange.

Table 7.4.:

	CLOSING RATE METHOD		CURRENT/ NON-CURRENT METHOD		MONETARY METHOD	
	Closing Rate	Hist. Rate	Closing Rate	Hist. Rate	Closing Rate	Hist. Rate
ASSETS:						
Cash/Securities	+		+		+	
Receivables	+		+		+	
Inventory	+		+			+
Fixed Assets	+			+		+
LIABILITIES:						
Current Payables	+		+		+	
Long-Term Debt	+			+	+	

Source: D. Walker, 'An Economic Analysis of Foreign Exchange Risk.' Institute of Chartered Accountants in England and Wales. *Occasional Paper No. 14 March 1978.*

The current/non-current method is declining in popularity and, as can be seen from Table 7.5, it is now the least commonly-used translation method, although it is used by some Commonwealth countries, notably Canada and South Africa.

The closing-rate method is now selected by the majority of U.K. companies. The survey of Institute of Chartered Accountants in England and Wales (ICAEW) of 1975/76 published accounts showed that it was adopted by 233 out of 257 (91 per cent) of the companies which disclosed their translation method.

The closing-rate method is also the most widely used method on the continent. As shown in Table 7.5, for instance, the majority of those French, Dutch and Swiss companies which consolidate their foreign subsidiaries use the closing-rate method.

Table 7.5
Translation Methods Used in 46 Countries

	Majority of Companies Use:		
Current/Non-Current Method	Closing Rate Method	Monetary/Non-Monetary Method	No Method Predominates
Bermuda	Denmark	Argentina	Bahamas
Canada	France	Australia	Belgium
Columbia	India	Brazil	Bolivia
Iran	Japan	Chile	Ethiopia
Pakistan	Netherlands	Fiji	Germany
S. Africa	Norway	Mexico	Greece
	Switzerland	New Zealand	Italy
	U.K.	U.S.A.	Jamaica
		Uruguay	Kenya
		Venezuela	Malaysia
			Nigeria
			Panama
			Paraguay
			Peru
			Philippines
			Rep. of Ireland
			Rhodesia
			Singapore
			Spain
			Sweden
			Trinidad
			Zaire
Total No.of Countries: 6	8	10	22

Source: Adapted from Price Waterhouse International – 'A Survey in 46 Countries: Accounting Principles and Reporting Practices', (Institute of Chartered Accountants in England and Wales, 1976), pp. 236–238.

In contrast, the closing-rate method is not even recognised as acceptable by the American Institute of Certified Public Accounts (AICPA).

In the U.S.A. FAS 8 requires that for fiscal years beginning on or after 1 January 1976 all U.S. companies must follow the 'temporal' convention[6].

The two main differences between the temporal and monetary/non-monetary methods are as follows:

(i) **Inventory.** Where inventory is stated in the original accounts at market value (i.e. where market value is less than historical cost) the temporal method requires that this should be translated at closing rates. According to the monetary/non-monetary method, however, inventory is always translated at the historical rate of exchange.

143

(ii) **Investments.** Where investments are stated in the original accounts at historical cost the temporal method requires that they should be translated at the historical exchange rate. According to the monetary/non-monetary method, however, investments should always be translated at the closing rate.

In contrast to the monetary/non-monetary method, in certain circumstances the temporal method treats inventory as an 'exposed' item and investments as 'non-exposed' items.

The impact of the translation method on accounting exposure

The choice of translation method can have a significant effect on the parent currency accounting 'value' of foreign subsidiaries, and hence on their accounting exposure. Indeed, identical firms could show different translation gains or losses merely because they used different methods of translating their foreign subsidiary's accounts. This can be demonstrated by the use of a simple example. A U.K. parent company sets up a subsidiary in West Germany on 1 January 1976. The underlying transactions are booked by the parent at the prevailing exchange-rate of £1 = DM 5. The opening DM balance sheet and its sterling equivalent are shown in columns 1 and 2 of Appendix III (*p. 167*).

The German subsidiary did not begin operations in the first quarter of 1976, so that at the 31 March 1976 year-end the Deutschemark balance sheet was exactly the same as at 1 January 1976. However, during this quarter sterling depreciated by 20 per cent vis-a-vis the Deutschemark, so that the closing rate of exchange is £1 = DM4. This rate is, therefore, applied in the consolidation of some or all of the subsidiary's items, depending on which translation method was used. The results, as measured by each of the three methods, are shown in columns 3, 4 and 5 of Appendix III.

This readily demonstrates the significance of the use of different translation methods, with results ranging from exchange gains of £325,000 (closing rate method) and £200,000 (current/non-current method), to a loss of £150,000 (monetary/non-monetary method).

Economic exposure

Having analysed the problems of exposure from the point of view of an accountant, exposure is now examined from the point of view of an economist. Accounting information is designed, among other objectives, to show the effects that currency changes have on a

company in the current period. It is not designed to   .
future effects currency changes may have.

Accounting records will not normally show:
  (i) the cash flow effect of a future exchange rate change;
 (ii) possibilities of price controls or high inflation in the f
(iii) reactions of the local labour force to wage and price changes
       following devaluation;
 (iv) effect of a future devaluation on the supply of loanable funds;
  (v) effect on price margins of higher future raw material costs;
 (vi) possibility of a more buoyant home market;
(vii) greater international competiveness in price.

Economic exposure is a means of allowing for these effects.
Economic exposure is based on the possibility that the parent
company's net present value of a foreign subsidiary's future cash
flow will be affected by exchange rate movements (*see Appendix* IV).

Professor Dufey has clearly illustrated that corporate reaction
to translation exposure, rather than economic exposure can be
contradictory[7]. Following the expected devaluation of the French
franc in 1968, the French subsidiary of a U.S. company greatly
reduced its exposed assets. Any policy to reduce exposure always
involves costs. In this case, the French subsidiary reduced its cash
holdings which had an adverse effect on its working capital and on
its efforts to develop the company. However, the devaluation may
increase the company's ability to export, thus improving the
company's position.

Devaluation, therefore, can have two opposing effects. Fearing
a large translation loss, the company may adopt defensive tactics,
which are costly, while the possibility of increased profitability may
call for greater investment. Devaluation should improve the local
currency revenues resulting from a firm's export sales. The firm
may either maintain its product prices in terms of foreign currency,
thereby increasing its local currency receipts by the devaluation
percentage, or it may lower the foreign currency price and attempt
to increase its sales volume. Similarly, firms producing goods which
compete with imports in the domestic market should normally see
an improvement in revenues, since the devaluation adversely effects
foreign competition. However, the devaluation causes a rise in the
local currency cost of inputs for most firms. Those companies
whose expenses include a high proportion of imported materials
are hardest hit. The price of imported inputs can increase by any
percentage up to the full amount of the devaluation rate, although
normally it is somewhat less, the final level depending on
competition.

The final effect of a devaluation on the profits received by the
parent company can be computed only after the expected local
currency revenue and costs have been brought into account. The
effect is determined by applying the new exchange rate to the

predicted net local currency profit. After translating the adjusted net local currency cash flows into dollars, the final devaluation gain or loss can be determined. The result will depend on whether the loss arising from the new rate exceeds, equals, or is less than, the change in the net local currency cash flow. It follows, therefore, that the outlook for some subsidiaries will actually improve after a devaluation, for some it will deteriorate, while for others the net changes will be close to zero.

Shapiro, like Dufey, also examined the accounting methods of measuring exchange risk[8]. He concluded by illustrating that, in contrast with accounting views, the major factors influencing a multinational firm's exchange risk include the distribution of its sales between domestic and export markets, the amount of import competition it faced domestically, and the degree of substitutability between local and imported factors of production.

The two ways of approaching the problem of the measurement of foreign exchange exposure, ie accounting exposure and economic exposure, are, however, linked in so much as economic exposure includes transaction exposure plus those items on the balance sheet which will actually be converted at market rates. Concentration on the two measures of exposure have resulted in two alternative systems of measuring the exposure. These two systems have been labelled the 'balance sheet approach' and the 'cash flow method'.

The 'balance sheet approach' starts by choosing a yardstick currency which, in the case of U.S. companies is the dollar. Current assets are then divided into 'exposed' and 'unexposed' according to whether the currency of denomination is 'softer' than the yardstick currency. Concern is only attached to imported inventories which have not been paid since only these can have a negative effect on dollar values in the event of a devaluation. Imported inventories already paid or local source inventories do not change in dollar value in the event of a devaluation. Fixed assets count entirely as unexposed because the real value of a fixed asset is the present value of the future stream of income that it will generate. Liabilities are accorded the same sort of classification analysis as current assets, again according to the effect on the payment cost of the liability as expressed in the yardstick currency. The sum of the exposed items result in an adjusted net worth measurement of exchange exposure. The deficiencies in this approach have already been enumerated (*p. 145*).

The cash flow approach recommended by Shapiro and Giddy emphasises that gains and losses arise not from assets and liabilities themselves but rather from the cash flows that these assets and liabilities generate[9]. Hedging should attempt to reduce the variability of cash flows by matching, whenever possible, each period's cash inflows with that period's cash outflows in a particular currency. Thus, whenever a firm has cash inflows from sales in a particular foreign currency it should seek to match those inflows by incurring contractual outflows in the same currency, either by borrowing in the same currency in which the firm has sales receipts, or by entering into a forward contract to sell the foreign currency at the time the foreign currency is received. As is explained in Chapters 3 and 10, if interest parity prevails, the additional (or lower) cost of foreign currency debt should equal the forward discount (or premium) and so the cost of either method should be the same.

Giddy, following the cash flow school, defines exchange risk as the variability of cash flows arising from currency fluctuations. These can be divided into contractual and non-contractual cash flows. Contractual cash flows arise from items like debts, payables and receivables. The risk here is in having excess outflows in a revalued currency or excess inflows in a devalued currency. Non-contractual cash flows are the expected revenues from sales and expected costs of purchasing inputs. Non-contractual exchange risk may occur following a devaluation with uncertainty attached to the rise in export revenues and the increase in import costs. He questions the importance of these two forms of exchange risk given the existence of two relationships. The first relationship is that between interest rate differentials and exchange rate differentials, the so-called 'Fisher effect'. The theory states that interest rates tend to reflect exchange rate expectations. If this is true, then the risk of exchange losses on contractual outflows or inflows in foreign currency may be small, since the Fisher effect also states that interest rates in 'strong' currencies tend to be low enough, and in 'weak' currencies high enough, to offset expected currency gains or losses. The second relationship is that between prices and exchange rates. According to the purchasing power parity theorem, gains or losses from exchange rates tend, over time, to be offset by differences in relative inflation rates. A firm buying inputs or with sales invoiced in a foreign currency may then find, that the net effect of devaluations and revaluations diminishes in the long run.

The 'Fisher effect' leads one to predict that contractual cash flows would not, in the long run, be subject to exchange risk. The purchasing power parity theory, if valid, means that, in the long run, non-contractual cash flows would not be subject to exchange risk.

Giddy then examines the empirical evidence for these relationships for the period 1972 to 1975 for four countries, Canada, France, the U.K. and Italy. His results show that over three-month periods the relationships are very poor but that over a three-year period the relationships are much more robust. This leads him to conclude that: 'except where some specific bias or market imperfection can be identified, the company that is prepared to

147

wait it out may save time and money by relying on the expectation that any exchange rate gains or losses will sooner or later be offset by interest rates and price changes'[10]. Other studies, notably by Robert Aliber, have confirmed Giddy's findings[11]. However, the question still remains as to what to do about short-term exchange risk. In the short run, contractual cash flows may be minimised by hedging or by increasing foreign currency debt. Eliminating non-contractual cash flows is more difficult. Giddy recommends that short-term exposure can be minimised by currency diversification. This reduces risk for three reasons. Firstly, exchange rate changes are imperfectly correlated, and frequently negatively correlated. If the pound sterling declines in value for example, the Deutschemark often increases in value when measured in some third currency such as the dollar. Secondly, business risk, defined as fluctuations in business conditions, are less than perfectly correlated between countries. Thirdly, for any given country, exchange rate changes and business conditions are less than perfectly correlated. He concludes by stressing that, in assessing exchange risk associated with cash flows in a particular currency, it is important to look not at the currency in isolation but rather at its contribution to the riskiness of the company's 'cash flow' portfolio as a whole.

IDENTIFICATION OF FOREIGN EXCHANGE EXPOSURES

The accounting definitions are, as they must be, deficient in that they are primarily concerned with what has already happened. Economic exposure, defined as the exposure resulting from the need to convert one currency into another in the future at what will be other than the present 'book' or 'planned' rates, is what is important. Economic exposure includes all transaction exposure and those items involved in translation exposure which will be converted at current exchange rates.

Transaction exposure is difficult to define quantitatively. A decision has to be taken in deciding how many months of sales or purchases should be included in the transaction exposure position. This varies between companies. It depends on each company's pricing flexibility and how fast it can increase selling prices to offset the effect of a currency change.

Economic exposure is the measure that most accurately describes the company's foreign exchange exposure. Once defined the next problem is that of identification. In identifying foreign exchange exposure it is necessary to identify both current and future positions. A company needs to develop a reporting system which provides information as to the firm's current and projected future exposure. The first step is to ensure that each subsidiary sends into the head office, on a regular basis, its balance sheet position delineated by currency.

Table 7.6

Balance sheet
(000)

Subsidiary:

Location:

Date:

Individual currencies
listed by column

Assets	$	£	DM	FF	etc.
Cash and short-term investments					
Accounts receivable: Third party					
Intercompany					
Short-term loans to affiliated companies					
Inventory					
Pre-paid taxes and other expenses					
Total current assets					
Long-term investments and advances					
Net property, plants and equipment					
Other assets					
Total assets					

Liabilities
  Short-term debt
  Current portion of long-term debt
  Accounts payable: Third party
                   Intercompany
  Accrued expenses
  Short-term intercompany debt
  Provision for taxes, other current
      Total current liabilities
  Other liabilities
  Long-term debt
  Long-term intercompany loans
      Total liabilities

Net worth
  Common stock
  Other equity accounts
  Retained earnings
      Total net worth

Total liabilities and net worth

Source. A.R. Prindl, *Foreign Exchange Risk,* John Wiley & Sons 1976

Table 7.6 shows how this can be done. This in turn needs to be supplemented by foreign exchange exposure forecasts and by cash flow forecasts. The company then has a broad picture of its present and future foreign exchange exposure.

Projections are essential for anticipatory exposure management. These projections need not necessarily be in detail for each item. Trends and basic changes in the most important positions frequently suffice.

Lamb and Ring have set out the necessary steps in reviewing these exposure forecasts[12].

(i) Review items which appear in the accounts at present, and which will not have been converted into cash by the next reporting period;

(ii) Review items which appear in the accounts at present, and which can be expected to have been converted into cash by the next reporting period;

(iii) Review items which do not appear in the accounts at present, but are budgeted to arise before the end of the next reporting period.

(iv) Review items which do not appear in the accounts at present, but will come and go by the end of the next reporting period.

(v) Review off balance sheet exposures. These include future commitments of sales and/or purchases, any leasing arrangements and forward exchange contracts.

RISK MEASUREMENT

In order to measure the degree of exchange risk faced by the company certain steps have to be followed:

1. Establish the total position in each currency according to both translation and economic exposure.
2. Undertake market analysis of the expected fluctuation range of exchange rates.
3. Establish the risk magnitude.
4. Introduce the decision format.

Once the risk magnitude is defined, the company can then decide, given the costs of hedging policies, whether to hedge or to leave the position open.

Establish the total position

This has already been discussed in detail earlier in this Chapter. Some of the new disclosure rules, such as FAS 8 in the U.S.A. and ED 21 in the U.K. which influence the company's translation exposure, are discussed later (p. 154 *et seq*).

Market analysis

An important step in measuring exchange risk is to identify accurately future exchange rate movements. Broadly speaking, two alternatives are open to the company. Firstly, the company can employ 'in-house' personnel. These forecast rates based on the ideas set out in Chapter 4. Alternatively, the company may use 'bought-in' exchange rate forecasts. Two major types of 'bought-in' exchange rate forecasts exist. One type is that provided by major banks; these include Citibank, Chemical Bank, European American Bank, N.M. Rothschild, Marine Midland and Harris Bank. Each offers principally subjective forecasts based on economic, political and psychological factors. Several use econometric models for background information. The second type consists of specialist forecasting services, such as those provided by Forex, Predex and Chase Econometrics. These tend to concentrate on forecasts based on an econometric model.

'Bought-in' forecasts differ in the sophistication of the services they offer. Some offer point estimates while others offer target ranges of future exchange rates. Forex Research for example provide forecasts based around the forward exchange rate. The latter have described their approach as follows:

At first sight, it seems a dauntingly difficult task to predict with total accuracy the future price of a currency. And so it is. But this is not what the corporate treasurer needs. What he requires is a correct signal. That is to say, if the price is going to weaken or strengthen more than the current forward price implies, the forecaster should pick this up. If he does do this, the client has then received accurate guidance on the central decision he has to take—whether to cover his forward currency requirements or not—and the forecaster will have earned his fee.

This point, which is crucial to grasp in unstanding the commercial value of a forecasting service, can be illustrated by an example. Suppose that a UK treasurer knows that he has to pay for a quantity of imports in US dollars in three months' time. The UK pound on day one is exchanging at $1.80, but on the 90 day forward market, it is worth only $1.75. The forecaster predicts that it will depreciate, not to $1.75, but only to $1.79, and he turns out to be right. The treasurer, following the forecaster's advice will not have covered, but buys spot when the imports are due. He thus receives $1.79 for his pound instead of $1.75, making 4 cents on every pound.

Again, suppose the actual price when the three months was up was not $1.79, but $1.76. The treasurer will still gain by following the forecaster's advice, i.e. not covering. The gain will be less (1 cent on every pound, the difference between the forward market and spot three months), but there will be a slight gain, and *this is* despite the fact that the forecaster in this example is actually less close to the actual outturn than the three month forward price was. The crucial fact is that the forecaster foresaw that the price was going to weaken less than the 90 day forward market view implied. In other words, the forecast was on the 'right' side of the market. The right signal had been given, and when the right signal is given, the corporate treasurer makes (or avoids losing) money[13].

Forecasts of this type provide an independent means of establishing the track record of the company. 'Bought-in' services may provide certain advantages. Firstly, they may help to provide a feel for the markets in both the short and long run. Secondly, they may be useful in helping the company to clarify its own thinking about many commercial decisions such as pricing and marketing policy. Thirdly, econometric services can be modified with a company's own judgment about non-econometric factors influencing exchange rates. Also a 'bought-in' service can be a way of collecting information on trade movements, interest rates, capital flows etc which can then be used for the 'in-house' forecast. Finally, 'bought-in' services can be used as scapegoats. Any multinational treasurer can use them to protect himself against often ill-informed criticism from those who do not understand the market. Thus he can claim to have taken the best advice he could obtain and, if this turned out incorrect, this is not his fault.

Despite these benefits professional exchange rate forecasting has been criticised on several grounds[14]. These criticisms are different from the criticisms made by efficient market theorists (which are discussed in Chapter 4). Firstly, the forecasts appear to be changed too often, particularly if rates are moving quickly. Secondly, it is easy to forecast the direction of an exchange rate but what companies need, and what is only occasionally accurately given, are point estimates for the times when covering may be necessary.

Establish the magnitude of the risk

The risk magnitude can be defined as:

CURRENCY POSITION × EXCHANGE RATE MOVEMENT.

One means of combining differing estimates of exchange rate movements is by the use of histograms. In this way the exchange rate forecasts may be weighted by their reliability. Thus, starting with a spot rate of $1.87, the following six-month forecasts of the dollar/sterling exchange rate can be obtained (Table 7.7):

Table 7.7
A CURRENCY HISTOGRAM

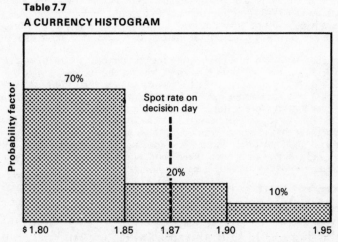

Assume that the foreign exchange advisors in this example were surveyed, their views can be summarised in the above histogram. Seventy per cent believed the rate would be between $1.80 and $1.85, twenty per cent between $1.85 and $1.90 and ten per cent between $1.90 and $1.95.

Assume also that a U.K. company had an import payable due in six months of $500,000. Using expected values, a loss expectation may be calculated as follows:

$500,000 (70% × 2.43% + 20% × 0% − 10% × 2.94%) = $6,965 or £3,724.

Thus, given the weighted expectation of the dollar appreciation, the position should only be totally covered if the cost of doing so does not exceed $6,965.

Introduce the decision format

Once the loss expectation has been established the company is then in a position to decide whether or not to cover. The company should then introduce a decision format, as outlined in Table 7.8, for its currency positions, its fluctuation factor and the expected loss or gain.

Table 7.8

Decision Format

(£000)

CURRENCY POSITIONS (±)	FLUCTUATION FACTOR (±)	EXPECTED LOSS/GAIN (±)
U.S. Dollars		
Deutschemarks		
Japanese Yen		
French francs		
Dutch guilders		

Given this information the company can decide what policy to undertake.

CORPORATE HEDGING STRATEGY

The hedging strategy depends on the corporate objectives and the attitude towards risk. This has been succinctly summarised by Prindl:

'If the firm considers its primary objective to be the maximisation of sales income from home and foreign operations and is otherwise adverse to risk taking, it may well wish to cover both translation and economic risks completely. If, on the other hand, the firm sees exchange gains as an additional component of income or determines that the cost of being fully covered outweighs the potential negative effects of any exchange rate movement it may establish a currency-by-currency strategy resulting in a policy to cover certain positions fully, but to leave others either partially or completely uncovered'[15].

A major company needs to choose between a policy of covering everything, i.e. taking out maximum insurance, and covering nothing, i.e. speculation. Of the many factors involved in this decision are the costs of alternative hedging policies (*see Chapters 8 and 9*). Other questions involve organisational implications, and the impact of disclosure rules on company results.

153

Centralisation versus decentralisation

The major organisational question for a company is of deciding whether to organise the exchange exposure from the headquarters or from the subsidiary. The advantage of allowing foreign subsidiaries to manage their exposure is that local managers are frequently in the best position to judge the timing of impending exchange rate changes and/or exchange control changes. Moreover, delegating this responsibility to local managers is a stimulus to their motivation. If they can consistently perceive the benefits of their actions they are likely to become more highly motivated. An advantage of centralised control is that a world-wide view of exposure can be achieved, thus preventing the previous situation occurring. Decentralisation, however, does have disadvantages. Due to large-scale intracompany payables and receivables the use of 'leads' and 'lags' may simply shift the exposure to another subsidiary.

Whether centralised or decentralised decision-making is introduced the company needs to use the expertise of a currency committee. This usually consists of economists, treasurers, planners, and marketing representatives. Basically, all major areas of the business need to be incorporated. The currency committee has a two-fold role; firstly, to establish the currency weights needed for the histogram analysis; and secondly, to educate the functional business areas as to currency developments and their likely corporate impact. The currency committee can provide guidance and consultation in the development of strategy and hedging options, bringing together knowledge and expertise outside the finance area and beyond the technical inputs dealing with tax, accounting and legal questions. It should consider long-term hedging options which may lie outside the treasurer's authority, or which may involve conflicts of authority.

An increasingly important variable influencing corporate attitudes to exchange risk is the effect of new rules affecting disclosure of profits.

THE U.S. ACCOUNTING POSITION

In the U.S.A., following FAS 8, upon consolidation U.S. companies must use the temporal method. The difference between the temporal method and the monetary/non-monetary method was outlined earlier (pp. 143–144)

The question of how to measure an exchange gain or loss is answered in FAS 8: Paragraphs 167 and 168.

167. 'In concept, exchange gains or losses from translating foreign statements are the direct effects, measured in dollars on existing assets and liabilities at the dates rates change, that are attributable solely to rate changes between the foreign currency and the dollar'.

168. 'In practice, however, the exchange gain or loss is usually determined at the close of a period by translating both the ending balance sheet and income statement accounts at the rates required by the translation method (that is, current or historical rates for assets and liabilities and weighted average rate for most revenue and expenses). When the translation is completed and the net income less dividends in dollars is added to the beginning dollar balance of retained earnings, the sum of those amounts will usually not equal the ending dollar retained earnings shown in the translated balance sheet. The difference is the exchange gain or loss from translating foreign statements.'

FAS 8 establishes a uniform accounting procedure for translating foreign currency transactions and foreign currency financial statements into dollars. It also requires firms to recognise in their quarterly income statements unrealised translation gains and losses arising from exchange rate fluctuations during the quarter. FAS 8 represents a marked departure from previous rules. Formerly, companies were free to choose from among several translation methods; usually they could also defer unrealised translation gains and losses by charging them against a reserve. Accordingly, in the past, firms were able to smooth the impact of currency movements on reported earnings flows in a way that they now are unable to do.

THE ACCOUNTING EFFECTS OF FAS 8

Before FAS 8, sixty per cent of American companies consolidated their accounts by using the current/non-current method. As previously stated they must now conform to the temporal convention. The basic translation rules of the temporal convention are as follows:
 (i) use the historic exchange-rate for items stated at historic cost; and
(ii) use the closing exchange-rate for items stated at replacement cost, market value or expected future value.

Table 7.9 illustrates the different exchange rates which FAS 8 imposes upon balance sheet items needing to be translated into dollars.

FAS 8 requires specific accounting treatment for forward exchange contracts. The accounting treatment is determined by the purpose of the contract. The FAS 8 accounting treatment of a forward exchange contract depends upon its purpose[16]:

PURPOSE	ACCOUNTING TREATMENT
Hedge of foreign currency commitments	Account for the commitment when it becomes a transaction at the exchange rate applicable to the hedge contract.

155

| Hedge of foreign currency exposed net asset (or liability) positions | Revalue hedge contract (and hedged assets or liabilities) at current spot rates; spread cost of hedge (difference between forward rate and inception spot rate) over life of hedge. |
| Other forward contracts (regarded as speculative) | Revalue at forward rate for remaining life. |

Since most multinational companies had a net asset position in their subsidiary, before FAS 8, as the foreign currency declined in value, they made a translation loss and, as the foreign currency appreciated, they made a translation gain. However, under FAS 8

Table 7.9

Translation Rules of the Temporal Method

Balance Sheet Items	Translation Rate	
	Closing	Historical
ASSETS:		
Cash on hand and demand and time deposits	+	
Marketable securities: carried at cost		+
carried at current market value	+	
Accounts and notes receivable	+	
Provision for bad debts	+	
Inventories: carried at cost		+
carried at current market value	+	
Prepayments		+
Property, plant and equipment		+
Accumulated depreciation of property, plant and equipment		+
Deferred income tax charges		+
Patents, trademarks and licences		+
Goodwill		+
Other intangible assets		+
LIABILITIES:		
Accounts and notes payable and overdrafts	+	
Accrued expenses payable	+	
Deferred income		+
Long term debt	+	
Unamortized premium or discount and pre-paid interest on bonds or notes payable	+	
Accrued pension obligations	+	
Obligations under warranties	+	
Deferred income tax credits		+

Source: adapted from Financial Accounting Standards Board - 'Statement of Financial Accounting Standards, No. 8: Accounting for the translation of foreign currency transactions and foreign currency financial statements'. (F.A.S.B., October 1975, p. 20) long-term debts are now exposed and this could place the multinational company in a net liability position. In this case, if the foreign currency depreciates, the company makes a translation gain and, if the foreign currency appreciates, the company makes a translation loss. The opposite is true if FAS 8 placed them in a net asset position. The essential accounting impact of FAS 8 is that the net exposed position translated at closing rates previously was positive and now is negative.

The effect of FAS 8 on the parent company of a change in the exchange rate influencing the subsidiary is summarised in Table 7.10

Table 7.10

THE EFFECT OF AMERICA'S FASB 8 ON THE PARENT OF A CHANGE IN THE EXCHANGE RATE INFLUENCING THE SUBSIDIARY

Before FASB 8	Assets > Liabilities	Assets = Liabilities	Assets < Liabilities
	Foreign currency long position	Neutral	Foreign currency short position
Devaluation	Loss	No impact	Gain
Revaluation	Gain	No impact	Loss
After FASB 8			
Devaluation	Gain	No impact	Loss
Revaluation	Loss	No impact	Gain

Source : RZ Aliber. *'Exchange Risk and Corporate International Finance'* Macmillan 1979.

As can be seen from paragraph 200, FAS 8 also introduced important income tax consequences of exchange rate changes:

200. The Board concluded that if an exchange gain or loss related to a foreign currency transaction of a foreign operation is taxable in the foreign country, the related tax effect shall be included in the translated income statement when the rate change occurs. Inclusion is appropriate regardless of the fact that the foreign operation's exchange gain or loss may be partially or completely (for a dollar denominated asset or liability) eliminated upon translation, because the rate change is the event that causes the tax effect in the foreign operation's financial statements. The fact that the exchange gain or loss does not exist (or exists only partially) in dollars should in no way affect the accounting for the tax effect, which does exist in dollars.

The majority of U.S. multinational companies are finding that exchange rate movements which previously produced accounting gains are now producing accounting losses, and vice versa. This also can have significant effects on non-American companies which are compelled on account of Securities Exchange Commission (S.E.C.) registration to conform to FAS 8. The results of the Royal Dutch/Shell Group of Companies for the first half of 1978 compared with the corresponding period in 1977 is given in Figure 7.1.

Table 7.11	First Half	
	1978	1977
	£ million	
Net income before currency translation effects	568	819
Net currency translation gains (losses) on stocks sold and on monetary items	(172)	(96)
Net income for the period	396	723

Source: Royal Dutch Shell Results for first half of 1978.

Table 7.11 shows that translation losses due to FAS 8 have a significant effect on net income for the period.

THE ECONOMIC EFFECTS OF FAS 8

The translation effect of FAS 8 may be the opposite of the economic effect of an exchange rate change. It has been established that, if the foreign currency appreciates and monetary liabilities exceed monetary assets there is translation loss. But if it is assumed that the subsidiary pays the same amount of foreign currency in, for example, dividends, because this is now worth more dollars there will be a postitive impact on the company's cash flow. Since FAS 8 requires the translation gains and losses be reported in the quarter in which they occur, with no possibility of smoothing the variations by the use of reserves, companies have great difficulties in determining exactly how they are fairing.

Companies must choose between accepting wide swings in their earnings figures or evening them out by hedging. If a U.S. subsidiary in Germany has exposed liabilities and expects a revaluation of the Deutschemark, it can hedge the liability by the parent company buying Deutschemarks forward. If the Deutschemark in fact strengthens, the parent company will have gained on the forward contract which offsets the translation loss, and thereby minimises the impact of exchange rate movements on reported earnings. If the company has acted in expectation of Deutschemark appreciation and instead the currency weakens, the firm will have a translation gain and an offsetting loss on the forward exchange contract, again neutralising balance sheet exposure. The translation gain is, however, merely a book-keeping entry, while the loss on the contract is a loss in real terms since at contract maturity the parent company owes more dollars for the Deutschemarks. The effect will be an impairment of cash flow. The economic effect is also affected by the 'grossing up' problem (*see* Chapter 9).

158

U.S. multinationals have, therefore, several problems with FAS 8. Firstly, when a company shows a translation gain now, in future time periods it may show a loss. Similarly, when a company shows a translation loss now it will show an improvement in future time periods. Secondly, it must decide whether to accept these wild swings in earnings and the effects this may have on the Stock Exchange value of the company or whether to adopt one or more of the strategies described in Chapters 8 and 9, which may be expensive, in order to reduce the variability of their earnings.

THE IMPACT OF FAS 8 UPON U.S. MULTINATIONALS

The U.S. Standards Board initiated and sponsored two studies concerning the impact of FAS 8. The first to be published (which appeared in December 1978) was carried out by T.G. Evans, W.R. Folks, Jr and M. Jilling, of the Centre of International Business and the Business Partnership Foundation of the University of South Carolina. It addressed itself to the question of changes in foreign exchange practices experienced by American multinational corporations which might have resulted from the implementation of FAS 8, and in particular, concerned itself with any attempts to avoid anticipated increases in the volatility of reported earnings arising from an increase in the use (or change in the nature) of foreign exchange risk management. A total of 156 U.S.-based corporations having 'significant direct investment in industrial operations in at least six foreign countries' was involved. Of these, 132 featured in the *Fortune 500* group of corporations. These firms were compared with a group of 107 companies which were studied by the authors in 1975 prior to the implementation of FAS 8.

The researchers found that FAS 8 had led a number of firms to reconsider their policies on dividends from foreign subsidiaries. Some indicated that the potential translation impact had caused them to refrain from at least one overseas investment which would otherwise have been acceptable. Others had adjusted their investment 'hurdle rate' because of the exchange risks now involved.

However, the study did point out that foreign exchange risk management objectives 'emphasise cash flows and asset value protection, and de-emphasise the importance of accounting earnings figures'. Moreover, 'there exists the belief that FAS 8 causes American financial management to over-emphasise the reported earnings impact of foreign exchange gains and losses, as compared to other financial considerations'. Nevertheless, the dilemma facing management remains clear as the study also found that almost 84 per cent of the firms questioned believe that application of FAS 8. 'misleads management, stockholders and security analysts because the cost of protection against exchange rate changes is not separately identified, whereas exchange gains and losses are highly visible in financial statements'. More than 55 per cent of the respondents agreed that their firms had greatly increased the resources devoted to exchange rate forecasting since the end of 1975.

This study complements another carried out by the U.S. Conference Board in which the financial executives of 117 top U.S. companies were asked whether FAS 8. should be retained, modified or repealed. The results of this study are summarised in Table 7.12.

Table 7.12

Respondents classified according to their companies' rank in sales of all US manufacturing companies	Retain	Repeat	Amend or modify	Company splits of no strong feelings	Total
Top 50	4	11	8	4	27
51–120	0	19	3	1	23
121–250	5	13	7	3	28
All other companies	8	17	6	1	32
Total	17	60	24	9	110

Again, the most frequently cited criticism of FAS 8 was that it distorts real operating results, providing misleading information; that it leads to uneconomic changes in financing methods; and that it results in non-productive activities. The method of valuing inventories at historical exchange rates, and the immediate recognition of foreign exchange gains and losses, were most frequently cited as the two provisions of FAS 8 which should be changed.

The second study published by the Accounting Standards Board involved a total of 497 multinational corporations. These were divided up into six groups according to their treatment of foreign exchange gains and losses prior to FAS 8. The groups were then compared with control sample firms over three different periods: January 1968 to December 1969 (relatively fixed exchange rates), January 1970 to December 1974 (floating exchange rates widely adopted), January 1975 to December 1976 (the period between the introduction of FAS 8 and the last date for which data was recorded). Using month-to-month changes in stock prices plus dividends as yardsticks for examining selected portfolios of firms over various test periods, the report concluded that the return on securities between the multinational and domestic groups was not significantly different beyond the '5 per cent probability level'.

Given widespread criticism of FAS 8 significant amendments are anticipated in 1979.

Joseph E. Connor, Senior Partner, Price Waterhouse and Company in December 1978 suggested the following reforms of FAS 8:

1. The use of a similar translation rate for both elements of a composite financing/investment decision, including the translation of inventories at the current rate.

2. The use of a totally pragmatic amortisation of gains and losses arising from debt translation, but in no event for a period longer than the life of the debt or the life of the financial asset.

3. The use of a technique . . . whereby the effects of changes in value of individual assets do not immediately affect results of operations pending realisation of the computed gains or losses. This could be achieved by suspending certain specific unrealised gains or losses in the equity section until the occurrence of an event or transaction approximating 'realisation', at which time they would be recognised in the income statement[17].

THE U.K. ACCOUNTING POSITION

The position in the U.K. is that the three methods of translation are recognised by the accountancy profession. Accountants are willing to prepare accounts using any one of the three methods. The only constraint that British accountants are obliged to follow in relation to foreign currency is to disclose in the accounts the basis on which foreign currencies have been converted into sterling. This requirement is contained in Schedule 2 of the Companies Act 1967.

The Institute of Chartered Accountants in England and Wales (I.C.A.E.W.) survey of 1975–76 published accounts (*see Table 7.13*) that the current/non-current method was adopted by less than ten per cent (24 out of 257) of the companies which described their method of translation. The closing-rate method was used by ninety per cent of the companies describing their translation method.

The situation whereby all three translation methods are acceptable is likely to change in the future following the publication of Exposure Draft 21 (E.D.21).

THE ACCOUNTING EFFECT OF EXPOSURE DRAFT 21

With regard to the method of translation, the use of either the closing-rate method or the temporal method of translation is allowed. As to the treatment of translation gains and losses however, companies using the temporal method must include

161

TABLE 7.13

Translation Methods Used By British Companies

	1975–76		1970–71	
Closing Rates	233	91%	205	90%
Other Methods	24	9%	24	10%
	257	100%	229	100%
Not applicable or no information given	43		71	
	300		300	

Source: adapted from: General Education Trust of Institute of Chartered Accountants in England and Wales - *Survey of Published Accounts, 1975 - 76,* (Curwen Press Ltd., London, 1977) Table 8, p.61.

translation gains and losses as part of the profit for the year from ordinary operations (unless the translation adjustment arises on an extraordinary item), in which case it will be classified as extraordinary. This follows the treatment of translation gains and losses which FAS 8. has imposed on U.S. companies.

The disposition of translation gains and losses as calculated by the closing-rate method is slightly more complex. The 'cover' method permits translation losses on foreign currency 'net' borrowings to be offset against gains on fixed assets. Translation gains and losses arising on uncovered fixed assets are to be credited or debited directly to reserves, unless these represent either:

(i) losses not covered by previous fixed asset translation gains (i.e. a negative fixed asset translation reserve is not allowed); or

(ii) the recovery of losses previously charged to the profit and loss account (as a result of (i) above).

Translation differences on uncovered net borrowings and other gains and losses on net current assets are to be reported as a separate item in the profit and loss account, after 'profit from ordinary items'.

THE ECONOMIC EFFECTS OF EXPOSURE DRAFT 21

Some expected economic effects of E.D. 21 have been outlined by Walker:

'The first main economic implication is that since ED21 does not attempt to regulate the translation methods used by UK companies (except by effectively prohibiting the current/non-current method, which is rarely used now anyway) it does nothing to alter the existing discrepancy between accounting and economic exposure. Moreover, it would appear that most UK companies (unlike their US counterparts) are not influenced by this discrepancy. In other words, UK companies do not include accounting exposure in their definition of exchange-risk. At the moment, then, the discrepancy between accounting and economic exposure is of little operational significance in the UK.[18]

One reason for this is that U.K. companies, because of exchange controls, are not allowed to hedge translation exposure.

The second principal economic implication concerns the possibility that the significance of translation gains and losses will increase as a result of ED21. Once again, however, the Accounting Standards Committee has not proposed any significant changes to the existing UK practices. The vast majority of UK companies already take such unrealised gains and losses either direct to reserves or as 'below-the-line' items in the profit and loss account.

In broad terms, then, ED21 has endorsed the prevailing methods of treating translation gains and losses. For the vast majority of UK companies (i.e., those adhering to the closing rate method) translation adjustment will continue to have no effect on the pre-tax figure. By showing translation adjustments either as movements on reserves or as separate 'below-the-line' items in the profit and loss account, it seems likely that the proposed new accounting regulation (unlike FAS 8 in the USA) will have little or no effect on the way companies define and hence manage their exposure to exchange risk. In other words, ED21 is unlikely to persuade UK companies to include accounting exposure in their definition of exchange risk.[19]

Comments so far received by the U.K. Accounting Standards Committee indicate corporate dissatisfaction with E.D. 21.

REFERENCES
[1] This is discussed further in B. Kettell, 'Business Decision Making under Floating Exchange Rates'. *Journal of the Society of Business Economists,* Vol 10 No. 1, Autumn 1978.
[2] S. M. Robbins and R. B. Stobaugh, *Money in the Multinational Enterprise. A Study in Financial Policy.* Longman Group Ltd. 1974. p22.
[3] M. Z. Brooks and H. L. Remmers, *The Strategy of Multinational Enterprise: Organisation and. Finance.* Longman Group Ltd. 1970. Page 167.
[4] D. P. Walker, 'An Economic Analysis of Foreign Exchange Risk.' Institute of Chartered Accountants in England and Wales, *Occasional Paper No. 14.* March 1978.
[5] Accounting Standards Committee, Proposed Statement of Standard Accounting Practice: Exposure Draft 21, *Accounting for Foreign Currency Transactions* (London: September 1977).
[6] Financial Accounting Standards Board. *Statement of Financial Accounting Standards Number 8: Accounting for the Translation of Foreign Currency Transactions and Foreign Currency Financial Statements.* Stamford, Connecticut: Financial Accounting Standards Board, October 1975.
[7] G. Dufey, 'Corporate Finance and Exchange Rate Variations' *Financial Management.* June 1972.
[8] A. Shapiro, 'Exchange rate changes, inflation and the value of the multinational corporation,' *Journal of Finance,* May 1975.
[9] ibid; I. Giddy, 'Exchange Risk: Whose View.' *Financial Management Summer 1977.*
[10] Giddy, *op cit.*
[11] R. Z. Aliber, *Exchange Risk and Corporate International Finance.* MacMillan, 1979.
[12] R. Lamb and T. Ring, 'Economic exposure does not always show up in the books.' *Euromoney.* June 1974.
[13] B. C. J. Hesketh, 'To What Extent can Forecasters 'Out-predict' the Forward Markets?' *Readings in Foreign Exchange Risk Management Vol. 4 No. 2.* Bradford University Management Centre.
[14] 'Mobbing up the Treasurer' *Euromoney.* August 1978. This article is a survey of the foreign exchange advisory business.
[15] A. R. Prindl, *Foreign Exchange Risk.* John Wiley and Sons. 1976. Page 38.
[16] This is discussed further in a series of articles: J. C. Donahue, B. Ant and A. C. Henry, 'The Implications of a Hedge,' *Euromoney.* July 1978. 'How to Hedge a Commitment,' *Euromoney.* August 1978. 'When a Forward Contract is call Speculative' *Euromoney.* December 1978.

[17] Adapted from 'Accounting for Exchange rate fluctuation: a review of recent developments.' *International Currency Review,* Vol II No. 1, 1979.

[18] Walker, ibid pp. 56–57.

[19] Walker *op cit.*

Appendix I

A Transaction Loss

The accounting effect on a U.K. company paying foreign currency at an exchange rate different from that which existed when the order was initially agreed upon is illustrated below. In this case a U.K. company purchases goods on three-months credit from a German supplier at DM 100,000. Following a change in the exchange rate from DM 4= £1.00 to DM 3.60= £1.00 the company makes a loss of £2,778.

	Account	Asset	Liability
Position at 1 April, 1978	Inventory	£25,000	
	Payable		£25,000
	Purchase for DM 100,000 at DM 4= £1.00		
Position at 1 July, 1978	Payable		£27,778
	Cash	£27,778	
	Settlement of Invoice for DM 100,000 at DM 3.60 = £1.00		

Realised loss on exchange of £2,778

Appendix II

A Transaction Gain

An Italian company is exporting goods on three months credit to Sweden. As most Italian companies invoice their export in foreign currencies, this company converted its selling price of lire 2,000,000 to Swedish Kroner 10,000 when the exchange rate was L.200 = 1 S.Kr. After three months the Swedish importer paid his Kroner but due to this being worth more Italian lire than before, the Italian company made a realised gain (an appreciation of the Swedish Kroner to L.220 = 1 S.Kr has been assumed in this example).

	Account	Asset	Liability
April 1, 1976	Receivable	L.2,000,000	
	sales		L.2,000,000
	Sale of goods for S.Kr. 10,000 at L200 = S.Kr. 1		
July 1, 1976	Cash	L.2,200,000	
	receivable		L.2,200,000
	Settlement of invoice at L.220 = S. Kr. 1		

Thus the Italian company makes a realised gain on exchange of L.200,000

Appendix III

Effects of the Use of Different Translation Methods on the Consolidation of Foreign Subsidiaries—An Example

	Subsidiary Balance Sheets at 1.1.76. and 31.3.76	Parent Balance Sheet at 1.1.76	Parent Balance Sheet at 31.3.76.		
			Closing Rate Method	Current Non-Current Method	Monetary Non-monetary Method
	DM '000	£ '000	£ '000	£ '000	£ '000
Cash	1,500	300	375	375	375
Inventory	4,000	800	1,000	1,000	800
Fixed Assets	5,500	1,100	1,375	1,100	1,100
TOTAL ASSETS:	11,000	2,200	2,750	2,475	2,275
Short-term payables	1,500	300	375	375	375
Long-term debt	3,000	600	750	600	750
TOTAL LIABILITIES:	4,500	900	1,125	975	1,125
Net worth	6,500	1,300	1,625	1,500	1,150
ACCOUNTING EXPOSURE: Positive or (negative)			1,625	1,000	(750)
TRANSLATION GAIN OR (LOSS) (20% of accounting exposure)			325	200	(150)

Source: D. Walker, 'An Economic Analysis of Foreign Exchange Risk'
ICA *Occasional Paper No. 14.* March 1978

Note. This example assumes an appreciation of the DM for £1 = 5DM to £1 = 4DM (a 20 per cent depreciation of sterling).

Appendix IV

It is now generally accepted that the value of an asset is equal to the discounted sum of the future after-tax cash-flows which the asset produces. This is known as the net present value (*NPV*) of future cash flows. In the valuation of foreign assets the only additional step required is that the *NPV* must then be translated into the parent currency at some rate of exchange. The *NPV* of a foreign subsidiary should therefore be defined as follows:

$$NPV_o = \sum_{t=o}^{n} \frac{(CIF_t - COF_t)_{ERt}}{(1 + d)_t}$$

where *NPV* = net present value (parent currency equivalent)

CIF = cash inflows (denominated in foreign subsidiary's local currency)

COF = cash outflows (denominated in foreign subsidiary's local currency), including corporate tax payments.

ER = exchange rate (parent currency value of one unit of foreign currency)

d = discount rate (the rate of return required by the parent company for its investment in the foreign subsidiary)

t = period *t*

n = the last period in which cash flows are expected.

Clearly, then, it is this value, the economic valuation of the foreign subsidiary, which is really affected by currency movements. The economic evaluation of exchange-risk should therefore be defined as the possibility that the parent currency-denominated *NPV* of the foreign subsidiary's future cash-flows will adversely be affected by exchange rate movements.

This impact will comprise two different kinds of effects, analogous to the price and quantity effects of basic economic theory. A change in the foreign subsidiary's exchange rate will not only have the automatic effect of altering the "price" at which future local currency (*LC*) cash flows are transformed into the parent currency (*ER* in the above equation), but it may also change the quantity (*CIF-COF*) and timing (*t*) of these cash flows. Hence the economic analysis of exchange-risk is essentially concerned with estimating these effects of currency movements on foreign operations' future *LC* cash inflows (sales revenues) and cash outflows (real input and financing costs). A conceptual framework will now be outlined for the economic analysis of the case of a devaluation of a foreign subsidiary's host currency (hereafter referred to as "the devaluation").

(i) *Cash inflows—sales revenues.* A change in the subsidiary's host country exchange rate (irrespective of whether it moves in relation to the parent currency) can have two types of effects on the subsidiary's sales revenues. It can alter the size of the market in which the subsidiary sells its output ("market size" effect) and/or it may alter the share of this market which the subsidiary holds ("market share" effect). The direction and incidence of these effects will vary according to the market characteristics of the subsidiary. These market characteristics can be categorised into three market types: the export sector; the import-competing sector of the domestic market; and the "pure" domestic market (i.e. zero import penetration). The devaluation (market size and share) effects will now be examined for each of these three market categories.

(a) *Export sector.* Whilst a devaluation will have little or no effect on the total size of the export market, it will have a favourable market share effect so that the *LC* revenues produced by the foreign subsidiary's exports should be increased. (This is the type of effect demonstrated in chapter VII of the impact of the French franc devaluation on the profitability of the French subsidiary of a US multi-national car manufacturing company.)

The export-orientated subsidiary may reduce its foreign (that is, "foreign" to the subsidiary's host currency) currency selling price by the devaluation percentage (maintaining the *LC* equivalent), which will presumably lead to a higher sales volume.

Alternatively, it can maintain its foreign currency prices (raising the *LC* equivalent), thereby increasing by the devaluation percentage the *LC* revenue per unit of an unchanged sales volume. In other words, devaluation should produce increased sales and/or higher profit margins—either way, export revenues should benefit from the devaluation. They may not benefit by the full devaluation percentage, however, since foreign markets may be the subject of increased competition from other exporters.

(b) *Domestic market, import-competing sector*. As in the export sector, the market share effect will be favourable because it will increase the competitiveness of local *vis-à-vis* foreign goods. Hence subsidiaries selling goods which compete with imports in the domestic market should also produce increased revenues, unless overseas exporters are willing and able to suffer a fall in revenue denominated in their own currencies. In all but the most competitive of markets, then, a devaluation will lead to an increase in the *LC* price of imported goods (in the short term, at least). Foreign subsidiaries located in the devaluing country and operating in the import-competing sector of the domestic market will therefore benefit, again in the form of increased sales volume and/or higher profit margins.

The rising price of imports and import-competing goods in the devaluing country may, however, reduce real income. More importantly, domestic demand is likely to be dampened by the Government deflationary measures which usually accompany devaluations. The favourable market share effects of a devaluation may therefore be partly offset by adverse effects on the total size of the domestic market.

(c) *Purely domestic market.* Companies operating in this market category are most likely to lose from a devaluation, since there will be no favourable market share effects to offset the adverse domestic income effect.

(ii) *Cash outflows.* For analytical purposes it is useful to make the distinction between "real" input (labour, raw material and plant) costs and "financing" (working capital and borrowing) costs.

(a) *Real sector.* Devaluation will increase the *LC* cost of real inputs for most firms operating in the devaluing country. Within this general pattern, Shapiro has proposed a threefold classification of the production function into imported, traded domestic and non-traded domestic inputs.

Clearly, those companies which import a large proportion of their inputs will be hardest hit by a devaluation. Their costs may not rise by the full devaluation percentage, however, if competition from domestic producers forces overseas suppliers to absorb part of the cost increase. Even firms using mainly domestic inputs will be subject to rising costs, since expansion in the export and import-competing sectors will force up factor prices. This will, of course, affect traded rather than non-traded input costs, which will be least affected by the devaluation. It should also be added that the extent to which devaluation-induced expansion leads to rising input prices will also crucially depend on the pre-devaluation employment situation, the effectiveness of the Government deflationary programme and the speed with which inputs can be shifted between different sectors of the economy.

(b) *Financial sector.* Devaluation will have a twofold impact on financing costs, since it will alter companies' working capital requirements as well as the cost of borrowing.

In terms of working capital requirements, it has been argued above that a devaluation may lead to increased sales revenues and rising input costs. If this is the case then larger cash and inventory balances will be required and customers' credit needs will be larger. Hence, devaluation may mean that additional working capital is required, thereby reducing the subsidiary's rate of return.

The effect on borrowing costs will depend on the currency-denomination of the company's liability structure. The obvious impact on the cost of foreign (that is, "foreign" to the subsidiary's host currency) currency-denominated loans, as most companies are now fully aware is that the effective interest rate will be increased by the devaluation percentage. Not so obvious, however, is the effect on domestic interest rates. These usually rise when a currency comes under pressure and a devaluation is expected. Hence the interest cost of all loans is likely to rise as a result of devaluation, although this increase will be greater the higher the ratio of foreign currency debt to *LC* debt.

After adjusting expected future *LC* cash inflows and outflows for the "quantity" effect of a devaluation, the economic analysis must finally take account of the "price" effect. The adjusted net *LC* cash flow which the subsidiary is now expected to produce is therefore translated into the parent currency at the new rate of exchange, giving the parent currency-denominated net cash flow. If the loss on translation at the new rate (the "price" effect) is more than offset by an improvement in *LC* cash flows (the "quantity" effect), then the parent company will benefit from the devaluation since the value of its foreign subsidiary is increased. If the reverse is true then the parent company should consider changes in the financing, sourcing and marketing structure of its subsidiary. Clearly, this is the correct approach to exchange-risk management.

Equally clear, however, is the fact that the economic analysis of future cash flows is a very difficult and complex task. It requires the estimation of such exogenous variables as the devaluation reactions of competitors (price elasticity of supply) and consumers (price elasticity of demand), and the efficacy of Government deflationary policies.

Abridged with the permission of David P. Walker from 'What is foreign exchange risk' in Readings in Foreign Exchange Risk Management *by D.P. Walker and T.W. Macrae. M.C.B. Publications Vol. 4 No. 2. 1978.*

8
Internal Techniques For Managing Foreign Exchange Exposure

Chapter 7 has outlined the distinctions between transaction, translation and economic exposure. In this Chapter the internal techniques open to the firm to reduce this exposure are examined. All exposure minimisation techniques involve costs of one sort or another and, clearly, only if the benefits outweigh the costs will the technique be worthwhile. The various costs involved are outlined throughout the Chapter.

First, some research results covering the management of foreign exchange are outlined. Bourguinat studied the behaviour of French firms[1]. Robbins and Stobaugh studied U.S. firms[2]. Unfortunately, these two researchers did not use similar methodologies nor did they ask exactly the same question. A comparison of their results can, however, be of interest.

Bourguinat concludes that:

(i) French firms billed in French francs during a period when the dollar was weak (May–December 1971) and billed in dollars when it was strong (1968–70).

(ii) Small firms hedge less than large firms as two-thirds of the small ones 'never covered'.

(iii) Large firms do not hedge systematically, but occasionally after an evaluation of the cost of cover against perceived risk.

Robbins and Stobaugh conclude that:

(i) small firms rarely cover;

(ii) medium-size firms cover systematically;

(iii) large firms cover selectively.

Bourguinat, and Robbins and Stobaugh reach similar conclusions in that small firms do not cover, and that large firms do so selectively.

The choice of currency hedging techniques by management is determined by the type of company making the choice. A company producing goods for export in foreign currency with import payables in foreign currency is one type, a multinational company with extensive international involvement is another. Naturally, the range of techniques open to the latter is greater than to the former. This choice is also determined by the structure of the company and by corporate policy towards exchange risk which, in turn, is constrained by hedging costs, tax effects, the method of translation adopted and by various regulatory bodies.

Two distinct types of technique exist: those which internally manipulate the composition of the exposed position and which may involve reorganisation of the company structure (internal techniques), and those techniques which involve the use of external institutional services and financial markets. Appendix I contains a summary of the main hedging techniques and indicates how these should be implemented, depending on whether a devaluation or a revaluation is expected.

Following Prindl, internal techniques can be broken down into:

1. Internal techniques affecting outstanding positions.

   (i) Prepayment of existing third party commitments.

   (ii) Intercompany term adjustment.

   (iii) Exposure netting.

2. Internal techniques affecting future positions.

   (i) Price adjustments:

      (a) local subsidiary price increases

      (b) export price increases

      (c) currency of billing changes

      (d) transfer pricing through the exchange rate

   (ii) Asset/liability management:

      (a) increase of net short-term assets

      (b) reduction of liabilities.

      (c) long-term asset/liability changes

3. Long-term structural changes.

   (i) Export financing vehicle.

   (ii) Reinvoicing vehicles[3].

INTERNAL TECHNIQUES AFFECTING
OUTSTANDING POSITIONS

Prepayment of existing third party commitments.

An importer expecting a revaluation of the exporting country's currency would be advised to pay for the goods immediately. By so doing the importer avoids the necessity, which would occur with a revaluation, of having to pay more of his own currency in the future. As this increases his need for working capital the importer will have to compare the cost of borrowing money (or its 'opportunity cost' if he already possesses finance) with the expected size of the revaluation. Similarly if a company has borrowed a strong currency which is expected to be revalued it would be advised to repay the liability as soon as possible. Again the cost of borrowing needs to be compared with the expected rise in the exchange rate.

These policies may however be complicated by exchange control regulations. An attempt to sell one's own currency for another, stronger currency is often interpreted as speculation by the official authorities and, rigorous exchange control regulations may severely limit a company's freedom to act as it wishes.

Intercompany term adjustment

Forty per cent of the world's trade is estimated to be undertaken by multinational companies[4]. This means that, even with exchange control restrictions, the scope for exposure minimisation by multinationals is much greater than for independent trading companies. Thus inter-company term adjustments, normally called 'leads' and 'lags', become feasible. 'Leads' are advance payments for imports to avoid the risk of having to pay more local currency if the supplier's currency revalues. 'Lags' involve the slowing down by exporters of foreign receipts into the local currency in the expectation that if a foreign currency appreciation occurs that it can then be converted into more local currency.

Einzig has outlined the situations under which 'leads' and 'lags' can operate[5]:

(i) changes in the timing of purchases and sales abroad.
(ii) changes (a) in the timing of payments for imports and in the timing of the collection of the foreign currency proceeds of exports, or (b) in the timing of the disposal of foreign currency proceeds.

(iii) changes in the country or currency in which imports and exports are financed.

(iv) changes in the currency in terms of which imports and exports are invoiced.

(v) changes in the purchase or sale of spot or forward exchanges arising from covering the exchange risk on the foreign trade transaction.

While practices under (i), (ii) (a) and (iv) can only be arranged in agreement with the trading partners concerned, practices under (ii) (b), (iii) and (v) can be arranged unilaterally by either of the two trading partners.

A U.K. exporter receiving foreign currency and expecting a foreign currency devaluation should 'lead' his receipts and the same exporter expecting a revaluation should 'lag' his receipts. A U.K. importer paying foreign currency and anticipating a foreign currency devaluation should 'lag' his payments and the same importer anticipating a revaluation should 'lead' his payments. A non-U.K. importer paying in sterling and anticipating a sterling revaluation should 'lead' his payments and the same importer anticipating a sterling devaluation should 'lag' his payments. A non-U.K. exporter receiving sterling and anticipating a sterling revaluation should 'lag' his receipts and the same exporter anticipating a sterling devaluation should 'lead' his receipts. Table 8.1 summarises these points.

Table 8.1

Foreign currency pending:	A U.K. exporter (receiving foreign currency):	A U.K. importer (paying foreign currency):
1. Devaluation	a. Leads	b. Lags
2. Revaluation	c. Lags	d. Leads
Sterling pending:	A foreign importer (paying in sterling):	A foreign exporter (receiving sterling):
1. Revaluation	a. Leads	b. Lags
2. Devaluation	c. Lags	d. Leads

Source: A. Watson *The Finance of International Trade*. The Institute of Bankers March 1976.

The scope for 'leading' and 'lagging' is still influenced by exchange control requirements. The benefits for the firms concerned depend on the size and timing of the exchange rate changes and the differences in local financing costs. Thus the subsidiary which is 'leading' import payments needs to finance these at the relevant interest rate. The subsidiary which is 'lagging' export receipts will have surplus cash which could be placed in the local money market.

In order to evaluate the constraints involved in 'leading' and 'lagging', some of which have already been mentioned, the firm should set them out systematically. Table 8.2 shows how this can be done. Thus the 'leading' firm needs to know the minimum number of days exchange controls permit the 'leading', the costs of borrowing and the opportunity cost of liquidating short-term investments. The 'lagging' firm needs to know the maximum number of days exchange controls permit 'lagging', what the position is on pre-paying debt and the returns available on investing the 'lagged' receipts.

Table 8.2

Summary of Leading and Lagging Constraints

Location	LEADING						LAGGING				
	Minimum Days	Total S.T. Credit Lines	Unused Credit	Cost	Short-Term Investments	Yield	Maximum Days	Prepayable Debt	Saving	Investment Availability	Yield
U.S.											
U.K.											
Italy											
Belgium											
France											
Canada											

For the U.K. shifts in 'leads' and 'lags', equivalent on average to a week's prepayment and a week's delay in payments, adversely affects the U.K. total reserves by about £1 billion. For economies with a shortage of foreign exchange reserves widespread 'leading' and 'lagging' can certainly induce the exchange rate changes that the policies are designed to avoid. It comes as no surprise that authorities make strenuous attempts to control these activities.

Exposure netting

Exposure netting involves leaving open positions in two (or more) currencies. Exposure netting may be based on the assumption that the activities of the companies involved are so large and varied that all the individual 'long' and 'short' positions will approximately cancel out.

Despite moving to a period of floating rates, there are still currencies which are closely linked together. Examples of this are the EMS Snake members, and the close link between the Deutschemark and the Austrian schilling. Thus a company with payables in Belgian francs and receivables of a similar magnitude in guilders may decide to leave these positions unhedged on the assumption that the currencies will retain fixed parity values. However, even within Snake-type arrangements this can be a risky business; witness the departure of the Italian lira, the pound sterling, the French franc and the Swedish kroner from the original Snake. Similarly, the intervention margins between the mark and the schilling have also been widened.

INTERNAL TECHNIQUES AFFECTING FUTURE POSITIONS

Two types of policies are possible which affect future positions. These involve pricing policies and changes in balance sheet positions. In discussing pricing policies, marketing considerations should predominate but currency issues can still be important.

Pricing policies

The immediate effect of a devaluation is to raise import costs. Any company anticipating a devaluation should, therefore, raise its domestic prices. This is even more important since devaluations are

Table 8.3

The effect of invoicing exports in sterling and
imports in U.S. dollars
combined with a sterling devaluation

	Due to receive	Due to pay
Month one:	£100	$200
£1 = $2		= £100
Month two:	£100	$200
£1 = $1.60		= £125

Fall in £/$ rate causes loss of £25:

(1) *If* the firm cannot pass the higher cost of its imports commitment on in a higher price to its customers, and

(2) *If* it has not hedged the foreign currency commitment in the forward market.

Reproduced from M. Crawford Currencies in a floating world, *Economist Intelligence Unit Ltd., 1977.*

often followed by price freezes. Between raising its prices and the devaluation occurring, discounts may be offered to lessen the impact of the rise and to maintain competitiveness locally. However, if a new price list is printed prior to a devaluation, a price squeeze which may follow a currency's depreciation can be circumvented. Moreover, when exporting to a weak currency area price rises can offset the effect of the exchange rate change.

Crawford has illustrated in Table 8.3 how companies, due to inappropriate pricing policies and exchange rate changes, can easily lose money[6]. In the example he gives, sterling is assumed to be a weak currency.

A study by Wood and Carse based on a sample survey showed that eighty per cent of U.K. exports were invoiced in sterling and ninety per cent of U.K. imports were invoiced in foreign currencies[7]. More generally a tendency for goods to be invoiced in the currency of the exporter was observed. Table 8.3 illustrates the effect on a company of invoicing its exports in a weak currency. The great majority of West Germany's export business is concluded in Deutschemarks while most of its imports are invoiced in weaker currencies. The initial effect of rises in the Deutschemark thus increases exporters' revenues, increases the West German trade surplus and also induces less pressure from imported inflation. A number of export markets would appear to have been lost in the 1960s by U.S. companies unwilling to invoice in any currency other than the U.S. dollar.

There are several advantages in invoicing in a foreign currency which is stronger than the local currency. Take the example of sterling and assume and it is at a discount in the forward market. Firstly, the existence of the forward exchange market enables the firm to sell that currency forward which, since it will be at a premium, gives the firm either a higher sterling profit on the transaction or enables it to increase turnover by reducing the foreign selling price of the product. Secondly, the firm could finance exports in a currency with interest rates lower than sterling interest rates. Thus, if the firm had a Deutschemark receivable, it could undertake Deutschemark borrowing, which may be cheaper than sterling, without it incurring any transaction exposure. Both of these advantages enable a more competitive price in overseas market to be quoted. Pricing in a currency which is stronger than sterling and which is appreciating also means that rises in domestic costs can be absorbed without the continual need to adjust the sterling list price.

Practical considerations may limit foreign currency invoicing. In a regular trading relationship a change in invoicing currency depends on the relative bargaining strengths of the exporter and importer and may be difficult to change. More sophisticated pricing and accounting procedures may be needed as well as expertise in managing the new system. Finally, if forward cover is not available or suitable, the company may be exposed to considerable risk due to the widespread gyrations taken by foreign exchange rates. A second method of manipulating the exposed position is by Transfer pricing. Approximately forty per cent of international trade is thought to be transfers between related multinational companies. Transfers within a multinational group enable tax burdens to be shifted from high tax to low tax countries as well as reducing exposure, by raising or lowering intragroup selling prices.

Transfer pricing operates by the arbitrary pricing of intra-company transfers of goods and services at a higher or lower figure than an arms-length evaluation would indicate. There is a considerable degree of subjectivity involved and consequently managements choice of a 'fair' price can lie between rather broad limits.

Transfer pricing can help to eliminate exchange losses in areas of the world where continual devaluations take place and can involve exchange gains where continual revaluations occur. Often countries with chronic inflation or balance of payments difficulties may limit capital outflows by various means. Transfer pricing may provide the only means for the investor to repatriate earnings from an economy experiencing devaluation and capital outflow controls. Intracompany transfers of goods and services to the subsidiary in question may be marked up in price; alternatively, its exports to affiliated companies may be priced as low as possible. Ideally, companies make high profits in strong currency low, tax areas and vice versa. However, even if as a result of the transfer pricing, earnings were increased in a country with a higher tax rate, this might well be more advantageous than having profits blocked, or eroded away by a continual depreciation of the local currency. Brooke and Remmers give an interesting example of transfer pricing where intracompany trading is virtually nil. They inter-viewed a company with extensive investments in Africa and South-East Asia. The company had periodically found that it could not repatriate the earnings of certain subsidiaries. Although there was little or no trading with these subsidiaries, the manufacturing plant was of a unique and complicated design available only from the parent company. Thus when explaining that they had not received a dividend from a couple of subsidiaries for a number of years, the financial director remarked: 'but do they ever pay through the nose when they have a mechanical breakdown!'[8]

Transfer pricing does, however incur costs. It is expensive to administer and it may cause the company to run foul of the tax and customs authorities at home and overseas. Generally, transfer pricing has become more difficult as the authorities, particularly in countries prone to devaluation, have insisted on arms-length pricing. Brooke and Remmers found that, if transfer pricing is to be used to shift earnings or funds within the company, the expected gain needed to be large for the extra trouble to be justified[9].

Asset/liability management

Asset and liability management for foreign exchange management is directly analogous to the management of working capital. The major components of current assets are inventories or stocks, debtors or accounts receivable, prepayments, short-term investments and cash and bank balances. Typical components of current liabilities include trade creditors or payables, accrued expenses, bank overdrafts, bank loans, proposed dividends, short-term loans and tax payments due. The major items of working capital are cash, receivables, inventories, payables and short-term debts and it is upon these that working capital management tends to concentrate.

Working capital management is desirable for several reasons. Firstly, there are costs involved in holding current assets. Inventories, cash and debts are idle assets and do not generally attract interest. The cost of holding these is the interest foregone which could have been earned. If everything is equal, inventories, cash and debtors should be reduced to nil balances. However, everything is not equal. This leads to the second benefit of managing working capital, namely the cost of having inadequate working capital. A company having a low level of inventory may find that customer requirements cannot be met. This reduces potential sales and may involve a long-term loss of customers. Sales may also be lost if the company is unable to provide competitive credit terms to customers, i.e. by not allowing receivables to rise. A further problem with inadequate working capital management is the inability to meet debts when they become due. A company may be very successful and yet may become bankrupt due to an inability to finance short-term debts.

The basic hedging strategies for assets and liabilities are summarised in Table 8.4.

Table 8.4
Hedging Strategies

	Assets	Liabilities
Hard currencies (unlikely to devalue)	Increase	Decrease
Soft currencies (likely to devalue)	Decrease	Increase

179

If a subsidiary is expecting a local currency revaluation it should increase its net short-term assets. This can be achieved by building up cash, short-term investments, receivables and inventories denominated in currencies likely to revalue. Thus cash can be allowed to accumulate in the bank, receipts for receivables speeded up and possibly, payment for raw materials slowed down. A similar result could be achieved by reducing the company's liabilities, i.e. by reducing the company's payables and hard currency borrowings. If a local currency devaluation is expected the company should decrease its assets, cash, receivables and inventories, and increase its liabilities, payables and borrowings.

The basic rule in working capital management of a currency which is likely to depreciate is to reduce assets and to increase liabilities. Similarly, if a revaluation is expected, the aim should be to increase assets in that currency and reduce liabilities. However, there are costs involved in working capital management. If a company reduces its cash in anticipation of a devaluation it will need to borrow locally to finance production. In some economies this may be heavily controlled or in others, notably South America, it may be extremely expensive. Interest rates in South America of over 100 per cent are not uncommon. Similarly, if receivables are reduced, customers, finding their trade credit greatly reduced, may refuse to undertake more business with the company. Finally, inventory reduction, in the face of an expected devaluation, may mean a loss of customers.

Long-term assets and liabilities are not so readily reducible, but the pre-payment of long-term debt is one method of reducing liabilities. Fixed assets, if their realisation is not apparent in the near future, are only exposed under the closing-rate method. Leasing of plant and equipment removes this exposure from the balance sheet, but is worthwhile only when the domestic currency is depreciating.

These actions must be undertaken in accordance with domestic exchange controls and may be limited in their implementation further by a creditor's or debtor's resistance to the variation of cash flow timing, and by the adverse tax implications which may result.

LONG-TERM STRUCTURAL CHANGES

Many multinational companies have altered their structure so as to improve their international currency management. Most multinationals have financing vehicles in countries which offer appropriate tax advantages in connection with borrowing activities. Some of these firms 'hive' off-part of their currency management functions to affiliates in tax havens. In some cases where a

European regional subsidiary with strong delegated powers exists, it is given charge of a currency management affiliate (usually located in Switzerland) with responsibility for certain aspects of all the European international transactions of the firm.

Local hedging is often constrained by exchange control requirements and the actual structure of the foreign exchange market. The cost of forward cover may be prohibitively expensive or it may simply be unavailable. As already mentioned, the advent of floating rates has seen a marked increase in the cost of forward cover[10]. A way of avoiding these problems is to create a finance company vehicle which buys the export receivables of the group and assumes the exchange risk. The export finance company provides certain advantages which are not always available to the local exporter. Firstly, there is the advantage of increased flexibility in sources of finance. The existence of the Euro-markets (see Chapters 10 and 11) gives an alternative source to the domestic market. Thus an export finance company can use domestic or external financing depending upon which is cheaper. Secondly, there may be the benefit of centralising an entire group's transactions risk onto the books of a single entity. Thirdly, there is a clear delineation of a group's transactions and translation currency risks that permit easier management. This is particularly important for U.S. multinationals since the advent of FAS 8 (see Chapter 7). Fourthly it provides a vehicle for netting or matching a group's currency transactions. One of the major benefits of matching is the saving in foreign exchange commissions.

In describing the benefits of central borrowing, raised either in the name of the parent company, or of some specially formed finance vehicle in Bermuda, the Netherlands, Switzerland, or the U.S.A. The treasurer of Imperial Chemical Industries, puts it as follows:

'The reasons are several – often subsidiaries, and particularly those growing at the fastest rates, cannot service large amounts of debt from their own cash flows; it is easier to ensure tax relief for interest payments at the centre of the group; it is also easier to ensure that terms – interest rates, maturities, etc. – are those appropriate to the group as a whole, and to fight for standardised 'group' convenants in indentures agreements, etc.; it is easier to build up and maintain a group repayment schedule – if subsidiaries are left to raise most of the debt finance in small, local operations, the resulting repayments can appear chaotic; economies of scale can obviously be achieved; bridging operations become virtually unnecessary – funds can be raised slightly in advance of actual requirements for the 'group' as a whole; much greater flexibility in the deployment of funds can be achieved – they can, in fact, be held in a central pool until needed in various parts of the world; better timing of the group's major money raising operations is also made possible; the link between debt and equity, via convertibles, warrant-attached issues, etc., is better facilitated; and finally a better mix of public issues and private placements is possible if most debt financing is 'centralised'. Putting all this briefly, if control of the overall financial plan and state of the group, in today's conditions, is to be achieved, central fund raising is a virtual necessity, and it brings with it the added benefits of mobility and flexibility in a number of ways.'[11]

Switzerland is generally preferred amongst European countries as a domicile for export finance companies. For many years Switzerland has had extremely good relations with all other countries and has not known any serious political crises. It has a stable social environment in comparison to other industrialised nations. The virtue of private property is held in high esteem by the population and is fully protected in the law. The Swiss franc is one of the strongest currencies and the Swiss have one of the lowest inflation rates in the world. The efficiency of the Swiss banking system is well known worldwide. Also Switzerland is outside the E.E.C. and as such is not subject to the Treaty of Rome. A negative point is the limited freedom allowed to foreigners who want to live and work within its borders.

REFERENCES

[1] H. Bourguinat, 'Exportation et risque de change.' *Revue Banque, No. 330.* June 1974, pp 581–86.

[2] Sidney M. Robbins, and Robert B. Stobaugh, *Money in the Multinational Enterprise.* Longman, London 1974, page 129–42.

[3] A.R. Prindl, *Foreign Exchange Risk.* John Wiley and Sons. 1976.

[4] G. G. Mueller, 'Accounting for Multinationals.' *Accountancy,* July 1975.

[5] P. Einzig, *Leads and Lags: The Main Cause of Devaluation.* Macmillan 1968.

[6] M. Crawford, *Currencies in a Floating World.* Economist Intelligence Unit. 1977.

[7] G.E. Wood and S. Carse, 'Financing Practices in British Foreign Trade.' *The Banker,* September 1976.

[8] M. Z. Brooke and H. L. Remmers, *The Strategy of Multinational Enterprise: Organisation and Finance.* Longman Group Ltd. 1970. Chapter 6.

[9] Ibid.

[10] A short survey of some of the empirical estimates of increased exchange rate variability since 1977 can be found in B. Kettell. 'The Impact of Floating Exchange Rates on Business Risk.' *International Currency Review.* March 1978

[11] A. Clements, Paper given to the 30th International Banking Summer School in Ronneby Brunn, Sweden, June 1877.

Appendix I
Exposure management techniques

Anticipation of a local currency devaluation	Anticipation of a local currency revaluation
Sell local currency forward	Buy local currency forward
Reduce levels of local currency cash and marketable securities	Increase levels of local currency cash and marketable securities
Tighten credit (reduce local receivables)	Relax local currency credit terms
Delay collection of hard currency receivables	Speed up collection of soft currency receivables
Increase imports of hard currency goods	Reduce imports of soft currency goods
Borrow locally	Reduce local borrowing
Delay payment of accounts payable	Speed up payment of accounts payable
Speed up dividend and fee remittances to parent and other subsidiaries	Delay dividend and fee remittances to parent and other subsidiaries
Speed up payment of inter-subsidiary accounts payable	Delay payment of intersub-sidiary accounts payable
Delay collection of inter-subsidiary accounts receivable	Speed up collection of intersubsidiary accounts receivable
Invoice exports in foreign currency and imports in local currency	Invoice exports in local currency and imports in foreign currency

Source: A.C. Shapiro and D.P. Rutenberg, 'Managing Exchange Risks in a Floating World'. *Financial Management,* Vol 5, No. 2 Summer 1976.

9

External Techniques for Managing Foreign Exchange Exposure

External techniques for exchange risk minimisation are those techniques which involve access to 'external markets'. The following range of techniques are open to companies with international operations:

(1) Use of forward exchange market.
(2) Taking out a foreign currency loan (used by an exporter with weak currency receivables).
(3) Borrowing/deposit arrangements in two currencies (used by an importer with strong currency payables).
(4) Discount/sale of foreign currency receivables.
(5) Retained currency accounts.
(6) Leasing.
(7) Exchange risk guarantees.
(8) Currency cocktails.
(9) Forfaiting.
(10) Other techniques: factoring and 'lock box' systems.

As with internal techniques these alternatives involve costs and the company must ensure that the benefits outweigh the costs before committing itself to one particular technique. The final section outlines some of the internal constraints which limit a firm's ability to use either internal or external hedging techniques.

Appendix 1 examines the use of parallel loans, back to back loans, and currency exchange agreements.

THE FORWARD EXCHANGE MARKET

The workings of the forward exchange market were outlined in Chapter 3. The existence of the forward market enables a contract to be made, usually with the foreign exchange department of a bank, to buy or sell a stated amount of a foreign currency on a stated day in the future at a known exchange rate. The rate of exchange quoted for the forward transaction is likely to differ from the 'spot' rate at which foreign exchange is bought or sold for immediate delivery.

The forward exchange rate depends on differences in Eurocurrencies, described in Chapter 10, and on foreign exchange market expectations as to whether a devaluation or a revaluation of the currency is likely to occur. If one currency, e.g. Deutschemark, is believed to be stronger than another, eg sterling, the price at which Deutschemarks can be bought for future delivery with payment in sterling will be higher than the spot rate. In other words, there will be a forward premium on Deutschemarks. This premium—the difference between the spot and forward rates—determines the cost of forward cover or 'hedging'.

Assume, for example, that a U.K. company orders a machine tool from a West German manufacturer. The equipment is to be delivered in six months from the date of order, and the price is quoted in Deutschemarks. At the present time the spot rate is £1=4D.M. The U.K. company believes, however, that the value of sterling is likely to fall in relation to the Deutschemark during the coming six months. If this happens the price that the U.K. company will have to pay in sterling to buy the Deutschemarks they need for the machine will increase. The company can cover itself against this risk by entering into a contract now to buy the required amount of Deutschemarks needed in six months time.

Assume that the rate quoted for six month Deutschemark is £1=3.75 D.M..The formula to calculate the annualised cost of cover is as follows:

$$\frac{\text{Forward rate} - \text{spot rate}}{\text{Spot rate}} \times \text{Time period} \times 100$$

$$\frac{(3.75-4.00)}{4.00} \times \frac{12}{6} \times 100 = 12.5\%$$

This means that if the U.K. company sells sterling forward to cover the exchange risk, it loses 12.5 per cent per annum compared with selling sterling for Deutschemarks now (i.e. a spot deal). The U.K. company has to decide whether the expected devaluation of sterling is likely to be greater than the cost of forward cover.

The formula above provides an accurate measure of the cost of forward cover under fixed exchange rates. However, the move towards floating exchange rates (*see Chapter 3*) has led to increased confusion over how to measure exactly the cost of using the forward exchange markets.

Bradford claims that a company treasurer, in calculating the cost of forward cover must take account of not only the relationship between the concurrent spot and forward rates but also the possible future spot exchange rate changes during the life time of the forward contract[1]. Pelli has argued that the usual formula to measure the cost of forward cover is the correct one and that since floating exchange rates primarily affect the future spot rate (which is not in the formula) this means that the cost of forward cover under floating rates has not changed[2].

Robert Ankrom, Treasurer (Europe) for Chrysler International reiterating Bradford's view, has demonstrated that in order to calculate the cost of forward cover since 1973 one has to forecast accurately the exchange rate at the end of the time period over which one is hedging[3].

The question of how to measure the cost of forward cover is tied in with the extent to which the forward market is a good predictor of the future spot market. Chapter 4 discusses purchasing power parity and relative monetary growth as predictors of future spot rates. Ankrom has given details of movements in spot and forward exchange rates for the period from the beginning of 1974 until mid-1977 for five currencies, all quoted against the U.S. dollar. The exchange rates in Table 9.1 indicate an answer to the questions of whether the forward rate is a good predictor of the future spot rate. It is assumed that a U.S. company has receivables in all these foreign currencies, and takes the decision to sell the foreign currencies forward and buy dollars.

Table 9.1

A comparison of the three-month forward rate with the actual change in the future spot rate.

	90 day Forward Premium (Discount)	Average 90 day change in spot rate. Increase (Decrease)	Profit (Loss) on forward coverage
Pound Sterling	(1.59)%	(2.47)%	0.88%
French Franc	(0.41)	(0.17)	(0.24)
Swiss Franc	0.94	1.60	(0.66)
German Mark	0.57	0.80	(0.23)
Japanese Yen	(0.67)	0.32	(0.99)

The first column indicates the average 90 day forward premium or discount. The second column gives the average 90 day change in the spot rate. The third column gives the profit or loss on forward cover taking account of the fact that a treasurer selling these currencies forward could have waited and dealt future spot.

The treasurer who computed his sterling cost of forward cover on the basis of looking at the forward discount would have concluded that it cost him on average 1.59 per cent to deal. However, if he had dealt future spot he would have lost 2.47 per cent. Thus in taking the decision to deal forward the treasurer gains

0.88 per cent. The sterling forward market appears to have under-anticipated the downward trend in sterling. Forward sale of French francs would appear to have a cost of 0.41 per cent, but again taking account of the spot market trend this gives an actual cost of 0.24 per cent. The French franc forward market appears to have overestimated the fall in the future spot market trend. The Swiss franc forward market gives a gain of 0.94 per cent but a future spot deal would have given a profit of 1.60 per cent. The Swiss franc forward market appears to have underestimated the rise in the future spot rate. The Deutschemark forward market gives a gain of 0.57 per cent but a future spot deal would have given a profit of 0.80 per cent, thus giving a cost of dealing forward of 0.23 per cent. Again, the Deutschemark forward market appears to have underestimated the rise in the future spot rate. The Japanese yen forward market gives a loss of 0.67 per cent but when account is taken of changes in the future spot rate there is a loss of 0.99 per cent. As before with the stronger currencies the Japanese yen forward market appears to have underpredicted future spot rate trends.

Figure 9.1

THE THREE-MONTH FORWARD RATE AS A PREDICTOR OF THE FUTURE STERLING/DOLLAR SPOT RATE

Source: JM Atkin. 'A path through the currency maze.' *The Guardian* 17 July 1978.

These results lead Ankrom to conclude that the 'true' cost of cover is the difference between the forward rate and the spot rate at the time the forward contract matures and not at the time the forward contract is taken out.

As can be seen from Figure 9.1, the forward rate for sterling, between 1973 and 1978, has provided little guidance to the future spot level of sterling.

A useful method of utilising the above information is to incorporate the histogram analysis (*see p. 152 et seq.*). The weighted future expectation of the spot rate can then be compared with the forward rate.

There are two reasons why the forward rate is a poor indicator of the spot rate. Firstly, the foreign exchange market tends to be guided by the past behaviour of the spot rate in fixing the forward rate. A traditionally weak currency (such as sterling) is usually traded at a discount on the forward market, which means that the foreign exchange market normally expects the pound to be lower in three or six months time than at present. This will result in the forward rate understating the spot rate, whenever the pound appreciates.

Figure 9.2
FORWARD STERLING RATE
3 month Premium/Discount against US Dollar

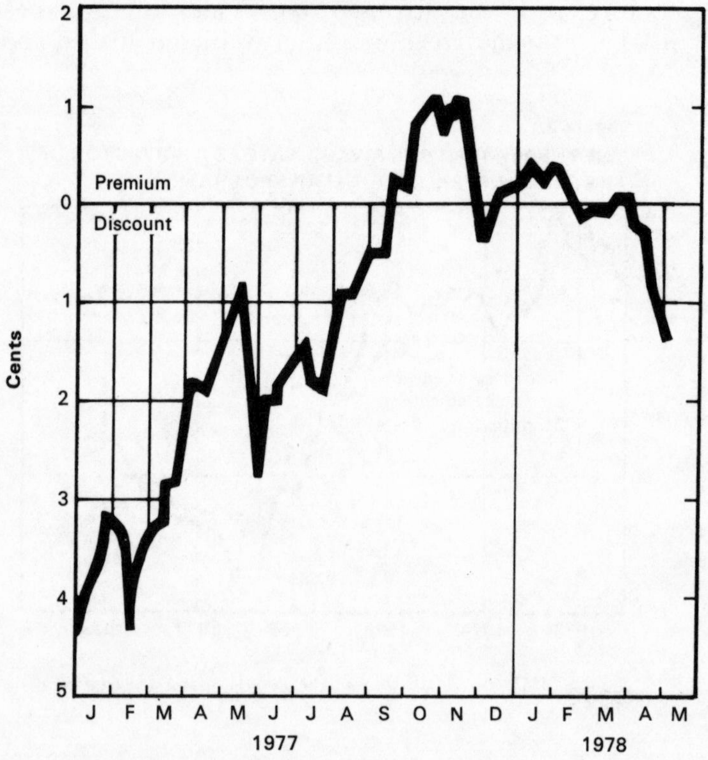

Source: *'Financial Times'* April, 1978.

The second reason is the inherent conservatism of the foreign exchange market. Large changes in the spot rate are rarely indicated by the forward rate. Even though the forward discounts on sterling widened in 1976, the spot rate fell much lower than had been indicated earlier by the forward rate; exactly the opposite occurred towards the end of 1977. In the case of sterling even though the pound moved to a premium on the forward market, a relatively rare recent phenomenon as can be seen from Figure 9.2, the spot rate rose much higher than had been indicated by the forward rate.

Howlett argues that for three reasons, use of the forward market, even though it is an unreliable forecaster of future spot rates, still has advantages[4]. Firstly, spot deals give only two days leeway. The existence of the forward market means that future liabilities can be exchanged on the most favourable day. Secondly, since the advent of floating rates, wide fluctuations in spot rates have taken place. Therefore, dealing spot may force one to deal on a day when the market is moving against one. Thirdly, Howlett stresses the insurance aspect of the forward market. This is particularly important for industries operating on fine margins.

Several studies have shown the degree to which the cost of spot and forward transactions has increased under floating rates. McKinnon examined the difference in 'bid—ask' spreads in the interbank market and found that the spreads were larger by a factor of 5 or 10 for both spot and forward transactions under the floating rate period covered[5]. Frenkel and Levich conclude that transactions' costs have risen dramatically during the managed float period as compared with previous periods and these results show, as do McKinnon's, that transactions' costs rose by a factor of 5 to 10[6].

As already outlined in Chapter 3, in order to minimise exchange risk, a firm with a future receivable or payable in a foreign currency can either undertake a forward transaction or deal future spot. Even if the forward rate is an unbiased predictor of future spot rates this does not necessarily mean that there is no extra risk under floating, rather than fixed, rates since there may be significant variation in the behaviour of the future spot rate. Aliber, using the forward rate as an estimate of the anticipated future spot rate, tests this relationship under fixed and floating rates[7]. The difference between the anticipated rates and the observed rates are considered 'forecast errors' and forecast errors in the pegged rate period are compared with those in the floating rate period. As a measure of risk Aliber uses the standard deviations of the differences between the predicted exchange rates and observed rates. The absolute mean deviations show that, except for France and Canada, under the floating rate period examined, these are ten times higher than under the fixed rate period. Similarly the standard deviation of the mean forecast error is generally from five to ten times larger in the floating rate period than in the pegged rate period. This means that under floating rates firms hedging their foreign exchange exposure incur higher costs in terms of forward discounts and firms not hedging incur much greater risk.

Although the forward rate may be a poor forecaster of future spot rates, indicating that the cost of measuring forward exchange contracts is unclear, the forward exchange market does provide great benefits which the future spot rate may not be able to provide.

Tax treatment of gains and losses arising on forward exchange contracts in the U.K.

In the U.K. the tax treatment of gains and losses arising on forward exchange contracts depends on whether the contracts are related to trading or capital items. Where the contract is undertaken to cover a trading transaction's exposure all forward exchange gains/losses are taxable/tax-allowable, just as with other trading profits and losses. If the forward contract is undertaken in respect of some capital item, however, the position may be very different. Suppose that a U.K. company borrowed Deutschemarks some years ago and that the cost of repayment in sterling terms is expected to rise. The company decides to hedge the position by buying Deutschemarks forward (presuming it can obtain exchange control permission for this). If the sterling cost of Deutschemarks in fact rises, the company may close its forward exchange contract and make a profit intended to compensate for the loss on having to repay a larger liability in sterling terms. The question is, however, whether these profits and losses in fact cancel out. There is a danger that the profit on the forward contract will be taxable while the loss on repaying the liability will not be tax deductible. In this case a full hedge would, at a fifty per cent tax rate, involve buying twice as many Deutschemarks as were apparently at risk. This problem is sometimes known as 'grossing up'. It is therefore important to know just how a transaction involving a change of parities will be treated for tax purposes.

FOREIGN CURRENCY LOANS

If an exporter sells goods to a buyer in a country whose currency is weak and has to invoice in the currency of that country, an alternative to a forward sale would be to offset the account receivable by local borrowing in the buyer's country.

Assume that a U.S. company has sold goods to France on 180 days credit, and believes that the French franc will devalue against the dollar during this period. The cost of covering by selling forward francs is likely to be very high. An alternative is simply to borrow francs on the French money market. Any loss on the dollar value of the francs obtained when the account receivable is collected will be offset by a corresponding fall in the number of dollars required to repay the French loan. In the meantime, the U.S. company converts the francs it has borrowed to dollars at the spot rate and lends them in the U.S. money market. Assuming that the U.S. company borrows the francs at ten per cent interest and is able to lend the dollars at six per cent, the cost of the operation is simply four per cent (ten—six)

A problem arises, however, if government restrictions on capital transfers make it impossible to take locally borrowed funds out of the country. This is true of the U.K., and other European governments have sometimes introduced similar restrictions. This problem can be circumvented by using the Euro-currency markets. It is usually possible to raise a sterling loan in the Euro-sterling market instead of in the U.K. domestic money market. Again the proceeds can be converted into dollars and used to make a dollar loan, and the cost of the operation is the difference between the interest rate on the Euro-sterling borrowed and the interest obtained when the dollars are deposited.

The choice of which currency to borrow can have a dramatic effect on the real cost of borrowing. Company treasurers have tended to argue that long-term borrowing in weak currencies at high interest rates tend through time to have similar costs to strong currencies lower interest rates. This is the so called 'Fisher effect' (see p. 147). To calculate the real cost of borrowing it is necessary to include the nominal cost of borrowing and the relevant exchange risk. Table 9.2 illustrates this problem. Assume that a company has the choice between four currencies at the stated interest rates and sterling depreciates against the dollar, the Deutschemark and the Swiss franc. Irrespective of whether the pre-tax redemption loss is allowable one can observe from Table 9.2 that the currencies with lowest nominal coupon rates are the most expensive in real terms.

Thus corporate treasurers in the period mentioned would have benefited from borrowing the currency with the highest coupon and with the highest probability of devaluation. Crawford has pointed out that, even if the currency borrowed does not appreciate faster (annually) than the percentage gain derived from borrowing at lower interest, the result may still be disadvantageous when borrowing on fixed interest terms[8]. When borrowing at a fixed rate of interest not only is the borrower locked into his interest obligation but he also needs a much bigger prospective saving on interest rates (even pre-tax) than appears at first sight. Suppose a firm can borrow dollars at ten per cent or Deutschemarks at five per cent, but is advised that the dollar might fall by five per cent per annum relative to the Deutschemark. If that happens, the borrower will not enjoy an interest rate more favourable on Deutschemark borrowings throughout the life of the loan (even ignoring the five per cent annual increase in the principal sum to be repaid) because the cost of interest payments on the Deutschemark borrowing will also appreciate gradually (in terms of dollars) and will erode the gain from the lower nominal interest rate in fourteen years.

Table 9.2

The Effective Cost of Borrowing Currencies

Currency of borrowing of 5 year loan	(1)	Millions			
		£	$	DM	Sw Fr
Nominal Coupon (%)	(2)	$9\frac{1}{2}$	$8\frac{1}{4}$	7	$5\frac{1}{2}$
Pre-tax Redemption loss allowable	(3)	9.5	13.8	16.0	16.8
Redemption loss not allowable	(4)	9.5	17.3	23.6	24.0

Notes: Line (1) indicates possible currency of borrowing which U.K. company could have undertaken in May 1972.

Line (2) indicates the interest cost of borrowing in the particular currencies.

Line (3) loss on repayment is allowable for tax purposes.

Line (4) loss on repayment is not allowable for tax purposes.

Round interest coupons and a 52 per cent tax rate have been assumed.

Exchange Rates Against Pound Sterling Used in Table 9.2

	US $	DM	Sw. Fr.
May 1973	2.5310	7.0691	8.025
May 1974	2.4140	5.9336	7.020
May 1975	2.3219	5.4532	5.814
May 1976	1.8101	4.6354	4.502
May 1977	1.7180	4.0591	4.337

Source: J. Chown and M. Finney, *Foreign Currency and Debt Management.* J. F. Chown and Company. 1977.

In discussing the tax effects of covering through the money markets it is important to distinguish between capital and revenue items. In the U.K. loans, particularly of a short-term nature used as working capital, are considered a normal part of trading activity and expenses occurred therein are normally tax allowable both as regards interest repayments and losses on repayment (either or both of which could change with exchange rate fluctuations).

If, on the other hand, the loan is used for any other purpose, especially that of funding the fixed assets of the business, then a different situation arises. Again, interest paid is normally allowable (including any change due to exchange rate fluctuation), but the difference between the original sterling value of the liability and the sterling cost of redemption is not tax allowable[9].

The countries with more sophisticated accounting systems (U.K., U.S.A., Canada and Israel) maintain the difference between capital and income items in determining the allowability of the extra cost of repaying a foreign currency loan. As is shown in Table 9.3 other countries by and large do not and as such it becomes easier to achieve the allowability of such an expense.

Table 9.3
General* Review of Taxation Treatment
—Realised Gains and Losses

	Gain	Loss	Gain	Loss
U.K.	I	I	NA	NA
U.S.A.	I	I	I/CGT	I/CGT
West Germany	I	I	I	I
Netherlands	I	I	I	I
Belgium	I	I	I	I
France	I	I	I	I

Key to Tables 9.3 and 9.4
* Subject, as always where tax is concerned, to numerous exceptions.
I = normal corporate tax rate.
CG = capital gains tax rate.
NA = no tax treatment applicable.

Source: A. J. Ring, *International Treasury Management: Accounting and Tax Aspects,* paper delivered at AMR International/Economy Conference, London, 5–6 June 1978.

Since 1 January 1976 Denmark has specifically provided that exchange losses or gains, whether capital or income in nature, are taxable or tax allowable as appropriate, though previously they had maintained the above distinction. The tax systems of Hong Kong, Canada and Sweden specify a transactions' basis and, as such unrealised profits and losses are not brought into account.

In West Germany and the Netherlands gains must be deferred until realised, whilst it is permissible to take account of unrealised losses, providing they are reasonably certain. This is illustrated in Table 9.4.

Table 9.4

General* Review of Taxation Treatment

Unrealised Gains and Losses

	Revenue transaction		Loan transaction	
	Gain	Loss	Gain	Loss
U.K.	I	I	NA	NA
U.S.A.	NA	NA	NA	NA
West Germany	NA	I	NA	I
Netherlands	I	I	I	I
Belgium	NA	I	NA	I
France	I	I	I	I

Source: A. J. Ring, *International Treasury Management: Accounting and Tax Aspects*, paper delivered at AMR International/Euromoney Conference, London, 5–6 June 1978.

BORROWING AND DEPOSITING FOREIGN CURRENCY

In the same way that an exporter with a receivable in a weak currency can arrange to borrow the weak currency so can an importer with a payable in a strong currency place the amount due on deposit. The importer buys the strong currency, e.g. Deutschemarks, spot in exchange for his own currency, say lire, and places the Deutschemarks on deposit. Exchange control permitting, the importer then possesses the Deutschemarks and is insulated from any appreciation of the Deutschemark which takes place. Again, the relevant interest rates to calculate the cost of this transaction are the Euro-rates. An importer can also prepay the liability and arrange for a cash discount.

The covering methods already described are not completely unrelated; they are linked together through the mechanism of interest rates (*see Chapter 10*). In theory, the cost of covering by these methods is always the same because the forward discount on one currency in terms of another is directly reflected in the interest rates between the two currencies. Thus, if the dollar is selling at a three per cent forward discount in terms of the Deutschemark, the interest rate on dollar loans will be about three per cent higher than the rate on Deutschemark loans. If there were no difference between the two interest rates, then money-markets arbitragists, realising the weakness of the dollar as shown by its forward discount, would start borrowing dollars and lending Deutschemarks. This arbitrage would quickly drive up the cost of dollar funds and drive down the cost of Deutschemark loans until the margin came into line with the forward market rates again. In the real world, however, there are three main factors which impede the working of the interest rate mechanism: government monetary and fiscal policies, central bank operations, and restrictions on convertibility and capital transfers. Moreover, there may be significant time lags in the adjustment of international interest rates.

DISCOUNTING FOREIGN CURRENCY RECEIVABLES

Foreign currency receivables can usually be discounted in local markets. The bank which discounts these bills will, in choosing the appropriate discount rate, combine domestic interest costs with the cost of forward cover. Under normal circumstances, exchange control permitting, local interest costs are related to Euro-rates, which in turn determine the cost of forward cover. However, divergences due, for example, to specific local banking reserve regulations may cause local rates to diverge substantially from Euro-rates and this in turn means that the relevant interest is higher or lower than would otherwise be the case. An additional advantage of discounting is that, if it is trade paper which is being discounted, the onus of collection falls on the bank.

FOREIGN CURRENCY ACCOUNTS

For companies involved in exporting and importing and thus having two-way flows of the same currency a foreign currency account provides distinct benefits. In the U.K. a company with foreign currency receivables and foreign currency payables may obtain permission from the Bank of England to receive and maintain them in a currency 'hold' account at a U.K. Bank. This means that the company does not need to convert foreign monies immediately into sterling. However, any currency balance not required for commercial purposes must be surrendered for sterling. The company thus avoids paying the bank a double commission for both selling and repurchasing foreign currency. This has become an increasingly important factor since the widening of spreads which occurred following the introduction of floating exchange rates. The company may also avoid the discount involved in selling the weaker currency in the forward market.

These foreign currency accounts may also provide an implicit hedge against import payables, as normally export receipts must be immediately converted into sterling.

LEASING

Leasing has long been used in connection with capital goods. A lease is a means by which a firm can acquire the economic use of an asset for a stated period of time. An exporter to a weak currency country may consider selling the goods outright to a leasing company which then leases them to the ultimate user. Since the exporter is paid immediately he can convert his weak currency receivables into a hard currency immediately and thus eliminate any exchange risk.

There are three principal types of lease financing. The first is sale and leaseback, in which a firm owning land, buildings or equipment sells the property and simultaneously executes an agreement to lease the property for a specified time under specific terms. Secondly, there is the service lease or operating lease, which include both financing and maintenance services, which are often cancellable, and call for payments under the lease contract which may not fully recover the cost of the equipment. Thirdly, there is the financial lease which does not provide for maintenance services nor is it cancellable; it fully amortises the cost of the leased asset during the basic lease contract period.

The cost of leasing an asset must be compared with the cost of owning the same asset. Leasing may be valuable for long-term contracts where the forward markets are very thin. As can be seen from the different types of leases the administrative problems for the major parties are likely to be considerable.

EXCHANGE RISK GUARANTEES

Most governments are willing to give some type of guarantee for certain types of exchange risks. Governments, perceiving the benefits of exporting, will normally assist the exporters in many ways, including the provision of exchange risk guarantees. These guarantees are often for official overseas borrowing, for projects with very long 'lead' times where forward market cover is not available, and traditionally, for hard currency countries.

In the U.K., nationalised industries, local authorities and other statutory bodies, such as the National Water Council, have in recent years raised substantial sums in foreign currency. Most of these loans have been raised under the exchange cover scheme which was in operation from 1969 to 1971 and which was reintroduced in 1973. This scheme provides borrowers with cover against exchange risk, against payment to the Exchange Equalisation Account (EEA) of a charge for cover. The charging arrangement provides that the borrower surrenders most of the interest differential between the rate on the foreign currency loan and the appropriate rate on sterling loans from the National Loans Fund (or in the case of local authorities, the Public Works Loan Board) but that he keeps an interest 'benefit' of about one per cent.

Since 1 October 1976 the U.K. Export Credits Guarantee Department (EGCD) cover has been improved for contracts expressed in certain major foreign currencies which were supported by use of the forward exchange market or foreign borrowing. Previously, an exporter who had protected himself against exchange rate changes by use of the forward exchange market or by borrowing against the expected receipt of foreign currency could suffer additional loss in meeting these currency obligations, if he did not receive payment from overseas. This loss would not have been covered by ECGD. Until recently, under ECGD Comprehensive Guarantees, claims have been paid by the ECGD at the rate of exchange ruling at the time ECGD cover commenced. From 1 October 1976 cover is related to the rate obtaining at the time the loss is incurred, if this is more favourable to the exporter. For business on credit terms up to six months E.C.G.D. will consider payment of up to ten per cent more than it would otherwise have paid on a valid claim, provided an exporter has suffered extra loss as defined above.

In Germany the export credit agency, HERMES, provides special policies for transfer and conversion risks for single or recurring sales. Cover is provided for exchange risks of more than three per cent. The scheme applies to contracts exceeding two years in duration. While HERMES bears the risk it also takes any profits which may arise, but it only covers major currencies.

In Holland, the Netherlands Credit Insurance Company Limited commenced insuring exchange risks in October 1973. Cover is eligible to any exporter from the Netherlands and is confined to contracts with maturities exceeding a period of two years which are denominated in currencies that are internationally marketable.

In France, the COFACE scheme provides for: (i) guarantees which cover the loss suffered by the exporter in the event of a reduction in the rate of the foreign currency in which an export contract is expressed; and (ii) guarantees which cover the loss incurred as a result of a rise in the exchange rate of the country in which the contract for the ·purchase of supplies or foreign loans necessary for the execution of the export contract is drawn up.

In the U.S.A., the Export-Import Bank (Eximbank), created in 1934, is an independent agency of the executive. It provides billions of dollars of credit to help foreigners import U.S. goods. The credits are often in the form of insurance or a guarantee. For a fee the Eximbank guarantees the payment of a receivable which the exporter has sold to a local bank, where the receivable is from a foreign customer. The guarantee covers all political risk and portions of normal business risk. The Eximbank also guarantees the direct loan by a U.S. bank to a foreign purchaser of U.S. goods. This guarantee is often used for capital equipment.

CURRENCY COCKTAILS

Currency cocktails are practical means of diffusing the effect of exchange rate fluctuations on international trade and investment. In addition they are used by various supra-national bodies, such as the EEC.

There are two main categories of currency units: firstly the official units of account including, particularly, the Special Drawing Right (SDR) and the European Unit of Account used in the Common Market. These are designed to provide a single medium of accounting for the transactions of international organisations where it would not be appropriate, for nationalistic reasons, to use a national currency.

The IMF created SDRs in 1968 to augment the world's international liquidity. In order to value the SDR sixteen currencies were chosen and prior to July 1978 the currencies were weighted as shown in Table 9.5:

Table 9.5

IMF SDR Formula

(% Weights of Each Currency)

United States	33	Belgium	3.5
Germany	12.5	Sweden	2.5
United Kingdom	9	Australia	1.5
France	7.5	Spain	1.5
Japan	7.5	Norway	1.5
Canada	6	Denmark	1.5
Italy	6	Austria	1
Netherlands	4.5	South Africa	1

Source: IMF

Because both weak and strong currencies are included in the 'basket', the movement of the SDR value of a specific currency over time would generally be less than the movement of one floating currency against another.

The EEC Unit of Account is the official denominator of the EEC Commission. It is defined as being equal to 0.88867088 grammes of gold and is used by the Commission, as the basis for its budget, for the common agricultural policy and for data collection. The EEC Unit may be expressed in dollars (using the official gold content of the dollar as a reference) but fluctuations in European currency parities have caused problems in using the unit as a means of settlement and payment.

The second major category of currency unit is the type of basket created in the private sector, chiefly for use in international bond issues, which attempts to provide a degree of protection against exchange rate changes to the borrower, lender or both. These include another European unit of account (EU) which is distinct from the official unit, as well as other variants of a European currency unit. Although mainly used for bond issues, currency cocktails can also be used for invoicing. The contract price may be linked to a unit of account, which means that the value of the contract is less susceptible to pronounced fluctuations than a contract linked to a single currency.

The official European unit of account (EUA) consists of a basket of fixed amounts of the currencies of the nine member countries. The amounts were assessed in such a way that when calculated at market exchange rates at the end of June 1974 the EUA was equal in value to the SDR, then still recognised as being equivalent to an underlying amount of gold.

The main difference between the EUA and the SDR is that the latter contains a much wider spread of currencies. In July 1978 the sixteen currencies which make up the SDR basket were changed to reflect the alterations in the relative importance of various countries in foreign trade and a system was established for revision at five-yearly intervals. The main effect of rebasing the SDR on statistics for the period 1972–76 was to take out the currencies of Denmark and South Africa and to substitute those of Iran and Saudi Arabia.

The EUA and the SDR are mainly used for official purposes though the latter has occasionally been adopted for international issues. However, for most purposes the private sector markets have tended to develop their own particular forms of currency units. Of these, the oldest and the most popular is the European Unit of account (EU). The value of the EU (which is not the same as the EUA) is identical to the account of the European Payments Union (EPU), i.e. 0.8886708 grammes of fine gold, which was, prior to the 1971 devaluations, equivalent to one U.S. dollar. Since the beginning of 1973 only the nine currencies of the Common Market members have been eligible to be used as reference currencies for the EU. This policy was later changed and, in its new formulation, a reference currency must have a par value and must participate in the European 'snake'.

Because it has a gold equivalent value, the value of the unit in terms of gold content changes only if all the reference currencies change their central rates with an absolute majority in the same direction. In effect, borrowers and lenders have to concern themselves with exchange risks only in relation to what happens to their own currency.

The relative equality of treatment which the EU accords to borrower and lender does not apply to the same extent to the European Currency Unit (ECU). The investor in ECU bonds can choose the currency in which the payment of principal and interest takes place. The effect of this is that the investor does not suffer when one of the component currencies is devalued, but does profit from any revaluation. For this reason, the formula has proved relatively unattractive to borrowers.

As mentioned earlier, the EUA is essentially a currency basket composed of fixed amounts of the currencies of the nine Common Market member states. These amounts were determined on 28 June 1974 when the value of the EUA was defined as 1 EUA = 1 SDR = \$1.20635. The relative weights accorded to each currency were calculated at that time on the basis of their official market exchange rates and the sum of the nine currency components, thus giving the value of the EUA. The ECU, which is at the basis of the new European Monetary System (EMS) is to be constructed in exactly the same manner as the EUA. The changing composition of the EUA can be seen from Table 9.6.

Table 9.6 ·
Composition of the European unit of account (EUA)

Currency	Units in EUA basket	Initial percentage at 30.6.1974	Percentage at 30.6.1978	Present EUA value at 30.6.1978
Deutschemark	0.828	27.3	32.1	2.58101
French franc	1.15	19.5	20.5	5.60057
Pound sterling	0.0885	17.5	13.2	0.66843
Italian lira	109	14.0	10.3	1062.79
Dutch guilder	0.286	9.0	10.3	2.77740
Belgian franc	3.66	7.9	9.0	40.6953
Danish krone	0.217	3.0	3.1	7.01962
Irish pound	0.00759	1.5	1.1	0.66845
Luxembourg franc	0.14	0.3	0.4	40.6953

When one or more of the currencies in the basket appreciates the EUA/ECU itself rises. For example the EUA was in mid 1976 worth \$1.10 but in early December 1978 its value was \$1.31.

Another feature is that the weight of the appreciating currency increases. When the EUA basket was put together in 1974, the Deutschemark accounted for 27.3 per cent of the weights. On 30 June 1978 that share had risen to 32.1 per cent. This results in one of the complications of EMS in that as currency cross-rates change so do currency weights within the ECU, thus complicating the problem of knowing whether a currency has reached its ECU intervention limits. Following the commencement of EMS the currency weights in the ECU are to be re-examined and, if necessary, changed within six months. Thereafter they will be revised every five years or, on request, when the trade weight of any currency changes by more than twenty-five per cent. Revisions have to be mutually accepted.

Another currency cocktail which has been used by Eurobond issues of the European Investment Bank is the European Composite Unit (Eurco). Eurco consists of the following currencies and weightings:

D.M.	0.9
+ F.Fr.	1.20
+ £ (U.K.)	0.075
+ £ (Irish).	0.005
+ Lira	80.00
+ B.F.	4.50
+ Lux F.	0.50
+ Guilders	0.35
+ D.Kr.	0.20

The weightings are based on a number of economic criteria such as GNP and balance of trade. As with all cocktails the loss to a borrower is limited in the event of a revaluation and an investor is only affected partially by a devaluation.

The Arab currency related unit (Arcru) is a unit of account based on the movement of the currencies of the following twelve Arab States against the U.S. dollar since 28 June 1974 (on which date the Arcru had a value of SDR 0.828948, or U.S. $1): Algeria, Bahrain, Egypt, Iraq, Kuwait, Lebanon, Libya, Oman, Qatar, Saudi Arabia, Syria, and the United Arab Emirates. To value the Arcru on any date, the two strongest and two weakest currencies against the U.S. dollar are identified, and a weighted average is taken of the changes in value against the dollar of the remaining eight Arab currencies. Clearly, the composition of the eight middle currencies will change over time as the relative strengths or weaknesses of the twelve component currencies shift over time vis-a-vis the U.S. dollar, which tends to stabilise the Arcru value in dollar terms.

There could certainly be benefits for importers and exporters in using currency cocktails to reduce exchange rate risks. This is particularly true for longer term contracts or in the less universally used currencies where exchange cover is not easy to obtain. The evidence, at present, is, however, that the unavoidable complexities of currency 'baskets' and their unfamiliarity have deterred companies from adopting this type of technique.

FORFAITING

Forfaiting means the business of bankers (or forfaiters) discounting, without recourse to the holder, a series of trade drafts or promissory notes with a final maturity of up to seven years. The 'without recourse' clause means that the endorser of a promissory note has the legal right to absolve himself of liability. This is not the case in many countries with a bill of exchange where the drawer is always legally open to recourse regardless of any declaration to the contrary.

The sources of forfaitable obligations are varied. The most important are countries where the traditional export credit system is inadequate, restrictive or uncompetitive. The U.K. and France, for example, are not high on the list, due to the generosity and all-embracing nature of their respective export credit institutions, ECGD and COFACE. However, Switzerland and West Germany, and more recently the U.S.A. and Italy, are countries where exporters require the assistance of private (i.e. non-governmental) financial institutions. In some cases, where governmental export credit programmes require the exporter to carry a sizeable recourse risk on his books, or require unreasonable conditions for documentation or difficult payment terms, exporters turn to forfaiting as a viable alternative. This is due particularly to the non-bureaucratic nature of forfaiting.

The cost of forfaiting i.e. the discount rate, is based upon a number of factors. The most important of these is, naturally, the refinancing cost to the forfaiting company, normally the Euromarket rate for similar credit periods for the currency used in the transaction. To this basic cost is added a premium to cover the commercial, currency, economic and political risks. The commercial risk concerns the possibility that commitments may not be honoured by the obligor or guarantor. The cost charged for the currency. risk being accepted by the forfaiter is reflected in the Euromarket cost of covering medium-term and thus in the Eurocurrency deposit rate. Economic risks arise when government intervention prevents or hinders payment of a debt. Political risks cover the non-financial difficulties which can occur, such as change of government, wars, blockades, boycotts and strikes which must be taken into account when fixing a margin for risk.

Forfaiting is normally possible for export debts with a longer period to maturity than one can obtain when factoring.

OTHER TECHNIQUES

Two other less important techniques for managing exposure are factoring and 'lock box' systems.

Factoring

The role of a factor is to buy debts incurred by business in the normal conduct of trade. For a U.K. based company there are two methods of international factoring:

(1) Factoring without recourse: The U.K. factor uses correspondent factors to guarantee debts and for collection. This method is restricted to exports to countries in which there is a chain member, i.e. mainly, most Western European countries and North America.

(2) Factoring with recourse: The exporter relies on an ECGD policy. The factor uses a chain member where possible and otherwise uses its own resources for collection. The factor is protected by an assignment of ECGD policy and a factoring endorsement.

The covering of exchange risk is not normally a part of the factoring service; the factor normally credits the value of debts purchased provisionally and adjusts the actual value on the basis of the amount collected in sterling. It is possible for the factor to arrange forward cover.

Apart from obtaining forward cover exchange risk protection can be arranged in two ways:

(i) Early payment might be arranged with correspondent factors against warranties issued by a U.K. factor on behalf of the exporter.

(ii) Subsidiary or associated companies might be set up in an importer's country through which export sales are effected. An importer may obtain factoring services locally and remit the proceeds promptly on arrival of goods.

Thus the benefit of international factoring is that, if the currency of a receivable is likely to weaken, one can obtain the equivalent amount denominated in a stronger currency.

'Lock Box' System

This system is very similar to the use of hold accounts. If a currency is expected to weaken, a basic principal of currency management is to hasten the receipts of weak currencies and then to convert them quickly into a stronger currency. One means of accelerating the flow of funds is a lock box system the purpose of which is to eliminate the time between the receipt of remittances by a company and their deposit in a bank.

A company rents a local post-office box and authorises its banks in the countries concerned to pick up remittances in the box. Customers are given instructions to mail their remittances to the lock box. The bank picks up the mail sent several times a day and deposits the cheques in the company's account.

The main advantage of a lock box system is that cheques are deposited at banks sooner and, therefore, become collected balances earlier than if they were processed by the company prior to deposit. In other words, the 'lag' between the time cheques are received by the company and the time they are actually deposited at the bank is eliminated. The higher the average amount deposited and the greater the probability of a devaluation, the greater are the benefits. Similarly, if only a small average remittance is involved and the lower the probability of a devaluation, the smaller are the benefits. The principal disadvantage of a lock box arrangement is the high cost.

CONSTRAINTS ON FINANCIAL OPTIMISATION

Robbins and Stobaugh pointed out that, theoretically, the net financial benefits from systems which optimise exchange risk minimisation, whereby the aims of the subsidiaries are deliberately subordinated to those of the multinational enterprise as a whole, may be quite substantial[10]. In actual fact, however, as Plasschaert has made clear, the opportunities for profit-maximising international financial management are seriously constrained by internal factors and, even more, by governmental exchange restrictions[11].

Any system designed to reduce internal constraints may have undesirable effects on the efficiency of the enterprise. Centralisation of financial management and exchange management implies that some powers of decision are taken at higher echelons, where a global view can be taken by sophisticated financial experts. Centralised financial management also subordinates the interests of the subsidiary to those of the multinational enterprise as a whole. The danger of this is that local managers are likely to resent intrusion on their prerogatives and become demotivated. Acceptance of the erosion of their decision powers calls, therefore, for adequate information and motivation.

Reshuffling of the internal payments flows through given techniques, in order to achieve systems optimisation, may distort the profit performances of subsidiaries. This occurs, for example, when transfer prices are used to obtain, say, a tax saving. Such manipulations cause discomfort in the local management teams, unless parallel, unbiased data are used to assess the real performance of a subsidiary. In addition, the rechanneling or recalibrating of financial flows, as when the 'leading' or 'lagging' gambit is practised, can affect the liquidity position of the subsidiaries involved and may necessitate expensive replenishment of working capital.

There are however inherent limits to the degree in which higher echelons (at the parent company, or at regional headquarters) can supplant local managers on routine financial decisions in the subsidiaries.

All in all, the internal impediments and costs involved in centralized financial optimisation are less serious obstacles to multinational enterprises than the panoply of exchange controls that governments imply. In recent years and in order to master the recurrent exchange troubles, even traditionally liberal countries, such as West Germany, Switzerland and Luxembourg, have at times expanded their exchange tool-kit and tightened regulations. These regulations mainly attempt to thwart the adverse impact of short-term capital flows i.e. the practices most likely to have a speculative impact on the reserve position and on the exchange rate level of the currencies concerned. The tools of exchange controls appear in almost infinite variety, as the IMF's Annual Reports on Exchange Restrictions witness.

In West Germany, domestic companies have in the past been discouraged from borrowing abroad through a cash deposit requirement (*Bardepôt*) which made foreign borrowing almost prohibitively expensive. Tight credit conditions in Germany and the large scope for borrowing in the Euro-currency market, with a weak dollar, would, without the *Bardepôt,* have made borrowing abroad quite attractive.

In a few countries, as in the U.K. and France, restrictions have been clamped on the forward market, especially with respect to the maximum term for which cover could be obtained. A forward exchange order does not directly affect the spot market. The counterpart in the forward contract, i.e. the bank, in order to square its own exchange position, will normally respond to its customer's forward purchase of, e.g. Deutschemarks, by a spot purchase of Deutschemarks. If the interim investment in Deutschemarks, which the bank will undertake within a swap arrangement, runs into difficulties, on account of negative interest rates or other restrictive measures, the efficiency of the exchange market is weakened. Deposit facilities at normal market rates in the parallel Euro-currency market(s) have, however, allowed banks to bypass the controls enacted in the domestic money markets.

Multinational enterprises cannot, it appears, operate in an unhampered fashion. Their freedom to effectuate short-term capital flows, either in covering an open position (e.g. borrowing to offset a long position in a weak currency) or for speculative purposes (e.g. borrowing in a weak currency for conversion in to a stronger one) is frequently severely circumscribed. One particular tool of exchange management, however, cannot easily be controlled by the monetary authorities. The central bank can prescribe a maximum length of time for payment terms (and, subsidiarily, impose the conversion of the foreign currency proceeds into domestic currency), i.e. control 'leading' and 'lagging', but too harsh prescriptions would stifle the freedom which international trade needs in the realm of credit terms. Besides, time-limits to the credit terms may be imposed on commercial transactions, but would be inappropriate with respect to some important non-commercial money flows, such as dividend remittances, which can also be modulated on the basis of exchange considerations through 'leading' and 'lagging'.

REFERENCES

[1] S. R. Bradford, "Measuring the Cost of Forward Exchange Contracts." *Euromoney*. August 1974

[2] G. Pelli, "Thoughts on the Cost of Forward Cover in a Floating System." *Euromoney*. October 1974.

[3] R. Ankrom, "Among their Hedgers, Treasurers may miss the obvious." *Euromoney*. December 1977.

[4] K. Howlett, "Forward Hedging does pay because the long run is too long." *Euromoney*. April 1977.

[5] R. I. McKinnon, "Floating Exchange Rates 1973–74: The Emperors New Clothes." *Mimeo,* November 1974.

[6] J. A. Frenkel, and R. M. Levich, *"Transactions Costs and the Efficiency of International Capital Markets."* A paper presented at the Helsinki Conference on the Monetary Mechanism in Open Economies. August 1975.

[7] R. Aliber, "The Firm under Pegged and Floating Exchange Rates." *Scandinavian Journal of Economics.* Vol. 28. No. 2. 1976.

[8] M. Crawford, Currencies in a Floating World. Economist Intelligence Unit. 1977.

[9] *See* J. Chown, and M. Finney, *"Foreign Currency and Debt Management."* J. F. Chown and Company Limited 1977.

[10] S. M. Robbins, and R. B. Stobaugh, *Money in the Multinational Enterprise. A Study in Financial Policy.* Longman Group Ltd. 1974.

[11] S. R. F. Plasschaert, "Multinational Enterprises, Exchange Markets and Monetary Crises." *Working Paper 76–19.* University of Antwerp. January 1976.

Appendix I
Exchange Financing—Parallel Loans, Back to Back Loans, Currency Exchange Agreements

Parallel loans, back to back loans and currency exchange agreements fall within the classification of exchange financing. They are techniques which companies with international operations can use to generate foreign currency for their overseas operations on a term basis and at preferential rates.

Why Consider Exchange Financing?

Exchange financing helps companies overcome difficulties experienced in the financial management of overseas operations, especially:

— the impact on earnings of foreign currency translation gains or losses;
— the mobilisation of world-wide intra-company liquidity, both in convertible and blocked currencies;
— the problems of obtaining medium/long term funds at reasonable rates in foreign capital markets;
— the thinness, when they exist, of forward foreign exchange markets beyond one year;
— the matching of assets and liabilities both in terms of currency and maturity;
— covering long term commitments in foreign currencies.

Optional Structures for Exchange Financing

A number of structures for exchange financing can be used. The choice will depend on factors such as exchange control, lending and borrowing regulations, and tax considerations. These structures can broadly be described as follows:

Parallel Loans—a pair of loans made simultaneously in two countries;
Back to Back Loans—reciprocal loans made in two different currencies between two companies;
Currency Exchange Agreements—a pair of foreign exchange contracts, one spot and one forward, between two parties in different countries;

PARALLEL LOANS

A parallel loan is a transaction where two parties simultaneously make loans of the same value to one another's foreign subsidiaries. These loans can be depicted as follows:

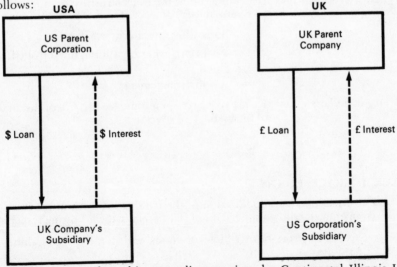

Permission to reproduce this appendix was given by Continental Illinois Ltd (London)

207

The main characteristics of a parallel loan are:

— two separate loans, with no *cross border* funds movements;
— normally some arrangement whereby the loans set off one another;
— payment of interest by both recipients of the loans;
— loans cannot be off-set in the parents' consolidated balance sheets.

The general terms of a parallel loan are as follows:

Counterparties:	Normally large, good quality companies
Term:	Between 5–15 years.
Amount:	Depends upon the parties' needs, however some flexibility is desirable. Amounts less than $5 million are not practicable.
Use of Proceeds:	Depends on local regulations.
Interest:	In deciding interest rates, parties essentially determine an acceptable differential. This reflects general market interest rate differentials between the two currencies, forward foreign exchange discounts, and what the parties believe their own opportunity cost is. Another factor is the absolute level of rates which normally depends upon Central Bank and tax considerations.
Security:	Each loan collateralises the other and the parties either take a formal charge over the loan, or agree to a right of set-off in the event of default. To maintain collateral in the event of exchange rate fluctuations it may be necessary to have a periodic realignment of the loans, or 'top up'. This is done by either increasing or decreasing the loans so that the two loans fully collateralise one another at current exchange rates.
Regulatory Permissions:	Depending upon the exact structure permissions may be required for:

— borrowing foreign currency;
— local borrowing by a foreign controlled company;
— set-off arrangements.

Arrangement Fees:	Each party pays a one-time fee of 1/2% of the amount of the loan.

BACK TO BACK LOANS

A back to back loan is a modification of the parallel loan. Although it is often used synonymously with parallel loans, it is different in the following respects:

— There is a cross-border flow of funds which raises withholding tax questions.
— There is only one loan document.

The back to back loan can be depicted as follows:

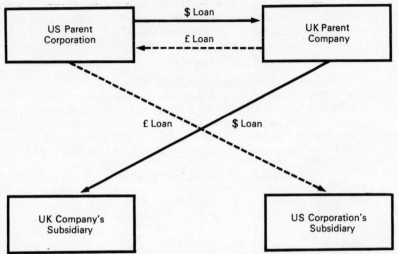

The general terms of such a transaction are the same as for a parallel loan, although the parties may need to seek relief from withholding taxes.

CURRENCY EXCHANGE AGREEMENTS

Currency Exchange Agreements ('CEAs') have become an internationally accepted mechanism for raising foreign currency. Set out below is some background information about these arrangements.

What is a CEA?

A currency exchange agreement is a modification of a back to back loan arrangement and overcomes certain disadvantages associated with the latter, especially with regard to right of 'set-off'. In a currency exchange, for example, a U.K. company would provide sterling to a U.S. company in exchange for U.S. dollars. At a later specified date, normally between five and ten years after the initial exchange, the two companies will have the option, or sometimes the obligation, to require the other to re-exchange the same amounts of currency as on the initial exchange day. In consideration for the exchange, one party, normally the provider of the stronger currency, pays to the other an annual exchange fee. In the case of a sterling/dollar exchange, the fee is currently payable by the provider of dollars to the provider of sterling, which is a reflection of the interest differentials and devaluation expectations between the two currencies.

Advantages Over Parallel/Back to Back Loans

Because they are similar to foreign exchange swap transactions, CEAs, in contrast to parallel loans:
— are reported off balance sheet;
— do not distort the profit and loss from the reporting of both interest income and expense;
— afford greater protection in the event of default;
— have simpler documentation.

Under a parallel/back to back loan, because of the ruling in the British Eagle case*, to be fully protected a right of set-off has to be registered. With a CEA, however, the obligation to re-exchange depends upon performance. Therefore, if one party defaults in the re-exchange, the other party has no obligation to return the currency it holds.

*British Eagle International Airlines Limited v. Compagnie Nationale Air France. All England Law Reports. (1975) 2ALL ER

Elimination of Foreign Exchange Exposure

Because CEAs can be revalued at current exchange rates they may be offset against other gains or losses arising from translation of foreign currency balance sheets. They can therefore be used to aid companies in eliminating translation losses and gains.

Development of Currency Exchange Agreements

Since the first currency exchange agreement was completed in August 1976, the product has been refined and become an acceptable international financing technique. For example, currency exchange agreements have now been written between non-residents in currencies where local regulations do not normally permit such an arrangement. These agreements can be completed without the necessity for either an initial exchange or re-exchange of currencies.

The following outlines the development of currency exchanges from those involving an initial exchange of currencies, to those which do not require any exchange at all. An example of a Belgian Franc/U.S. Dollar exchange is used since the Bank of England does not permit CEAs without an initial exchange of currencies.

Initial Exchange—Traditional Method

Diagram 1 represents the traditional structure of a currency exchange. In the example we have assumed that B Co and US Co enter into a currency exchange agreement for five years whereby B Co will exchange BF30 with US Co in return for US Co providing B Co with $1. Normally the dollars and BFs would be onlent to the respective subsidiaries unless the proceeds were to be used directly by the parent. Diagram 1 assumes inter-company loans.

Re-exchange—Traditional Method

Diagram 2 represents the re-exchange in five years with B Co. and U.S. Co. having agreed to re-exchange currencies in the initial amounts *no matter* what the future exchange rate, i.e. B Co. gives us Co. $1 in exchange for U.S. Co. giving B Co. BF30.

Diagram 1

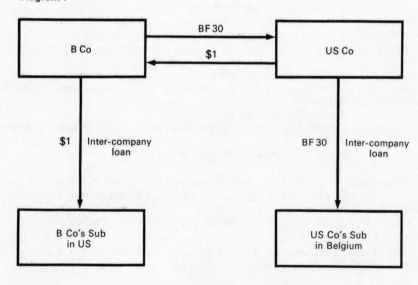

210

Diagram 2

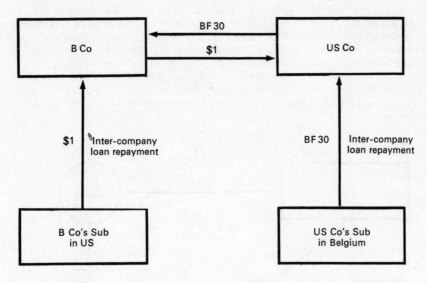

KEY
B Co	Belgian Parent
U.S. Co	US Parent
BF	Belgian Franc
$	US Dollar

Re-exchange only

The most important part of a currency exchange agreement is the re-exchange in five years between B Co. and U.S. Co. Diagram 3 shows this re-exchange without the inter-company loans which are separate transactions from the currency exchange agreement. The importance of this re-exchange is that exposure arises in B Co.'s case, for example, when it acquires dollars assets with the dollars received. If the asset acquired, when translated, is worth less than BF30 the B Co. would incur a translation loss. However, the above re-exchange means that no matter what the exchange rate is in the future, someone (the U.S. Co.) will give B Co. BF30 in return for $1. Consequently, any loss arising on the translation of the dollar asset will be off-set by B Co.'s revaluation of the currency exchange agreement.

Diagram 3

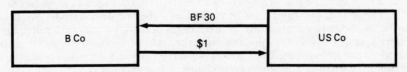

No Initial Exchange

Let us assume that U.S. Co. only wants to cover its BF exposure through the re-exchange, i.e. Diagram 4 (b), then if B Co does require dollars, it can achieve this through a spot sale of BF's for dollars as represented in Diagram 4 (a). In this diagram we have assumed B Co would lend the dollar proceeds to its U.S. subsidiary after the spot transaction by way of a dollar inter-company loan. Again, B Co would have exposure when translating the dollar assets acquired but similarly as mentioned above under "Re-exchange Only", the currency exchange agreement (Diagram 4 (b)) can be revalued to off-set any translatable exposure.

Diagram 4 (a)

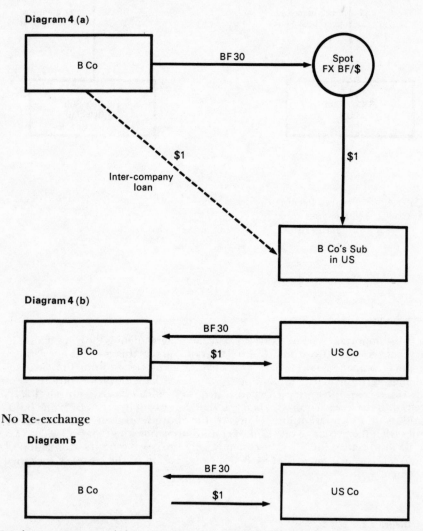

Diagram 4 (b)

No Re-exchange

Diagram 5

We have now covered the situation where no initial exchange of currencies takes place. If required, this can be accomplished by a spot BF/$FX transaction. It can also be demonstrated that no re-exchange need take place. Under these circumstances, a provision allowing for 'alternate performance' can be incorporated in the agreement. Then following three cases explain what is meant by alternate performance and why a re-exchange is not necessary.

212

Case 1

Let us assume that in five years B Co. could buy $1 for BF30. In this case it could be agreed between the two parties that no re-exchange take place. B Co. could keep the $1 and U.S. Co. the BF30 as B Co. could sell that $ for BF30, the initial amount it sold to generate $1. Conversely, the U.S. Co. could buy BF30 for $1. In this case both companies are in exactly the same position as they were on the date of entering into the agreement five years earlier and neither would incur a gain or loss if they agreed to waive the re-exchange.

Case 2

Let us assume that B Co. and U.S. Co. decide to buy one another's currencies for the re-exchange but that B Co. could buy $1 for BF28. Obviously B Co. has a gain of BF2, after the re-exchange when it would receive BF30. However, its dollar asset would now only be worth BF28, therefore the gain on the conclusion of the exchange contract is offset by the loss on the dollar asset. Rather than both parties re-exchanging, the U.S. Co. could pay the difference between the CEA re-exchange rate and the current spot rate, a net amount of BF2 to B Co.

Case 3

Alternatively, if B Co. could only buy $1 for BF32 B Co. would have to pay BF2 to U.S. Co. However this loss on the exchange contract is once again off-set by the gain on the dollar asset which would now be worth BF32.

Summary

From the above three cases, it can be concluded that, provided in the fifth year one party pays the BF difference to the other party (depending on whether the dollar has appreciated or depreciated vis-a-vis the BF), the result would be exactly the same as if B Co. had given U.S. Co. $1 in return for U.S. Co. giving B Co. BF30. The payment of only the difference is referred to as 'alternate performance'.

Conclusion

We have now moved from agreements where there is an initial exchange and re-exchange of currencies to cases where 1) there is no initial exchange, but only a re-exchange of currencies, and 2) where there is no initial exchange or re-exchange, but only payment of the difference as described above.

10

The Euro-Currency Markets

WHAT ARE EURO-CURRENCIES?

The Euro-currency market is the market in which Euro-banks accept deposits and make loans denominated in currencies other than that of the country in which they are located. Like domestic savings banks, Euro-banks provide depositors with safe, interest-bearing and relatively short-term financial assets, while they lend for considerably longer maturities to borrowers. This is in contrast to the Euro-bond market where there is no intermediary between the borrower and the lender. In the Euro-bond market the investor holds a claim directly on the borrower instead of on a financial institution.

Table 10.1

Euro-currency market
($ billions)

based on foreign-currency liabilities of banks in major European countries, the Bahamas, Bahrain, Cayman Islands, Panama, Canada, Japan, Hong Kong, and Singapore.

	1970	1971	1972	1973	1974	1975	1976	1977	1978
	Dec	Dec	Dec	Dec	Dec	Dec	Dec	Dec	Dec
Estimated size:									
Gross	110	145	200	305	370	455	560	695	795
Net	65	85	110	160	215	250	310	380	450
Euro-dollars as % of all Euro-currencies—gross	81	76	78	73	77	78	79	76	n/a.

p—preliminary

Source: Morgan Guaranty Trust Company: *World Financial Markets*. Various Issues.

Examination of Table 10.1 shows, firstly, that the growth of the Euro-currency market between 1970 and 1978 has been phenomenal; secondly, that the dollar has consistently accounted for 80 per cent of the market during this time period. A Euro-dollar deposit is a dollar deposit held with a bank outside the U.S.A. The question of location is of paramount importance in understanding the Euro-currency market. The only difference

215

between a Euro-dollar deposit and any other dollar deposit is that with a Euro-dollar deposit the original owner of the dollars no longer looks to the U.S.A. for repayment but to a bank located outside the U.S.A. Euro-dollars come into existence when 'dollars are transferred from a U.S. bank to a foreign bank or to the overseas branch of a U.S. bank, or when foreign currencies are converted into dollars which are then deposited in a bank located outside the U.S.A. The dollars underlying the Euro-dollar system never leave the U.S. banking system. A Euro-bank, accepting dollar deposits, acquires a dollar deposit in a U.S. bank, and when it lends Euro-dollars it draws down its U.S. dollar balances.

The term 'Euro-dollar' is something of a misnomer. Euro-dollars can be traded anywhere as long as it is not in the U.S.A.; the majority, however, of Euro-dollars are traded inside Europe. Euro-currency markets exist for several currencies apart from the dollar, e.g. Euro-Deutschemarks, Euro-sterling, Euro-guilders, Euro-Swiss francs. Thus Euro-sterling, for example, is sterling which is traded outside the U.K. In the same way that Euro-dollars are tied to a deposit in the U.S.A., Euro-guilders are tied to deposits in the Netherlands, Euro-Swiss francs to deposits in Switzerland etc.

WHY DO EURO-CURRENCY MARKETS EXIST?

The answer to this is quite simple. They exist because of government regulations. Euro-dollars have been defined as financial assets and liabilities denominated in dollars but traded outside the U.S.A. The Euro-dollar market offers the opportunity for trading dollars outside the control of government regulations imposed on residents within the boundaries of the U.S.A. When regulations started to limit Americans' ability to borrow and lend money in the U.S.A. an alternative market evolved which enabled their financial needs to be met abroad. Indeed, the growth of the Euro-dollar market has paralleled the growth of controls on the U.S. banking system.

The U.S. banking system was faced with two needs in the mid-1960s. Firstly, U.S. monetary policy forced the banks to finance domestic operations abroad. Secondly, the widespread growth of multinational companies meant that, if U.S. banks were to satisfy their clients, overseas expansion was needed.

The U.S.A. has used traditional monetary control measures of changing interest rates and reserve requirements. Regulation 'Q' imposed by the Federal Reserve during the 1960s limited the interest rates that banks could pay on deposits. This was an anti-inflationary measure. The restrictions did not apply to Euro-dollar deposits, even when they were in the European branches of U.S. banks. Hence, once Regulation 'Q' became effective there was an incentive to withdraw funds from the U.S.A. and to invest them in Euro-dollar deposits.

At the same time as dollars were leaving the U.S.A. profitable opportunities for dollars arose in the U.S.A. This was due to Regulation 'M'. This regulation specified the amount that U.S. banks were required to keep as a reserve against deposits. However, until 1969 this regulation did not affect the amount of reserves to be kept against deposits from foreign banks or from their own foreign branches. Hence, dollar-denominated accounts in European branches (Euro-dollar accounts) had no reserve requirements and the branch could deposit (lend) the funds with its parent company which was then free to lend against the full amount of the account. In contrast, had the same customer deposited the funds in the U.S. head office in the first place, the bank would have been forced to keep a certain percentage of the funds on reserve against the deposit.

It was in periods of 'tight money' in the U.S.A. that the Regulation 'Q' ceiling acted as a major stimulus to the Euro-dollar market. In 1966 and in 1969 the Federal Reserve reduced the rate of growth of the money supply, with the inevitable effect that interest rates rose. Since Regulation 'Q' prevented banks from raising their interest rates on deposits, deposit rates became extremely unattractive and banks experienced withdrawals of deposits. In order to try and regain those deposits U.S. banks increased their borrowings of dollars in the Euro-dollar market which forced up interest rates in that market. This raising of Euro-dollar rates, in turn, persuaded more and more investors who had held deposits in the U.S.A. to redeposit those funds in the Euro-dollar market and take advantage of the attractive yields available. However, although Regulation 'Q' did influence the growth of the Euro-dollar market the basic reason for the market's growth was the lack of government controls.

As from 5 October 1978 the reserve requirement on foreign borrowings of Federal Reserve Board member banks, primarily Euro-dollars from their foreign branches and other foreign banks, was reduced from four per cent to zero. Since 1969 the reserve requirements have ranged from four per cent to twenty per cent. Because U.S. banks have had to maintain these reserves, while their foreign-owned counterparts did not, U.S. banks had been at a competitive disadvantage in Euro-banking.

Another set of regulations which contributed heavily to the fast growth of the Euro-dollar market were those designed to limit capital outflows from the U.S.A. These regulations were threefold. Firstly, there were controls on foreign direct investment which made it necessary for multinational companies to finance foreign direct investment from outside the U.S.A. Secondly, the interest equalisation tax (IET) imposed a penalty on U.S. residents who bought securities issued by foreigners. Thus, if a U.S. resident obtained a higher yield on a foreign security than he would have received on an equivalent U.S. security, he paid the difference in tax. Thirdly, the voluntary credit restraint programme limited the amount of credit that U.S. banks could extend to foreigners. All these restrictions attempted to move the demand for funds for use abroad from the U.S.A. to elsewhere. The Euro-dollar market provided a perfect 'elsewhere'. All these regulations were eliminated in 1974.

Exchange control restrictions designed for balance of payments reasons have stimulated the growth of the Euro-markets. Thus a multinational company wanting to obtain sterling, lire, or French francs for use in the respective economies and prevented from so doing by local regulations could freely obtain these in the Euro-sterling, Euro-lira and Euro-French franc markets.

HOW DOES THE MARKET OPERATE?

The Euro-dollar market is entirely of a wholesale nature and transactions are typically of a minimum size of $1 million although deals of $500,000 and $250,000 also occur. Amounts up to $10 million are not infrequent; during 1969–70 there were transactions of $100 million and even more. Like the foreign exchange market, the Euro-dollar market is confined to inter-bank dealings. Even the largest non-banking firms have to deal with banks. The market is confined to deals between banks with the highest 'names' with low credit risks. The market operates within an international framework with a network of international banks connected by correspondent relationships and linked by telephone and telex.

The market developed during the 1960s and during this time the number of participating banks grew very quickly. Large numbers of U.S. banks in response to the needs of the overseas subsidiaries of U.S. multinationals have entered the market via the establishment of branches in Europe.

London plays an important role in the Euro-currency market. In 1978 some fifty per cent of Euro-dollar business and some thirty-five per cent of Euro-currency business as a whole was transacted in London. The pre-eminence of London largely stems from the long tradition of international banking in the U.K., originating from the time when sterling and not the dollar was the world's main trading currency and reserve asset. With the skill of knowing how to conduct business, and having established customers, the U.K. banks were able to switch from sterling to the dollar in financing international transactions. U.S. banks were encouraged to move to London due to political stability, a common language, lack of controls and a supply of experienced personnel.

Banks operate as intermediaries between lenders and borrowers. Since Euro-dollars are not used as a medium of exchange chequeing facilities do not exist. This means that banks do not acquire dollars without having to pay interest on them as do banks acquiring interest-free current account deposits. All deposits are interest bearing whether they have a maturity of one day or several years. The standard maturities are similar to those of the forward market. Thus, deposits can be for one day, two days, seven days, one month, three months, six months or one year. Deals transacted at other time periods within one year are known as 'broken dates'. These deals tend to be transacted at somewhat unfavourable rates. Euro-currency dealing for time periods over one year tends to take place within a very thin market.

Banks which are large dealers in Euro-dollars find it possible at times to easily lend to one customer a deposit given to them by another customer. Much more often, however, they have to find the counterpart in the market. This can be done either by contacting a bank in a foreign centre (or by being contacted by them) or, locally, mostly through the intermediary of a foreign exchange broker. Some banks prefer to deal direct with each other, not only to save brokerage but also because it is felt that direct contact gives their dealers some idea of how keen the other party is on transacting business at the rate suggested. On the other hand, by dealing through brokers, banks find it less awkward to refuse 'names' or to quote higher rates than those quoted to borrowers of first-class standing.

In foreign exchange dealings brokers confine themselves to indicating the type of bank that is offered as a counterpart and do not disclose 'names' until after the deal is concluded. In Euro-currency dealings they have to disclose the borrowers identity to the lender before the deal is concluded, as soon as they are satisfied that the latter really intends to proceed with the transaction and does not want to sound out the market. The reason why banks usually insist on knowing the actual potential borrower's name even if the broker assures them that he has regularly dealt with the bank is that, conceivably, their limit for that 'name' may have been completely used up. All banks place limits on the amount they will lend to other banks. This limit is based on formulae designed to measure the certainty with which the bank will repay the deposit upon maturity. The limits placed on each 'name' by most banks are a closely-guarded secret and are subject to change in either direction. All Euro-currency transactions are unsecured credits, hence the importance attached to 'names' by would-be lenders.

Banks deal directly with each other in foreign exchange transactions between two foreign centres, but a certain amount of Euro-currency deposit business between foreign centres is now transacted through international money brokers.

The entire money market is rationalising itself into four main regional centres. These are London, New York, Singapore and Bahrain. Money brokers when expanding internationally will either forge a trading relationship with existing local brokers or will open a subsidiary office of the mother company.

WHAT FACILITIES DO THE EURO-CURRENCY MARKETS PROVIDE FOR MULTINATIONAL COMPANIES?

Certainty of ability to borrow or lend funds

A multinational company's ability to raise funds in the domestic money markets in which they are operating may be limited in two ways. Firstly, domestic money market rates may be high. Secondly, foreign companies may not be permitted access to domestic money markets. Many governments argue that if they are to permit multinationals to enter their domestic market the multinationals should use their own sources of finance and not pre-empt the local money market. The Euro-markets provide a source of finance which may be cheaper than local finance and which will most certainly be available irrespective of local market conditions. This is not to say that Euro-currency borrowing is regulation-free. Indeed in the U.K. Euro-currency borrowing may involve a significant exchange risk as multinational companies are allowed to hedge forward the interest on their borrowings but not the principal itself.

If the subsidiary of a multinational in Switzerland desires Swiss francs without incurring any exchange risk it has two choices: firstly, to borrow Swiss francs in the local money market; or secondly, to borrow another currency, e.g. the dollar, sell the dollars spot for Swiss francs and then re-purchase the dollars forward in exchange for Swiss francs. The dollar liability would then be repaid. This second option is normally called a 'swap'. The cost of borrowing local Swiss francs is the local interest rate for the relevant maturity date. The cost of the swap is the cost of the borrowed Euro-currency less what is lost on the forward transaction. Clearly, the multinational should choose the cheapest alternative. What is important here is that the existence of Euro-markets when combined with a swap transaction may yield funds at a lower interest cost than using the domestic money market. The Euro-markets are clearly even more important when access to domestic money markets is either forbidden or severely limited. Many money markets are very 'thin' and consequently a small

220

increase in the demand for funds may result in a large increase in interest rates. The majority of Euro-currencies regularly traded have fairly 'thick' markets. Multinational companies are always keen to reduce their dependence on one source of finance. The Euro-markets have provided them with an ideal way of diversifying their reliance on one single source.

In the same ways that Euro-markets enable companies to borrow funds so they provide an arena for investing surplus funds. In the case of excess dollars these could· be placed directly into Euro-dollars or could be exchanged for another currency, invested in the relevant money market, and the forward cover provided by the swap. Again the advantage of thick markets becomes evident.

Related to the above points is the role of exchange controls. Exchange controls have as their objective the limiting of the ability of private organisations to move capital from one financial centre to another. There are many types of controls. Spot exchange rates may be controlled by having a two-tier system, as in Belgium, where access to the controlled section is limited. Restrictions can be placed on usage of the forward market. Interest rate measures may involve direct control over interest rates allowed on external bank deposits. Exchange controls placed on banks can take many forms. There may be reserve requirements on external liabilities of up to one hundred per cent, prohibition of acceptance of external deposits, ceilings on gross or net external liabilities, or conversion limits from foreign to domestic currency. There may also be restrictions on repatriation of external assets, control of the term structure of external liabilities, and penalties on banks' excess foreign liabilities. Measures on non-bank financial institutions could include, as well as some of the above mentioned measures, limits on overseas borrowing. Direct primary measures have also become more common as controls on banks and other financial institutions have gradually been circumvented. The adoption of the *Bardepôt* in Germany in 1970 is an example of this. Other controls include a prohibition on foreign borrowing for internal use, prohibition on advance payments for exports and/or imports, i.e. 'leads' and 'lags', controls over access to domestic capital markets by foreign firms and controls on inter-company transactions.

Given the widespread existence of foreign exchange controls the Euro-markets provide access to an accessible, uncontrolled source of, or market for, funds.

SUPPLY AND DEMAND STRUCTURE OF THE EURO-DOLLAR MARKET

By far the most important aspect of the Euro-currency market, some eighty per cent, can, as shown in Table 10.1, be accounted for by the Euro-dollar market. It is instructive to examine who supplies and who demands these funds.

The supply of Euro-dollars come from several sources. Firstly, there are those placed by multinational companies and individuals, both resident and non-residents. These funds, in turn, derive from existing deposits held in the U.S.A., from conversions of local and other foreign currency holdings into dollars, or from dollar proceeds from sales of goods, services and capital assets. Euro-dollar balances represent deposits placed in order to earn interest but some, notably in Switzerland and Canada, are held for transaction purposes. Many holders of Euro-Swiss francs and Euro-Deutschemarks earn very low interest rates on their investments but these holdings are based on an expected up-valuation of the currencies concerned. Secondly, commercial banks supply Euro-dollars on a large scale. They convert excess cash reserves into dollars and place them directly into the Euro-dollar market. Thirdly, central banks and other official institutions provide an important source. A large number of central banks in developing countries and a few in Europe have for several years been depositing dollar balances in foreign banks. Some have done so only where their own commercial banks were withdrawing dollars from the market, notably during periods of 'window-dressing' pressures. Central banks have on occasion used the Euro-dollar market as a means of regulating domestic money market conditions. In an attempt to neutralise the effect on the German money supply of continual intervention in the foreign exchange market the German central bank has occasionally offered German commercial banks attractive swap arrangements (*see Chapter 3*) in order that banks would borrow dollars from the Bundesbank. Under these arrangements commercial banks buy spot dollars for Deutschemarks and the central bank agrees to buy the dollars back at an attractive rate at a future date. The combination of the interest yield on the dollar asset obtained by investing in the Euro-dollar. market and the spot-forward exchange deal gave the banks a more attractive return than could be obtained within Germany.

Finally, the Bank for International Settlements (BIS), the central bank for central bankers, has been a major supplier of funds to the Euro-dollar market, employing dollars from various sources. Substantial funds are received by BIS as deposits from some central banks. At times, in order to stabilise the market the BIS has employed dollars obtained with swaps from the Federal Reserve System.

Who are the demanders of Euro-dollars? When Euro-dollar deposits are accepted they may be used immediately by the bank but often they are redeposited in other banks. When the funds are finally used a major portion goes into loans to non-banks for financing commercial transactions. Among these, loans for financing foreign trade are the most important. If the borrower does not need dollars for payment purposes he sells them for whichever currency he needs. A substantial portion of the dollars deposited in foreign banks is sold for third currencies either by the recipient banks or by the ultimate borrower.

Another major demander of Euro-dollar balances are the overseas branches of U.S. banks for the express purpose of improving the parent bank's liquidity position and credit base. Also, sizeable amounts of Euro-dollars are employed in loans to U.S. companies for financing the needs of overseas affiliates. Corporate usage of the Euro-currency market was examined in a earlier section (*p. 220 et seq.*). Other users of Euro-dollars are the New York agencies and branches of foreign banks for commercial loans and loans to securities dealers and brokers. Recently the end-users of funds have been local or municipal authorities or public utilities such as the U.K. Electricity Council or Gas Board. The exchange risk with official U.K. borrowers is occasionally guaranteed by the U.K. government.

Banks may use the Euro-markets as a means of adjusting their liquidity positions, i.e. taking deposits when their balance sheet becomes illiquid and putting the deposits out when the liquidity structure becomes excessive. Again, banks may borrow or lend depending on their view of the future movements of interest rates. In this case they will increase their level of deposits if interest rates are expected to rise at some future date, or reduce deposits when the opposite movement is expected. Also banks will increase their position in currencies to increase in value and decrease their position in currencies expected to decrease in value.

STRUCTURE OF EURO-CURRENCY INTEREST RATES:

Examination of the Euro-currency interest rates taken from the *Financial Times*, (Table 10.2) gives an indication of the range of Euro-currencies regularly traded. In each case the first rate quoted is the bid, or borrowing rate, i.e. the rate which the banks pays for deposits. The second rate quoted is the offer, or lending rate, i.e. the rate at which the banks will lend the currency. Clearly, the difference between the borrowing and lending rate, the spread, is the bank's profit on the deal.

Table 10.2

Euro-Currency Interest Rates

Jan. 29	Sterling	U.S. Dollar	Canadian Dollar	Dutch Guilder	Swiss Franc	West German Mark	French Franc	Italian Lira	Asian $	Japanese Yen
†Short term	$11\frac{1}{2}-11\frac{5}{8}$	$10-10\frac{1}{4}$	$8\frac{1}{2}-9\frac{1}{2}$	$7\frac{3}{8}-7\frac{5}{8}$	par–$\frac{1}{8}$	$1\frac{3}{8}-1\frac{5}{8}$	$7-7\frac{1}{4}$	8–12	—	—$2\frac{9}{16}-3$
7 day's notice	$11\frac{7}{8}-12\frac{1}{8}$	$10\frac{1}{8}-10\frac{3}{8}$	$8\frac{1}{2}-9\frac{1}{2}$	$7\frac{3}{8}-7\frac{5}{8}$	par–$\frac{1}{8}$	$2\frac{5}{8}-2\frac{7}{8}$	$7\frac{1}{8}-7\frac{3}{8}$	10–11	$10\frac{3}{8}-10\frac{1}{2}$	—$\frac{7}{16}-1$
Month	$11\frac{7}{8}-12\frac{1}{8}$	$10\frac{1}{4}-10\frac{1}{2}$	$10\frac{5}{8}$	$7\frac{3}{8}-7\frac{5}{8}$	par–$\frac{1}{8}$	$3\frac{3}{8}-3\frac{1}{2}$	$7\frac{3}{8}-7\frac{7}{8}$	13–14	$10\frac{5}{8}-10\frac{3}{4}$	$\frac{9}{16}-1\frac{3}{8}$
Three months	$13\frac{1}{8}-13\frac{1}{4}$	$10\frac{11}{16}-10\frac{15}{16}$	$10\frac{7}{8}-11\frac{1}{4}$	$7\frac{3}{8}-7\frac{5}{8}$	$\frac{1}{16}-\frac{5}{16}$	$3\frac{3}{4}-3\frac{7}{8}$	$8\frac{3}{8}-8\frac{5}{8}$	$13\frac{1}{2}-14\frac{1}{2}$	$11\frac{1}{4}-11\frac{3}{8}$	$1\frac{13}{16}-2\frac{5}{16}$
Six months	$13\frac{1}{8}-13\frac{1}{4}$	$11\frac{1}{8}-11\frac{3}{8}$	$10\frac{7}{8}-11\frac{1}{4}$	$7\frac{3}{8}-7\frac{5}{8}$	$\frac{5}{16}-\frac{7}{16}$	$4-4\frac{1}{8}$	$8\frac{3}{4}-9$	$13\frac{3}{4}-14\frac{3}{4}$	$11\frac{1}{2}-11\frac{5}{8}$	$2\frac{11}{16}-3\frac{1}{16}$
One year	$12\frac{1}{4}-12\frac{7}{8}$	$11\frac{1}{8}-11\frac{3}{8}$	$10\frac{7}{8}-11\frac{1}{4}$	$7\frac{3}{8}-7\frac{5}{8}$	$\frac{5}{8}-\frac{3}{4}$	$4\frac{1}{8}-4\frac{1}{4}$	$9\frac{1}{4}-9\frac{1}{2}$	14–15	$11\frac{7}{16}-11\frac{9}{16}$	$3-3\frac{1}{2}$

Source: *Financial Times*, 30 January 1979

A striking feature of the interest rate structure, or yield curve, is that in normal circumstances, in order to allow for the fact that money now is worth more than money in the future, interest rates tend to be higher the more distant the maturities. Another striking characteristic is that interest rates on weak currencies, notably sterling, the U.S. and Canadian dollar and the Italian Lira are higher than interest rates on strong currencies, notably the Swiss franc, and the Deutschemark. As can be seen from Table 10.2 the supply of Euro-yen was, on 29 January 1979, so high that interest rates, not for the first time, became negative. Weak currencies have high Euro-rates since speculators attempt to acquire a liability in a weak currency which they hope will decrease in value enabling them to repay the debt and make a profit. Strong currencies have low Euro-rates since speculators have bought these currencies with the hope that they will be revalued thus giving them a profit. As the Euro-market is a free market, if demand exceeds supply, prices, i.e. Euro-rates, rise and if supply exceeds demand prices, i.e. Euro-rates, go down. Forward rates can also influence Euro-rates. (see pp 226 *et seq*).

As Dufey and Giddy have shown analysis of the relationship between domestic interest rates and external rates gives a clear understanding of what the Euro-currency market is all about[1]. Using the U.S.A. and its currency for illustration, the external (Euro-dollar) and internal (domestic) market are merely competing segments of the total market for dollar denominated credit, intermediated by financial institutions operating either internally (domestic banks) or externally (Euro-banks). The Euro-dollar market competes with the domestic U.S. bank market in the same way that commercial paper competes with bankers' acceptances.

It has been suggested that the Euro-dollar interest rate structure is quite independent from that in the U.S.A. but, given that both markets are dealing in the same currency and that there is considerable freedom for capital to move between the two markets in response to interest rate differentials, it is to be expected that the interest rate structure in fact is closely linked. Arbitrage between the domestic and external segments of the dollar money market assures close correspondence both in terms of rate levels and in terms of rate changes in the absence of specific barriers and obstacles.

Examination of Table 10.3 indicates that the difference between the Euro-dollar rate and the U.S. Certificate of Deposit Rate (C.D.) remains low. A similar finding occurs for the Euro-Deutschemark rate and the German interbank rate. This correlation for the dollar reflects arbitrage activities on the part of U.S. banks, which adjust their borrowing between U.S. C.D.s and Euro-dollar deposits until the effective cost of funds is equalised in the two markets. A very high correlation also exists between movements in the U.S.C.D. and Euro-dollar rates, on the one hand, and changes in the Federal Fund rate on the other.

Table 10.3

INTERBANK RATES ON 3 MONTH EURO-CURRENCY DEPOSITS AND DIFFERENTIALS OVER DOMESTIC RATES

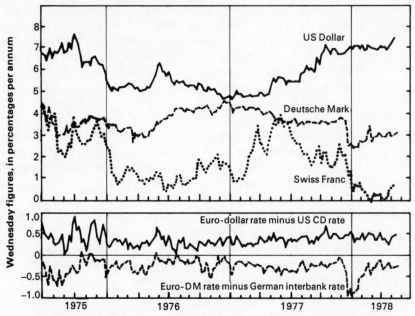

Source : *'Bank for International Settlements. 48th Annual Report'* 12th June 1978.

Despite this close correlation between Euro-dollar rates and equivalent U.S. rates, especially after 1973, there have been persistent rate differentials which exhibit a certain pattern of fluctuations. Dufey and Giddy explain these differentials by the existence of controls on international credit transactions, special risk factors and differences in competitive conditions in the respective markets.

Legal restrictions on international credit flows cut the external (Euro) market off from its internal (domestic) base and, to the extent that they are effective, controls tend to insulate Euro-market rates from the influence of domestic credit conditions. Under these conditions, Euro-dollar rates become a function of (a) external credit demand/supply, and (b) the effectiveness of the controls.

Johnston has confirmed that, in the absence of capital market imperfections such as capital controls, there is at the margin a very close relationship between the effective cost of loanable funds to banks in the Euro-dollar and U.S. domestic markets[2]. Again, this finding is due to domestic banks arbitraging between the domestic and Euro-currency markets.

THE RELATIONSHIP BETWEEN EURO-MARKETS AND FOREIGN EXCHANGE MARKETS

In order to appreciate how multinational companies and banks can maximise their use of Euro-currency markets it is essential to understand how the Euro-markets and foreign exchange markets interrelate.

The forward discount or premium of a currency in terms of another is directly related to the difference in interest rates prevailing in the Euro-currency markets of the two countries (*see Chapter 3*). The currency with the highest Euro-rate sells at a discount in terms of the currency of a lower interest rate. The currency with the lowest Euro-rate sells at a premium in terms of the currency of a higher interest rate.

If the interest differential in favour of a given currency is higher than the discount in the forward market for that currency, there is an incentive to invest funds in the high interest rate currency and to cover the investment in the forward market. If the interest differential in favour of a given currency is lower than the discount in the forward market for that currency, there is an incentive to invest funds in the low-interest currency and to cover the investment in the forward market.

An example illustrates this. If the money markets are in equilibrium this is termed 'interest parity'. For simplicity, it is assumed that bid and offer rates are identical.

Euro-currency Rates
(Three month maturity)

Euro-pound sterling	=	9 per cent
Euro-dollar	=	6 per cent

Foreign exchange market

Three month forward pound sterling	=	3 per cent discount against the dollar

In this example the high interest currency, the pound sterling, is at a 3 per cent per annum discount in the forward market against the dollar and this fully reflects the interest differential between the Euro-currency rates. A company or a bank would be indifferent between investing in sterling at 9 per cent and covering forward, giving a total return of 6 per cent, or of investing in dollars at 6 per cent. In other words interest parity prevails. However, assume now that the cost of forward cover is 2 per cent. In this case there is an advantage to be derived from investing in sterling at 9 per cent and covering forward at 2 per cent, giving a return of 7 per cent. This gives a better return than the 6 per cent available by investing in dollars. In this example the interest differential (3 per cent) is greater than the cost of forward cover (2 per cent) giving an incentive to invest in the high interest currency. However, this situation will not last long as the increased investment in sterling reduces sterling interest rates and increases dollar interest rates. Similarly, the increase in forward sales of sterling causes the discount to widen. Eventually, interest parity again prevails.

Assume now, that the Euro-rates remain the same but the cost of forward cover has risen to 4 per cent.

Euro-currency rates
(Three months maturity)

Euro-pound sterling	=	9 per cent
Euro-dollar	=	6 per cent

Foreign exchange market

Three month forward pound Sterling	=	4 per cent discount

In this case, investing in sterling and covering forward gives a total return of 5 per cent (9 – 4 per cent) which compares unfavourably with investing in dollars. The interest differential is lower than the discount in the forward market and this gives an incentive to invest funds in the lower interest currency and to cover the investment in the forward market. Thus an investor could borrow covered sterling for 5 per cent and invest in dollars for 6 per cent. Yet again this situation is unlikely to last for long. Continued sterling borrowing combined with large placements into dollars soon raises sterling rates and reduces dollar rates until interest parity prevails. Arbitrage along these lines always ensures that the Euro-currency interest rate differential equals the forward premium, or discount.

The second major relationship between the Euro-markets and the foreign exchange market is that the Forward premium or discount tends to be related to the expected rate of change of exchange rates (*see Chapter 9*).

The third major relationship, again developed by Dufey and Giddy, is that the expected rate of change in the exchange rate is related to the Euro-currency interest rate differential[3]. This can be illustrated by an example where the three month Euro-dollar interest rate is 6 per cent per annum and the Euro-mark rate is 4 per cent per annum. In this case an investor will prefer to hold his funds in Euro-dollar deposits unless the lower Euro-mark rate is offset by an expected depreciation of the dollar against the Deutschemark at an annual rate of 2 per cent or more.

Similarly, borrowers of three month funds will prefer Deutschemarks unless the Deutschemark is expected to appreciate at a rate of 2 per cent per annum or more. Assuming that a corporate treasurer expects the Deutschemark to rise by 1 per cent per annum his actions, and those of many other companies, will tend to bid the Euro-mark rate up (as depositors move funds out of Euro-marks into Euro-dollars and borrowers borrow more Euro-

Deutschemarks and fewer dollars). At the same time, the sale of Deutschemarks to obtain dollars by both sets of transactors will bid the dollar/Deutschemark spot exchange rate down. Ignoring transactions costs the incentive for this choice of depositing and borrowing currencies will disappear only when the Euro-Deutschemark rate has been bid up and the dollar/Deutschemark exchange rate bid down to the point at which the Euro-Deutschemark rate plus the expected rate of appreciation of the Deutschemark approximates the Euro-dollar rate.

In conclusion, the borrowing, lending and hedging actions of banks and corporations tend to ensure that the interest rate differential between two Euro-currency markets equals the forward premium, or discount, and that this same interest rate differential also equals the expected exchange rate change expressed as an annual rate.

POSSIBILITIES OF ARBITRAGE AND SPECULATION

An alert treasurer is always able to take advantage of deviations from interest-rate parity outlined above. Indeed it is the reaction of corporate treasurers which guarantees that interest-rate parity normally prevails. In addition to this however, the Euro-markets also provide an opportunity for speculation. There are many misunderstandings and misconceptions with regard to speculation. Whenever a foreign exchange position is left 'open' it is subject to gains or losses arising from changes in exchange rates. Speculation in the narrow sense would be if such open positions were established for the sole purpose of making money. In a wider sense maintaining open positions (arising from commercial or financial transactions) and intentionally not hedging them is also speculation. An importer who knows that he will later need foreign currency and does not purchase it forward is a speculator in the wider sense. The same is true of an exporter who has foreign currency receivables and still does not sell them forward. The same is also true of a company which borrows in a foreign currency but neither has income in that currency nor buys the currency forward.

Foreign exchange controls severely limit the use of domestic funds for speculative activities. However, the Euro-markets are not subject to these controls. The two most frequent types of speculation are speculation about changes in future spot rates and speculation about future interest rate changes. Speculation about changes in forward discounts and premiums is also possible.

If a speculator anticipates a depreciation in a currency he can speculate by borrowing the weak currency and then waiting for the depreciation. A profit will be made if the depreciation is greater than the interest differential obtained by borrowing an expensive currency and investing in a low yielding currency plus the transaction costs. If a speculator anticipates a revaluation of a currency he will acquire assets denominated in the currency expected to appreciate by borrowing in softer currencies. The cost here is the interest differential between the interest on the loan and the return plus transaction costs. The speculator will expect that the expected revaluation compensates for holding a low yielding asset.

If an interest rate fall is expected within six months a speculator could lend dollars for six months and cover his shortage by borrowing on a day-to-day basis. If an interest rate rise is expected a speculator could borrow dollars for six months in the hope of lending them out at a higher rate later.

The ability of multinational firms to speculate becomes evident when one realises the size of their reserves. The US Commission on Tariffs calculated that the liquid reserves of multinational firms in 1971 amounted to $268,000 million, or more than double the total currency reserves of all the central banks put together. However, a report commissioned by the West German Ministry of Finance and published by the Hamburg Economic Research Institute pointed out that the potential inflow of foreign currency to West Germany in 1972 was DM. 54,000 million and that, had it materialised, it would have increased the money supply by nearly forty per cent. In the event the total inflow was only some DM. 14,000 million of which scarcely a third came from multinationals.

THE RISE OF CONSORTIUM BANKING

The objective of consortium banking is syndication, i.e. the participation of several banks in a 'loan syndicate'.

The typical Euro-currency loan is quite sizeable in relation to a bank's capital and deposit base, so that most credits are syndicated with a number of other banks. A consortium provides a permanent syndicate of banks, although most loans are also syndicated outside the consortium as well. More generally, one could say that a consortium bank provides a means of pooling resources. For small banks, such as the seventeen shareholders of Allied Bank International, this meant generating an additional capability in international banking which none of them could achieve individually; for large banks, such as Chemical Bank, which acquired a thirty per cent holding in London Multinational Bank, it offered a vehicle for enlarging both management expertise, through cross-fertilisation with the merchant bankers Baring Brothers (20 per cent), and its deposit base, through Credit Suisse (30 per cent). Manufacturers Hanover Limited, although 25 per cent controlled by Manufacturers Hanover Trust Company, had as minority shareholders the prestigious N.M. Rothschild and Sons (10 per cent), the Long-term Credit Bank of Japan (5 per cent) and the Italian insurance concern,

Riunione Adriatic di Sicurta (10 per cent), thereby combining the dollar, lira, and yen resources of three banks with the financial expertise of Rothschilds. In practice, the performance of these banks has depended to a large extent upon the personality of their chief executive officers and the support given by the shareholders, and not so much upon the apparent strengths of a particular grouping. However, the difficult Euro-bond market in 1974 terminated the life of many consortia.

Consortium banks were also designed to afford shareholders access to sophisticated foreign capital markets which they previously lacked. In practice, due to problems of communicating between distant locations and among diverse shareholders, the benefits to shareholders have been small.

The growth of the Euro-dollar market combined with a steep growth in US multinational companies operating in Europe has led to many American banks opening branches in Europe. European banks responded to this by forming major partnerships, such as the EBIC group, the CCB group, and SFE (Société Financière Européenne). Another group, Orion, includes both European and non-European banks.

Table 10.4

Consortium Bank Results

	Pre-tax profits			Attributable profits			Balance sheet total		
	1977	1976	% change	1977	1976	% change	1977	1976	% change
Orion Bank	10.18	9.71	+5	5.24	4.65	+13	1,025.55	999.95	+3
Scandinavian Bank	7.25	6.50	+12	3.74	3.19	+17	851.89	729.81	+17
International Commercial Bank	6.08	4.57	+33	2.75	2.13	+29	487.75	504.98	−3
Nordic Bank	2.21	0.91	+143	1.02	0.36	+183	457.86	323.41	+42
UBAF Bank	3.24	2.63	+23	1.36	1.04	+30	431.36	373.16	+16
Saudi International Bank	1.41	1.79	−21	0.56	0.76	−26	416.50	227.65	+83
Japan International Bank	3.05	2.99	+2	1.43	1.39	+3	381.15	379.32	0
European Banking Company	1.82	3.16	−42	0.83	1.51	−45	318.02	257.35	+24
Libra Bank	5.10	4.15	+23	2.43	2.03	+20	307.00	273.85	+12
United International Bank	1.60	1.70	−6	0.76	0.80	−5	222.51	215.84	+3
International Energy Bank	2.08	1.85	+12	0.99	0.88	+13	151.84	125.24	+21
International Mexican Bank*	2.07	2.15	−4	0.95	1.01	−6	145.44	149.09	−2

*London bank only

Source: *The Banker*. Supplement, April 1978.

London's consortium banks, as can be seen from Table 10.4 have been under increasing difficulties following a very bad year in 1977. Profit increases were modest and balance sheets showed only slight improvements over 1976. Since the banks do the bulk of their business in foreign currency but draw up their accounts in sterling, both profit and balance sheet totals, as translated into sterling in the accounts, were adversely affected by the pound's sharp recovery at the end of 1977. Exchange rate volatility in 1977 also resulted in severe disruptions in the fields of accounting, planning and taxation. Moreover, the 1977 experience has highlighted the consortium banks' dependence on the London Euro-currency market and, in an attempt to diversify, the banks are pursuing three types of policies: firstly, to improve the maturity structure of their portfolios; secondly, to build up fee earning services; and thirdly, to widen the geographical spread of their business.

THE EURO-CREDIT CREATION PROCESS

A much commented-upon feature of the Euro-markets is their seeming ability to create credit. Appendix I (*p. 233*) illustrates how this credit creation process can take place.

In a domestic banking system, there is a fixed reserve requirement imposed by the authorities. There is also a relatively fixed leakage from the currency holdings of the public. In addition, it is a feature of closed banking systems that their deposits cannot be extinguished by transfer to competing institutions such as building societies. In the Euro-dollar market on the other hand, there are no compulsory reserve requirements, no cash holdings, and there is no reason to suppose that funds lent in this market will automatically return to it.

In trying to estimate the value of the credit multiplier in such a market it is necessary to know by how much the market would grow given some initial inflow of funds. If the total size of the market increased by only the size of the inflow, then the multiplier would be one. If it expanded as a result of credit multiplication by twice the amount of the inflow, the multiplier would be two. In fact, what limits the expansion to little more than the amount of the inflow, apart from the low deposit ratio, is the fact that it has to compete, in regard to interest rates with the US market. An inflow of funds tends to reduce interest rates, and the resulting fall in the differential in favour of Euro-dollars vis-a-vis US domestic deposits and other domestic deposits tend to cause other funds to flow out of the market. Effectively the banks, in order to loan out the additional funds, have to make loans more attractive, which means lowering the loan rate as well as the deposit rate. The market suffers heavy leakages when borrowers convert from Euro-currencies into domestic currencies. In practice, given the low deposit ratio and the interest rate effect discussed above, the multiplier in the market is unlikely to be much more than one.

There are two theoretical objections to the textbook description of a multiple expansion of credits and deposits on a given reserve base. The first objection is put forward by Friedman who observed:

'For example, if Euro-dollar banks held zero prudential reserves 100 per cent of outstanding deposits would be created deposits and the potential multiplier would be infinite. Yet the actual multiplier would be close to unity because only a small part of the funds acquired by borrowers from Euro-dollar banks would end up as additional time deposits in such banks'[4].

The second objection is that the multiplier is misleading even in a national system under a regime of reserve requirements. Tobin has pointed out:

'an individual bank is not constrained by any fixed quantum of reserves; depositors' performance preferences do matter, so that an increase in reserves does not lead automatically to an expansion of deposits'[5].

To sum up, the application of bank reserve multipliers to the Euro-currency market is not a realistic approach because the reserve multipliers can only show potential creation processes which say nothing about actually created deposits.

Despite these criticisms of the credit creation process there is no doubt that the Euro-dollar system has gone a long way towards meeting increased liquidity requirements for routine financing of international trade in normal conditions. The Euro-dollar market does tend to make for expansion through increasing the velocity of circulation of deposits. Formerly idle deposits become active deposits. By changing hands more frequently they finance a larger volume of trade.

References
[1] G. Dufey and I. H. Giddy, *The International Money Market*. Prentice Hall 1978.
[2] R. B. Johnston, "Some Aspects of the Determination of Euro-currency Interest Rates. *Bank of England Quarterly Bulletin*. Vol. 19, No. 1 March 1979.
[3] G. Dufey and I. H. Giddy, Ibid.
[4] M. Friedman, "The Euro-Dollar Market: Some First Principles." *The Morgan Guaranty Survey*, New York, 1969, p.11.
[5] J. Tobin, "Commercial Banks as Creators of Money", in *Banking and Monetary Studies*, Ed. by Deane Carson, Homewood, Ill., 1963, p.417.

Appendix I

In order to demonstrate an example of multiple deposit creation with respect to the Euro-dollar market an example of monetary expansion as a result of a transfer of funds from a U.S. bank to a London bank is examined. An Arab sheik transfers $1,000,000 from his New York bank, Morgan Guaranty in Friedman's example, to his London bank, Bank H. Bank H will then show an increase of deposit liabilities of $1,000,000. At the same time, it will gain an asset, ie a claim on a U.S. bank for $1,000,000. For simplicity Friedman assume that Bank H's correspondent bank is Morgan Guaranty. As Morgan Guaranty will decrease its liabilities to the Arab sheik by $1,000,000 and increase its liabilities to Bank H by $1,000,000, the change in their accounts can be numerized as follows:

| Morgan Guaranty | | Bank H | |
Assets	Liabilities	Assets	Liabilities
	−$1,000,000 to Arab Sheik +$1,000,000 due to Bank H	+$1,000,000 due from M.G.	+$1,000,000 to Arab Sheik

The total deposit liabilities of Morgan Guaranty have not changed while both total assets and total liabilities of Bank H have gone up by $1,000,000. If Bank H normally retains ten per cent of its assets and prudential preserves, it now will have an additional $900,000 to lend out, while keeping $100,000 on demand at Morgan Guaranty. Assuming the recipient of the loan, a British import company, U.K. Ltd., requires the funds for future use in the U.S.A. and so holds the money in a demand deposit at a U.S. bank, conveniently, Morgan Guaranty, Bank H has now replaced its $1,000,000 deposit with Morgan Guaranty by a $100,000 deposit with Morgan Guaranty, and a $900,000 loan to U.K. Ltd. The total liabilities of Morgan Guaranty are again unchanged.

| Morgan Guaranty | | Bank H. | |
Assets	Liabilities	Assets	Liabilities
	−$900,000 due to Bank H +$900,000 to U.K. Ltd.	−$900,000 due from Morgan Guaranty +$900,000 loan to U.K. Ltd.	

A quick summary of the total change is now in order. Morgan Guaranty's position is fundamentally unchanged: it had a $1,000,000 liability to the Arab Sheik; now it has a $100,000 liability to Bank H and a $900,000 liability to U.K. Ltd. However, Euro-dollars are up by $1,000,000. There has been no balance of payments deficit and no monetary expansion. The increase in Euro-dollars occurred as a result of a transfer of funds. However, because these funds were transferred from a non-bank to a bank (from an Arab Sheik to Bank H) there is a potential for expansion. The expansion will take place if the borrowed funds are redeposited in the system, i.e., redeposited in a Eurobank.

Suppose that U.K. Ltd., rather than holding the $900,000 in the U.S.A., uses it to purchase timber from a Russian company, and this company chooses to hold the money in dollars at Bank R, another bank in London which again conveniently holds its dollars on deposit with Morgan Guaranty in New York.

Again Morgan Guaranty's position is fundamentally unchanged with a $100,000 liability to Bank H and a $900,000 liability to Bank R rather than a $1,000,000 liability to Bank H. There have been 900,000 more Euro-dollars created in this instance as Bank R's liabilities are up by $900,000.

Morgan Guaranty (M.G.)		Bank H.		Bank R.	
Assets	Liabilities	Assets	Liabilities	Assets	Liabilities
	−$900,000 due to Bank H +$900,000 due to Bank R	−$900,000 due from M.G. +$900,000 loan to U.K. Ltd.		+$900,000 due from M.G.	+$900,000 to Russian company

If this process continued, the proceeds of Euro-dollar loans always being redeposited in Eurobanks, the final volume of obligation of Eurobanks denominated in dollars would be $10,000,000 all based on the $1,000,000 liability of Morgan Guaranty. The Euro-dollar multiplier (the rate of the increase in Euro-dollar deposits to the initial primary deposit) in the first case is one and in the second case, ten. In the first example, there was a maximum leakage and in the second, zero.

Source. Adapted from M. Friedman, The Euro-Dollar Market: Some First Principles. *The Morgan Guaranty Survey,* New York. 1969, p.11.

Chapter 11

THE INTERNATIONAL BOND MARKETS

Raising money internationally can be done in the same two ways that companies and governments regularly borrow from domestic lenders: by bond issues and by bank loans. The only difference is that the money often comes in a currency which is different from that normally used by the borrower. The international bond market is characterised by the fact that the bonds are always sold outside the country of the borrower. It is important to distinguish between three types of bonds, of which two are international bonds. A domestic bond is a bond issued in a country by a resident of that country. A foreign bond is a bond issued in a particular country by a foreign borrower. Euro-bonds are bonds underwritten and sold in more than one country. A Euro-currency bank credit is a bank loan in a currency which is not native to the country in which the bank office making the loan is located.

Table 11.1
The International Financial Markets
($ Billions)

	1973	1974	1975	1976	1977	1978
Net Euro-currencies market	160	215	250	305	350	450(a)
Euro-credits	21.8	29.3	21.0	28.8	41.7	65.48 (b)
International Capital market						
Euro-bonds	4.2	2.1	8.6	14.3	17.7	14.7 (b)
Foreign bonds (inside and outside the United States)	3.6	4.7	11.1	18.2	16.1	19.2(b)
Total of Euro-bonds and foreign bonds	7.8	6.8	19.7	32.5	33.8	33.9

Source: Morgan Guaranty Survey. *World Financial Markets* – Various issues.
(a) Provisional estimate up to September 1978
(b) Provisional estimate up to December 1978

235

Appendix I (p. 255) gives a breakdown of international bond issues from 1970 to 1978. An impression of the size of the international financial markets can be obtained from Table 11.1. As can be seen, the Euro-currency market has been significantly larger than the international capital markets. Both the Euro-currency and the international capital markets have had significant growth rates between 1973 and 1977. This expansion of the Euro-currency market continued throughout 1978, although the international capital market stabilised around its 1977 level.

The Euro-bond and the Euro-credit markets have virtually doubled between 1975 and 1977. Between 1973 and 1977 the Euro-bond market increased by 316 per cent, the foreign bond market by 302. per cent and the Euro-credit market by 84 per cent. While the Euro-credit and foreign bond markets continued to increase throughout 1978, the Euro-bond market in fact declined by 17 per cent over this time period. Table 11.2 illustrates the growth of the international bond market between 1973 and 1978.

Table 11.2

International Bonds
($ million)

	1973	1974	1975	1976	1977	1978 (a)
TOTAL	7,779	6,832	19,913	32,518	33,976	34,169
Issued by:						
Industrial countries	5,770	5,065	15,213ᐧ	24,082	23,851	24,879
Developing countries	664	603	827	1,810	3,671	4,227
International organisations	1,345	1,164	3,873	6,626	6,454	5,033

Source: Morgan Guaranty Survey. *World Financial Markets* – various issues.
(a) Provisional estimate up to December 1978

THE FOREIGN BOND MARKET

A foreign bond is an international bond sold by a foreign borrower but denominated in the currency of the country in which it is placed. It is underwritten and sold by a national underwriting syndicate in the leading country. For example, a U.S. company might float a bond issue in the German capital market, underwritten by a German syndicate and denominated in Deutschemarks. The bond issue would be sold to investors in the German capital market where it would be quoted and traded.

Foreign bonds are issued inside the U.S.A., so called 'Yankee bonds' or issued outside the U.S.A. Foreign bonds issued in Japan are called 'Samurai bonds.' Examination of foreign bonds issued inside the U.S.A., given in Table 11.3, which are obviously always in dollars, indicates that between 1973 and 1978 Canadian entities were very significant borrowers because Canada needs abundant capital in order to exploit its natural resources.

Table 11.3
Foreign Bonds Issued Inside the United States
($ million)

	1973	1974	1975	1976	1977	1978 (a)
TOTAL	960	3,291	6,462	10,604	7,428	5,689
By category of borrower:						
Canadian entities	865	1,962	3,074	6,138	3,022	3,142
International organisations	–	610	1,900	2,275	1,917	459
Other	95	719	1,488	2,191	2,489	2,088

Source: Morgan Guaranty Survey – *World Financial Markets*, Various Issues.
(a) Provisional estimate up to December 1978

The market for foreign bond issues inside the U.S.A. rose by 673 per cent between 1973 and 1977. This reflects the depth of the U.S. capital market. The year 1976 did, however, mark a peak for this market and total issues since have been well below the 1976 level.

The market for foreign bond issues outside the U.S.A. grew by 419 per cent between 1973 and 1978 with a growth rate of 57 per cent between 1977 and 1978. Examination of Table 11.4 indicates that US firms are very small borrowers in this market while international organisations are significant borrowers. However, the largest borrowers are foreign companies, state enterprises and governments who constitute the 'other' category. In 1978 Government borrowing was $5771 million.

THE EURO-BOND MARKET

A Euro-bond has been defined by Morgan Guaranty Trust as an international bond underwritten by an international syndicate and sold in countries other than the country of the currency in which the issue is denominated[1]. A typical example of a Euro-bond transaction is the issue by a Dutch company of dollar denominated bonds through a consortium of British merchant bankers, a large Dutch bank, and the overseas affiliate of an American investment bank[2].

Faced with a rising balance of payments deficit the U.S. authorities, in 1964, introduced the interest equalisation tax. The objective of this was to close off the New York capital market to borrowers from abroad. Restrictions were also placed on the amount of funds that U.S. multinational corporations could raise

237

Table 11.4

Foreign Bond Issues Outside the United States

($ millions)

	1965	1966	1967	1968	1969	1970	1971	1972	1973	1974	1975	1976	1977	1978[c]
Total	$376	$378	$403	$1135	$827	$378	$1538	$2060	$2650	$1212	$4884	$7586	$8777	$13776
By Currency														
German Mark	123	0	10	674	531	89	308	509	386	328	1089	1288	2181	3376
Swiss Franc	78	94	153	238	196	193	669	815	1526	709	3297	5359	4870	5489
Italian Lira	24	139	24	72	24	0	32	163						
British Pound	62	76	102	19	0	12	138	0	736[b]	175	497	939	1626	4921
Other[a]	89	69	114	132	76	84	391	586						
By Borrower														
U.S. Firms	10	24	48	139	223	55	200	215	546	72	61	28	40	245
International Organizations	156	200	133	611	271	171	709	1074	941	140	1358	2158	2846	2664
Other	110	154	222	385	333	152	629	771	1163	1000	3465	5400	5891	10867

Source: Morgan Guaranty Trust Company, *World Financial Markets*, various issues.
(a) Includes £/$ option issues.
(b) Includes approximately $300 million worth of issues in yen.
(c) Provisional estimate to Dec. 1978.

in the U.S.A. for overseas. These restrictions, which have been since lifted, caused borrowers and lenders to shift their activities from New York to Europe. The stage was then set for the rapid growth of the Euro-bond market.

Table 11.5 shows that the two most important currencies of denomination are the dollar and the Deutschemark. For most of the 1970s the dollar accounted for approximately 60 per cent of the market with the Deutschemark accounting for approximately 20 per cent. However, in 1978 the combination of a weak dollar with a strong Deutschemark resulted in the dollar share falling to 50 per cent and the Deutschemark share rising to 40 per cent. Since 1974, despite the predominance of the dollar, U.S. companies have only accounted for about 5 per cent of the Euro-bond borrowers. It is to be noted that foreign companies and state enterprises are the main Euro-bond issuers.

In the Euro-bond market the investor holds a claim directly on the borrower instead of on a financial institution. Euro-bonds are generally issued by corporations and governments in need of secure, long-term funds and sold through a geographically-diverse group of banks to investors around the world.

Euro-bonds are similar to domestic bonds in that they can be issued with a fixed coupon. However, they do possess four distinctive features:

(i) The issuing technique for Euro-bonds takes the form of placing rather than formal issuing, in order to avoid national regulations on new issues.

Table 11.5

The growth of the Eurobond Market from 1970 to 1978

($ millions)

	1970	%	1971	%	1972	%	1973	%	1974	%	1975	%	1976	%	1977	%	1978(a)	%
Eurobonds, total ($ million)	**2986**		**3842**		**6335**		**4193**		**2134**		**8567**		**14328**		**17735**		**14704**	
by category of borrower:																		
U.S. companies	741	24	1098	30	1992	31	874	21	110	5	268	3	435	3	1130	6	1122	8
Foreign companies	1065	35	1119	31	1759	27	1309	31	640	30	2903	33	5323	37	7284	41	4641	32
State enterprises	594	20	848	23	1170	18	947	22	542	25	3123	36	4138	28	4707	26	3388	23
Governments	351	11	479	13	1019	16	659	16	482	22	1658	19	2239	16	2936	16	3643	24
International organizations	215	7	98	3	395	6	404	9	360	16	615	7	2193	15	1678	9	1910	13
by currency of denomination:																		
U.S. dollar	1775	60	2221	60	3908	62	2447	58	996	46	3738	43	9125	63	11628	63	7350	50
German mark	688	23	786	22	1129	18	1025	24	344	16	2278	26	2713	19	4109	23	5747	40
Dutch guilder	391	13	298	8	393	6	194	5	381	18	719	8	502	3½	361	2	431	3
Canadian dollar	0	0	0	0	15	1	0	0	60	3	558	6	1407	8	674	9	0	0
French franc	0	0	20	1	491	7	166	4	0	0	293	3	39	0	0	0	0	0
European unit of account	54	1	166	5	0	0	99	2	174	8	371	4	99	½	28	1	165	5
Other	58	2	151	4	398	6	262	6	179	6	610	7	443	3	935	3	1011	5

Source: Morgan Guaranty Trust Company of New York World Financial Markets. Various Issues.
(a) Provisional estimate up to December 1978.

(ii) Euro-bonds are placed simultaneously in many countries through multinational syndicates of underwriting banks, who sell them to an international investment clientele throughout the world.

(iii) Unlike conventional foreign bond issues, Euro-bonds are sold principally in countries other than that of the currency of denomination (e.g. in the case of dollar-denominated Euro-bonds, outside of the U.S.A.)

(iv) The interest on Euro-bonds is not subject to withholding tax, an advantage over domestic bonds on which withholding tax is charged before interest is paid.

For the interest on a Euro-bond to be free of withholding tax it is usually necessary for the issuing company to form a special financing subsidiary, often in Luxembourg. The subsidiary then issues the bonds with a parent company guarantee usually in the form of bearer bonds.

If the Eurobonds are issued with a fixed interest coupon (in terms of Deutschemarks, dollars or whatever) then their capital value·will change as interest rates change. An extreme example makes this clear. Assume a $100 bond is issued, paying $5 annual interest, which gives ·an interest rate of 5 per cent, in line with market rates at the time of issue. Now assume interest rates generally double: a bond paying $5 interest is now worth only $50. This kind of capital loss is unusual and is anyway only temporary because, when bonds are redeemed, it is at their original issue price. Even so, lenders are naturally put off by the prospects of losses in the short term. New issues are therefore rare when interest rates are expected to rise and are plentiful when they are thought to be coming down. In order to avoid this problem floating rate notes have been introduced. Expectations of currency movements and interest rate changes are the dominant features of the Eurobond market.

Operation of the market

There are several types of Euro-bonds. A straight bond is a bond having a fixed interest coupon and maturity date. Straight bonds can be issued with a floating rate of interest. Such bonds have their interest rate fixed at six-monthly intervals at a stated margin over the London Interbank Offered Rate (LIBOR) for deposits in the same currency. Thus, if the bond is a Euro-dollar bond then the interest rate will be LIBOR for Euro-dollar deposits. Floating rate notes have come to represent an increasing proportion of new issues on the Euro-bond market accounting for about 20 per cent of Euro-dollar bond issues in 1977. Interest on these bonds is paid at the end of each six-month period. It is usual for such bonds to have a guaranteed minimum interest. Thus, if a bond has an interest rate of LIBOR plus 1 per cent with a minimum of 7 per cent and LIBOR falls below 6 per cent the coupon will remain at 7 per cent. The basic rationale for floating rate notes is that they help to eliminate risk for investors by imposing a time limit for the yield to be out of line with current short-term interest rates.

A convertible Euro-bond is a bond having a fixed interest coupon and maturity date, but including an option for the holder to convert his bonds into an equity share of the company at a conversion price set at the time of issue.

Medium-term Euro-notes are shorter-term Euro-bonds (maturities range from three to eight years) with an issuing procedure that is less formal. Interest rates on Euro-notes can be fixed or flexible. Medium-term Euro-notes are similar to medium-term rollover Euro-dollar credits. The difference is that in the Euro-dollar market lenders hold a claim on a bank and not directly on the borrower.

In order to tap the widest possible market the issue of Euro-bonds is normally undertaken by a consortium of banks. The borrower which could be a government or a large company usually asks a major international bank to arrange the issue. A managing syndicate normally including at least four or five leading banks plus a bank from the borrowing country is then organised. As mentioned earlier, Euro-bonds are placed rather than formally issued. A record of the transaction called a 'tombstone' will be published in the financial press. An example of a tombstone is given in Figure 11.1

Those banks, whose names appear at the top of the 'tombstone' agree to subscribe to the issue. At a second level a much larger underwriting syndicate is formed. The banks in the managing syndicate make arrangements with a worldwide group of underwriters, mainly banks and security dealers. After arranging the participation of a number of underwriters, the managing syndicate makes a firm offer to the borrower, who obtains the funds from the loan immediately. At a third level the underwriting group usually arranges for the sale of the issue through an even larger selling group of banks, brokers, and dealers. The selling group are not normally mentioned in the tombstone.

A list of the lead managers and co-managers of internationally syndicated bond issues in 1977 is given in Table 11.6.

Euro-bonds are usually expressed in a currency other than the currency of the country of domicile of the borrower. However, U.S. borrowers usually borrow in American dollars. Euro-bond issues have been made in U.S. dollars, Deutschemarks, pounds sterling,

241

Figure 11.1

FINASA

Financiera Nacional Azucarera, S.A.

(a National Credit Institution of the United Mexican States)

DM 100,000,000

medium term loan at a fixed rate of interest

This financing was arranged by

BAYERISCHE LANDESBANK GIROZENTRALE

as Manager

and

LANDESBANK RHEINLAND-PFALZ GIROZENTRALE
NORDDEUTSCHE LANDESBANK GIROZENTRALE
WESTDEUTSCHE LANDESBANK GIROZENTRALE

as Co-Managers

and provided by

BADISCHE KOMMUNALE LANDESBANK —GIROZENTRALE—	BAYERISCHE LANDESBANK —GIROZENTRALE—
HAMBURGISCHE LANDESBANK —GIROZENTRALE—	HESSISCHE LANDESBANK —GIROZENTRALE—
INDUSTRIEKREDITBANK AG DEUTSCHE INDUSTRIEBANK	LANDESBANK RHEINLAND-PFALZ —GIROZENTRALE—
LANDESBANK SAAR —GIROZENTRALE—	NORDDEUTSCHE LANDESBANK —GIROZENTRALE—
WESTDEUTSCHE LANDESBANK —GIROZENTRALE—	WURTTEMBERG'SCHE KOMMUNALE LANDESBANK —GIROZENTRALE—

French francs, Swiss francs, Belgian francs, Luxembourg francs, Dutch guilders, Lebanese pounds, Kuwaiti dinar, European currency units, units of account, European composite units, special drawing rights and Arab currency related units. The last five are cocktails of various currencies (discussed in Chapter 9) which are designed to give the investor a hedge against foreign exchange movements. Euro-bonds are normally issued in amounts varying between U.S. $10 million and U. S. $600 million.

Denominating a Euro-bond in a particular currency does not mean that investors receive their interest and principal in that currency; the currency of issue simply determines how much will be repaid at prevailing exchange rates. Despite the introduction of these currency cocktails, examination of Table 11.5 indicates the overwhelming importance of the dollar and the Deutschemark.

Table 11.6
Lead Managers and Co-Managers of Internationally Syndicated Bond Issues in 1977
($ millions)

Manager	$	Can $	DM	Dutch Florins	Other currencies	Total	No. of issues	No. of issues as lead manager
1 Deutsche Bank	4,733.00	139.16	2,562.36	125.06	173.59	7,733.17	110	30
2 Credit Suisse White Weld	6,045.00	261.96	997.66	29.60	161.06	7,495.28	109	17
3 Union Bank of Switzerland (Securities)	5,040.00	256.41	1,179.29	—	55.17	6,530.87	94	10
4 Swiss Bank Corporation (Overseas)	4,385.00	382.61	760.53	74.49	120.46	5,723.09	103	6
5 Westdeutsche Landesbank Girozentrale	2,675.00	151.73	2,423.30	59.76	69.86	5,379.65	94	26
6 Dresdner Bank	2,795.00	23.89	1,653.97		93.61	4,566.47	63	19
7 Amsterdam-Rotterdam Bank	3,085.00	38.57	237.51	331.12	82.06	3,774.26	54	8
8 S. G. Warburg, Co	2,885.00	76.57	443.28	60.77	183.97	3,649.59	62	19
9 Commerzbank	1,540.00	78.48	1,803.23	29.82	56.54	3,508.07	56	11
10 Kredietbank SA Luxembourgeoise	2,155.00	42.80	946.71	80.73	106.38	3,331.62	63	3
11 Banque Nationale de Paris	2,185.00	37.81	584.31	—	93.32	2,900.44	42	3
12 Banque de Paris et des Pays-Bas	2,180.00	143.96	389.88	—	127.62	2,841.46	49	3
13 Société Générale de Banque	2,280.00	126.33	—	—	90.76	2,497.09	39	—
14 Algemene Bank Nederland	1,605.00	—	434.71	331.12	44.78	2,415.61	38	3
15 Crédit Lyonnais	1,525.00	—	658.80	—	72.86	2,256.66	41	5
16 Société Générale	1,840.00	14.68	286.07	—	69.60	2,210.35	31	1
17 Morgan Stanley International	1,740.00	48.64	42.48	—	24.28	1,955.40	34	17
18 Salomon Brothers International	1,533.00	100.60	105.30	—	78.98	1,817.88	26	—
19 Orion Bank	845.00	126.38	710.04	—	21.17	1,702.59	34	10
20 Banca Commerciale Italiana	1,375.00	42.82	197.03	—	82.06	1,696.91	20	—

Source: Credit Suisse White Weld.

Redemption of Euro-bonds

Until 1974 Euro-bonds were usually issued for a term of fifteen years. Occasionally this was exceeded but, more often, these terms were for shorter period, e.g. six, seven or eight years. The shorter term Euro-bonds are usually referred to as 'notes' although they are identical in form to bonds.

Redemption provision can be broadly divided into three categories:

1. Normal-bonds are either repayable in one amount at maturity or, more often, in stages during the life of the bonds. In the latter case redemptions may be mandatory, as in the case of a Sinking Fund, or conditional, as in the case of a Purchase Fund.

   With a Sinking Fund the borrower is obliged to redeem a specified amount within preset time limits, e.g. the borrower may have to retire 10 per cent of the issue in each of years three and four, 20 per cent in each of years five and six and the balance at maturity. If the bonds are trading at a discount the borrower will usually buy the required number of bonds in the market but in other cases the bonds will be drawn and repaid at par.

   With a Purchase Fund the borrower is only required to buy up to a specified amount of bonds if the bonds are trading in the market at a price below par during any particular year. From the investor's viewpoint this is advantageous in that he has the assurance that, if his bond is trading at a premium, it will not be liable to be drawn and repaid at par (as it might be if there is a Sinking Fund). On the other hand if the bond is trading at a discount he is assured of some support in the secondary market.

   Convertible bonds are usually (but not always) repaid in one amount at final maturity.

2. Optional-issuers often reserve the right to accelerate repayment of the bonds in part or in whole in which case they usually pay a premium varying with the length of time repayment is accelerated. The premium is imposed to dissuade them from repaying an existing issue with a new issue made when coupon levels fall.

3. For tax purposes issuers usually reserve the right to repay bonds at par (or at a small premium) if there is a change in the law which forces them to deduct tax from interest payments.

THE ADVANTAGES OF EURO-BONDS TO BORROWERS

Euro-bonds, as outlined by Giddy, provide the following advantages to borrowers:

(i) Absorptive capacity: the market has the capacity to absorb large and frequent issues. The foreign bond markets of European countries could not handle the financing needs of governments, international institutions and large corporations once New York became inaccessible. The U.K. has a deep capital market but foreign borrowers are excluded by exchange controls. The annual volume of new issues on the Euro-bond market compares favourably with all national markets except New York.

(ii) Freedom and flexibility: the Euro-bond market has a freedom and flexibility not found in domestic markets. The issuing technique makes it possible to bypass restrictions such as requirements of official authorisation 'queuing' arrangements, formal disclosure, exchange listing obligations and so forth, which govern the issue of securities by domestic as well as foreign borrowers in the individual national markets. All the financial institutions involved in Euro-bond issues are subject to at least one national jurisdiction; national authorities, therefore, can and sometimes do make their influence felt, especially when their own currency is used to denominate the issue. In contrast to national bond markets, however, Euro-bond issuing syndicates are made up of financial institutions from all major financial centres which often operate and are incorporated in many countries. This ensures that the market will not succumb to restrictions or a temporary funds shortage in one country.

(iii) Costs of issue: the costs of issue of Euro-bonds, around 2.5 per cent of the face value of the issue, are also relatively low.

(iv) Interest costs: interest costs on dollar Euro-bonds appear to be competitive with those in New York. There have been several periods when U.S. multinationals could raise funds at a slightly lower cost in the Euro-bond market than in the U.S. domestic market.

(v) Maturities: maturities in the Euro-bond market are particularly suited to long-term funding requirements. Maturities can reach thirty years, although fifteen year Euro-bonds are more common. In the medium-term range, say five to ten years, Euro-bonds run into competition with medium-term Euro-dollar loans. The longer maturities provide the assurance of funds availability at a known rate.

(vi) Institutional framework: an important feature of the Euro-bond market is the development of a sound institutional framework for underwriting, distributing and placing of securities. The basis for Euro-bond issues has developed to a high degree over the last decade. Since the same issuing houses act for many borrowers and serve largely the same group of investors, the volume of borrowing can be tailored to the capacity of the market[2].

245

THE ADVANTAGES OF EURO-BONDS TO INVESTORS

Giddy has outlined the following characteristics which make Eurobonds attractive to investors:

(i) Taxes and anonymity: two particular features of Euro-bonds make them attractive to investors. Firstly, Euro-bonds are issued in such a form that interest can be paid free of income or withholding taxes of the borrowing countries. Secondly, the bonds are issued in bearer form and held outside the country of the investor, enabling him to evade domestic income tax. However, exchange control regulations may limit an investor's ability to purchase Euro-bonds. In the case of the U.K. Euro-bonds cannot be bought by residents of the Scheduled Territories without payment of the investment dollar premium unless they arrange for a foreign currency loan for this purpose. Although such loans can be arranged this is only worthwhile for convertible bonds or equities.

(ii) Safety: issuers of Euro-bonds have, on the whole, an excellent reputation for creditworthiness. Most of the borrowers, either governments, international organisations, or large multinational companies have first class reputations. Since 1975 investors have been able to judge Euro-bond issues through Moody's Investor Services and Standard and Poors.

(iii) Convertibles and warrants: a special advantage to borrowers as well as lenders is provided by convertible Euro-bonds. Holders of convertible debentures are given an option to exchange their bonds at a fixed price and within a specified period for the stock of the parent company of the financing subsidiary.

A warrant gives the bondholder an option to buy a certain number of shares of common stock at a stated price. The more the price of the underlying stock rises, the more valuable the warrant becomes, and since the warrants are usually detachable, the bondholder may retain the bond while selling the warrants if he wishes.

(iv) Liquidity: an essential feature of a successful primary market is an efficient and resilient secondary market. The more active the secondary market, the more marketable and liquid is any investment in Euro-bonds and hence the more willing are investors to buy newly issued bonds[3].

An active secondary market developed during the late 1960s and early 1970s. Euro-bonds are traded over the counter both locally and internationally between financial institutions that are ready to buy or sell Euro-bonds for their own accounts or on behalf of their clients. In the same way as telephone and telex linkages have integrated the foreign exchange market so have they integrated the secondary market in Euro-bonds.

Since 1968 trading internationally in Euro-bonds has been greatly facilitated by a clearing-house arrangement formed by Morgan Guaranty Trust Company in Brussels and called 'Euro-clear'. Participants in Euro-clear can complete transactions by means of book entries rather than time-consuming physical movements of the securities. This removed the main barrier to secondary market trading, which had been the inability to deliver bonds on time. The other major clearing arrangement in Europe is CEDEL, and in 1971 a 'bridge' between the two systems was established as a result of pressure from the market's self-regulatory body, the Association of International Bond Dealers (AIBD).

THE EURO-CREDIT MARKET

The Euro-credit market is sometimes called the medium-term Euro-credit market, or the medium-term Euro-currency market. Morgan Guaranty define a Euro-currency bank credit as a 'loan in a currency which is not native to the country in which the bank office making the loan is located'[4]. The Euro-credit market is concerned with medium and long-term loans with banks being the major lenders and the major borrowers not being banks but large multinational companies, international organisations and governments frequently in developing countries. Examination of Table 11.7 gives an indication of the size and growth of the Euro-currency bank credit market.

Park has outlined five ways in which banks can obtain Euro-currency funds:

(i) Accept short-term Euro-dollar deposits.
(ii) Buy three to six-month Euro-currency inter-bank loans from other Euro-banks.
(iii) Issue short and medium-term Euro-dollar Certificates of Deposit (CDs) in London. These were first introduced in 1966, in London, by First National City Bank and White, Weld and Company and are now issued by over 100 banks. A strong secondary market exists in these and CDs are now very liquid assets.

There are two types of Euro-dollar CDs: Tap CDs are issued on an 'as required' basis by banks, with maturities from one month to five years; so-called 'tranche CDs' are marketed in amounts of between $15 million and $30 million, in small denominations of about $10,000, are widely distributed and have some of the characteristics of a Euro-bond issue.

Table 11.7
Euro-currency bank credits
by country of borrower ($ millions)

	1970	1971	1972	1973	1974	1975	1976	1977	1978(a)
Industrial countries	**4246**	**2601**	**4097**	**13783**	**20683**	**7231**	**11254**	**17201**	**26604**
Australia	53	239	155	3	127	124	12	360	0
Canada	45	25	29	51	30	113	885	3292	5705
Denmark	27	171	41	254	393	341	607	868	2224
Finland	36	47	20	433	308	399	300	314	475
France	19	40	176	50	3224	719	586	2325	1915
Greece	10	65	270	510	419	239	323	204	509
Ireland	30	0	0	0	321	338	433	440	616
Italy	1387	317	928	4761	2321	120	355	1024	2375
Japan	5	35	80	195	372	448	370	112	27
New Zealand	80	30	32	0	490	313	0	538	0
Norway	0	15	128	265	402	159	472	182	1339
South Africa	60	226	149	333	587	510	650	0	0
Spain	230	317	136	479	1151	1147	2037	1973	2171
Sweden	48	38	115	99	203	302	440	1446	1872
United Kingdom	48	462	689	3150	5655	160	1671	1992	2399
United States	1827	428	864	1649	2221	764	677	826	1116
Yugoslavia	10	0	226	303	551	73	125	443	0
Other[1]	330	145	60	1248	1905	961	1310	872	3861
Developing countries	**446**	**1286**	**2414**	**7288**	**7318**	**11098**	**15017**	**20852**	**35198**
Non-OPEC countries	300	936	1481	4537	6252	8199	11019	13427	25158
Argentina	41	185	20	87	499	72	957	849	1421
Brazil	87	257	579	740	1672	2152	3232	2814	5354
Chile	0	0	0	0	0	0	208	591	975
Hong Kong	0	0	10	72	67	533	85	408	0
Ivory Coast	0	22	0	95	63	50	154	265	0
Korea	25	49	100	205	133	347	738	1265	2605
Malaysia	0	24	50	0	140	425	207	212	858
Mexico	56	295	196	1588	948	2311	1993	2700	7126
Morocco	0	0	0	0	0	200	641	772	605
Peru	0	0	139	434	442	334	395	188	0
Philippines	5	0	50	187	843	363	970	698	1992
Taiwan	0	0	0	0	297	135	219	524	255
Other	86	104	337	1129	1146	1276	1218	2140	3967
OPEC countries	146	350	933	2751	1067	2899	3999	7424	10040
Algeria	0	50	172	1302	0	500	643	691	2515
Indonesia	0	0	93	192	668	1347	469	817	1118
Iran	123	211	335	722	114	265	1411	1209	1107
United Arab Emirates	0	0	18	310	151	156	55	1085	706
Venezuela	23	79	200	137	57	38	1185	1666	1866
Other	0	10	115	88	75	593	235	1955	2728
Communist countries	**38**	**66**	**285**	**779**	**1238**	**2597**	**2503**	**3394**	**3517**
Germany (East)	0	0	35	0	12	280	215	832	642
Hungary	30	50	50	90	150	250	300	300	700
Poland	0	0	0	430	509	475	525	19	374
Soviet Union	0	0	0	0	100	650	282	234	400
COMECON institutions	0	11	140	50	120	480	600	1100	0
Other	8	5	60	209	347	462	581	909	1401(b)
International Institutions	**0**	**10**	**0**	**0**	**24**	**65**	**74**	**190**	**160**
TOTAL	**4730**	**3963**	**6798**	**21851**	**29263**	**20992**	**28849**	**41637**	**65479**

[1]Includes multinational organizations

Source: Morgan Guaranty *World Financial Markets* various issues.
(a) Provisional estimate up to December 1978
(b) Includes COMECON institutions

(iv) Short and medium-term Euro-dollar notes are sold by Euro-credit banks and some banks issue medium-term Euro-bonds to finance their lending.

(v) All consortium banks have lines of credit with their parent banks, whose power and prestige also protect the financial integrity of the consortium banks. Thus consortium banks can draw on secure sources of funds denominated in several major currencies[5].

A Euro-credit is generally extended not by a single bank but by a large group of banks from many countries. Thus the risk of loan default can be spread among many banks. These banks are usually called consortium banks (*see Chapter 10*).

TECHNIQUES OF EURO-CREDIT LENDING

Park has admirably set out the techniques in an article 'Structure and Function of the Euro-Credit market', *Euromoney*, April 1974, from which the following has been abstracted.

The most frequent size of a Euro-credit is between $20 million and $50 million while loans larger than this are quite common. In view of the large size of average Euro-credits it may be financially unsound or physically impossible for one bank to take up the whole amount. For this reason loans exceeding a certain amount are spread among a number of banks. There are two distinct methods of spreading a loan among banks. The first is the 'participation method', whereby an originating bank first commits singly the total loan to a borrower, and then offers participations in the loan to other banks. Participation certificates of Euro-credits are documents which enable a creditor bank to liquidate its position and hand on its creditors role to another bank.

Selling participations is a fairly controlled operation: invitations to participate are telexed to various banks and followed up sometimes by a visit giving details of the borrower and the terms of the loan. Participation is established by a letter, which summarises the relevant parts of the loan agreement, and the participant is usually issued with the photocopy of a promissory note, which may be renewed at each interest date. A variation of this type is what has been described as the 'broadcast system'. First, a Euro-credit bank singly commits itself to the entire amount of the loan. Then the bank offers, by telex, participation more or less indiscriminately to any number of other Euro-credit banks. A share in the loan, which can be as low as $25,000, is denoted by a participation certificate. Even if only 5 to 10 per cent of the telexed banks respond, most of the loan can be placed.

The second way of spreading a loan is straight syndication, which is probably the more regular practice. In this case the manager sets up the loan and then selects, usually with considerable care, a syndicate. The approach to potential members is probably verbal. Criteria for picking a member include geographical expertise, exposure in terms of lending to that area, knowledge of the borrower, availability for possible future syndicates, likelihood of reciprocal business, etc.

Terms of loan

As explained above, interest rates of most Euro-credits are 'floating rates', tied usually to the six-month inter-bank rate for the same Euro-currency on the London market. Depending upon the borrower's creditworthiness, a premium (or spread) of 0.375 to 2.5 per cent is added to the inter-bank rate. This spread allows the lending banks a profit margin related to the risk involved, and also allows the lenders to avoid the risk that they will be obliged to finance further renewals with funds whose cost exceeds the interest rate paid by the borrower. Certain credit agreements provide an option for the borrower to change the currency in order to benefit from more favourable interest rates, provided that the currency requested is available on the market in sufficient quantities. This option may be of considerable importance in a regime of widely fluctuating exchange rates, since a judicious choice of currency significantly alters the cost of the loan to a borrower. In some cases the borrower also has the right to terminate the loan upon payment of a penalty and, in other cases, even without any penalty payment. A pre-payment without penalty clause permits a borrower to refinance the loan later if market conditions change in his favour. Management fees, which traditionally amounted to 0.5 per cent of the amount syndicated, have been cut significantly and in some cases eliminated, as borrowers such as public agencies or national governments find that they themselves can syndicate their major loans among many financial institutions without having to pay a fee for the service.

THE SIMILARITIES AND DIFFERENCES BETWEEN THE EURO-CREDIT MARKET THE EURO-CURRENCY MARKETS AND THE EURO-BOND MARKET

All three Euro-markets are similar in terms of their transactions (or trading) currencies. The transaction currencies in the three Euro-markets are Euro-currencies such as Euro-dollars, Euro-Deutschemarks, Euro-Swiss francs, etc. The Euro-currency market is defined as the market in which Euro-banks accept deposits and make loans denominated in currencies other than that of the country in which they are located. Several characteristics distinguish the Euro-credit market from both the other two markets.

The Euro-currency market is overwhelmingly a short-term money market with most loans maturing within a year or so. However individual banks will extend Euro-currency medium term loans to their own corporate customers. Inter-bank trading is very important for the Euro-currency market where both lenders and borrowers are Euro-currency banks themselves. In contrast, the Euro-credit market is concerned with medium and long-term loans with banks as lenders but multinational companies, governments and international agencies as borrowers.

The Euro-credit market and the Euro-bond market are similar both in terms of transaction currencies and maturity of loans. However, the lenders in the Euro-bond markets are individual investors, although banks may hold Euro-bonds. Also, Eurobonds are bonds, not bank credits, with all the characteristics of bonds, such as underwriting syndicates, bond indentures, listing and trading on stock exchanges, fixed coupon rates, etc. By contrast, Euro-credits are basically bank loans and most Euro-credits carry a floating interest rate usually tied to LIBOR. The floating interest rate of a Euro-credit is in reality 'fixed' for six months and after each six month period a new interest rate is adopted based on the LIBOR at the time of roll-over, for another six month period. Thus the interest rate of a Euro-credit floats only at the end of each roll-over period, while it is fixed during a roll-over period of six months.

CURRENT DEVELOPMENTS IN THE EURO-MARKETS

A bank's spread must cover at least three elements: firstly, a risk premium to cover losses; secondly, a contribution to the banks cost of capital related to the loan; and thirdly, the out of pocket and overhead operating costs involved.

The medium-term Euro-market has been increasingly tilted in favour of borrowers. Banks lending spreads over Euro-interbank offer rates have fallen sharply, as Table 11.8 indicates. From an accepted minimum norm of one per cent over LIBOR spreads by the first half of 1978 had fallen for very best quality borrowers to around 0.5 to 0.625 per cent over LIBOR. For other borrowers the decline has been very steep indeed.

In some cases a borrower's creditworthiness has been upgraded because of country stabilisation efforts and improved external payments positions. In addition, domestic bank loan demand in many industrial countries has remained modest. The recession of the 1970s has reduced the opportunities for bank lending, resulting in increased pressure between competing banks.

Table 11.8

Average loan rate spreads on new Euro-currency bank credits to governments and state enterprises in selected countries

(spreads in percentage points over LIBOR)

	1977 QI	QII	QIII	QIV	1978 QI	QII
Industrial countries:						
Denmark	1.32	1.19	—	0.96	0.75	0.72
Finland	—	1.09	—	—	0.71	0.75
France	0.92	0.94	—	0.69	0.57	0.56
Ireland	1.41	—	—	0.88	—	0.75
Italy	—	1.38	1.34	1.19	1.12	1.01
Sweden	0.93	—	0.99	0.88	—	0.70
Spain	1.63	1.39	1.54	1.00	0.94	0.87
Non-oil LDCs:						
Argentina	1.65	1.70	1.56	—	1.57	1.22
Brazil	1.93	1.88	2.00	2.08	1.97	1.63
Korea	1.88	1.44	1.89	1.72	1.13	0.88
Malaysia	1.13	0.88	—	—	0.78	0.70
Mexico	1.57	1.53	1.70	—	1.30	1.11
Philippines	1.75	1.75	1.63	1.63	1.32	1.00
OPEC countries:						
Algeria	1.63	1.63	1.63	1.57	1.44	1.41
Indonesia	—	—	1.70	1.38	1.38	0.88
Iran	1.13	0.95	0.88	0.92	0.80	0.71
Venezuela	1.00	—	0.88	—	0.75	0.79
Communist countries:						
Bulgaria	—	1.13	1.13	1.08	—	0.85
East Germany	1.25	1.19	1.25	1.13	1.08	0.75
Hungary	—	—	1.05	1.00	—	0.70
Weighted averages:						
7 industrial countries	0.99	1.17	1.35	0.92	0.85	0.78
6 non-oil LDCs	1.76	1.61	1.76	1.99	1.30	1.22
4 OPEC countries	1.04	1.18	1.15	1.31	0.98	0.95
3 communist countries	1.25	1.18	1.15	1.10	1.08	0.75
TOTAL: 20 selected countries	1.21	1.32	1.52	1.22	1.09	1.03

Average loan rate spreads over LIBOR are calculated by weighting the average spread on each loan by the size of the loan. The average spread on an individual loan with a split spread is calculated by weighting each spread by the number of years it is in effect.
Source: Morgan Guaranty. *World Financial Markets,* June 1978.

The only real exception to this is the U.S.A. where loan demand has been buoyant and the U.S. banks have frequently stayed out of some of the finest margin deals. As maybe seen from Figure 11.2, lending margins for prime Euro-market borrowers have steadily fallen from 1975.

Controversy over these margins stems from the fact that LIBOR and quoted lending spreads, represent no more than a convenient indication rather than a true reflection of returns. This counter-argument has been well summarised.

Figure 11.2

LENDING MARGINS FOR PRIME BORROWERS IN EUROMARKET

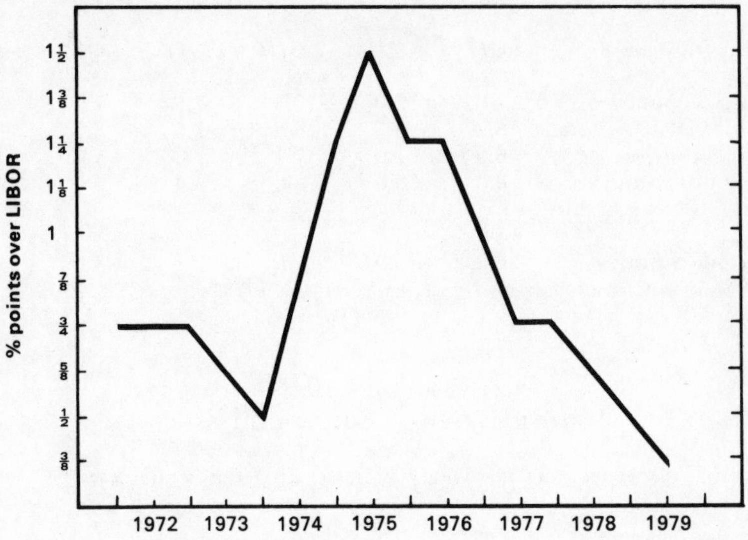

Source: *'Amex Bank Review'* March 1979.

Base LIBOR deemed to apply to members of a Euro-credit syndicate does not in fact apply equally to all; strong banks can secure inter-bank funds below the commonly quoted LIBOR while lesser banks have to bid more. Nor do banks finance themselves at LIBOR alone. Large commercial banks secure funds below LIBOR from official depositors from developing countries, partly industrialised countries and communist countries, and from lesser commercial banks outside the 'inner circle' of the Euro-market, as well as from corporate depositors. Moreover, large commercial banks obtain some of their funds in the form of interest-free sight deposits from their branch networks. This applies particularly to the biggest banks which dominate the Euro-credits market and whose direct return is therefore well above quoted spreads over LIBOR, bolstered further by front end fees[6].

Another current feature of the Euro-markets has been that final maturities of new Euro-credits have lengthened steadily. Average loan maturities have moved out from six and a half to nine years. This can be seen from Table 11.9.

As in the case of Euro-currency credits there has been a perceptible lengthening of the maturities of Euro-bond issues. As shown in the Table 11.10 the proportion of issues with final maturities of more than ten years has risen substantially since mid-1977.

253

Table 11.9

Average final maturities on new Euro-currency bank credits to governments and state enterprises in selected countries

maturities in years	1977				1978	
	QI	QII	QIII	QIV	QI	QII
7 industrial countries	7.0	7.0	6.3	7.2	7.0	8.9
6 non-oil LDCs	6.2	6.7	6.5	7.6	8.2	9.6
4 OPEC countries	6.9	7.0	7.1	7.0	8.9	8.4
3 communist countries	6.0	6.0	6.2	6.4	6.0	6.8
TOTAL:						
20 selected countries	6.8	6.9	6.6	7.1	8.0	9.0

Source: Morgan Guaranty . *World Financial Markets* June 1978.

Table 11.10
Maturities of new Euro-bond issues

(per cent of total new issue volume in each maturity category)

	1977				1978	
	QI	QII	QIII	QIV	QI	QII
years to maturity:						
3 to 5	23	20	24	16	29	40
over 5 to 7	32	36	25	21	19	19
over 7 to 10	28	33	18	23	34	16
over 10 to 15	15	9	26	39	17	25
over 15 to 20	1	2	7	1	1	1

Source: Morgan Guaranty. *World Financial Markets,* June 1978.

Other developments have been that longer grace periods have been allowed, the terms of new loan documents have been eased, and re-negotiation of old loan agreements has occurred in several instances.

References
[1] Morgan Guaranty Trust. *World Financial Markets*. August 1978.
[2] I. Giddy,, 'The blossoming of the Eurobond market.' *Columbia Journal of World Business*. Winter 1975.
[3] Ibid.
[4] Morgan Guaranty Trust. *op. cit.*
[5] Dr. Y.S. Park, 'Structure and function of the Euro-credit market.' *Euromoney*. April 1974.
[6] *The Banker* Supplement June 1978.

Appendix I
International bond issues

by country of borrower, (*$ million*)

	1970	1971	1972	1973	1974	1975	1976	1977	1978 (a)
Industrial countries	**3800**	**4930**	**7415**	**5829**	**5390**	**15214**	**24200**	**22554**	**24879**
Australia	106	120	247	28	117	690	1056	1074	1218
Austria	14	37	82	142	488	855	682	1295	1027
Belgium	2	0	25	135	20	31	134	277	0
Canada	1046	849	1501	1195	2080	4499	9336	5229	4764
Denmark	92	141	317	170	124	206	994	721	928
Finland	47	96	262	132	43	353	342	329	970
France	242	286	255	92	385	1825	2720	1663	1286
Germany	120	62	97	58	106	194	374	567	—
Greece	0	0	60	15	0	0	0	0	—
Ireland	42	100	30	95	134	70	20	86	—
Israel	0	0	20	0	300	2	119	111	—
Italy	340	149	110	77	50	106	85	312	—
Japan	120	121	106	77	237	1739	2084	1935	3443
Netherlands	261	279	235	206	467	686	486	533	251
New Zealand	11	92	64	0	33	467	413	567	624
Norway	94	100	111	97	76	944	1406	1649	2806
South Africa	99	215	281	216	50	446	77	33	—
Spain	30	97	86	88	0	117	244	298	—
Sweden	65	87	225	171	75	1000	1111	1500	836
Switzerland	0	52	35	0	49	152	301	135	—
United Kingdom	258	654	861	1234	221	275	1036	1905	1365
United States	796	1298	2207	1420	187	329	463	1289	2973
Yugoslavia	0	0	0	30	0	0	71	120	—
Multinational companies	15	84	152	105	91	194	559	749	—
Other	0	10	47	46	56	32	87	177	—
Developing countries	**74**	**98**	**564**	**664**	**263**	**585**	**1595**	**3565**	**4227**
Non-OPEC countries	74	98	479	565	201	517	1456	2752	2684
Argentina	69	0	0	0	0	16	0	93	—
Brazil	0	6	116	63	25	35	268	732	843
Chile	0	0	0	0	0	53	0	0	—
Hong Kong	0	15	0	83	50	24	0	129	—
Ivory Coast	0	0	0	9	0	0	10	0	—
Korea	3	12	0	0	0	0	59	69	—
Malaysia	0	0	25	17	0	0	10	43	—
Mexico	0	47	207	176	50	293	448	1159	568
Morocco	0	0	0	0	0	28	44	28	—
Peru	0	0	0	0	0	0	0	0	—
Philippines	0	0	0	25	17	30	367	118	170
Singapore	0	10	51	60	0	12	162	314	—
Taiwan	0	0	0	0	20	0	0	0	—
Other	2	8	80	133	39	25	87	67	—
OPEC countries	**0**	**0**	**85**	**99**	**62**	**67**	**139**	**813**	**1543**
Algeria	0	0	25	71	60	35	109	239	721
Indonesia	0	0	0	0	0	17	0	0	—
Iran	0	0	20	21	0	0	30	81	—
United Arab Emirates	0	0	0	0	0	0	0	42	—
Venezuela	0	0	40	7	2	0	0	433	588
Other	0	0	0	0	0	15	0	18	—
Communist countries	**0**	**25**	**50**	**0**	**40**	**239**	**96**	**248**	**30**
Germany (East)	0	0	0	0	0	0	0	0	—
Hungary	0	25	50	0	40	102	25	174	—
Poland	0	0	0	0	0	21	71	74	—
Soviet Union	0	0	0	0	0	0	0	0	—
COMECON institutions	0	0	0	0	0	0	0	0	—
Other	0	0	0	0	0	117	0	0	—
International Institutions	**686**	**1231**	**1719**	**1345**	**1165**	**3873**	**6626**	**5839**	**5033**
TOTAL	**4560**	**6284**	**9748**	**7838**	**6857**	**19911**	**32516**	**32208**	**34169**

Source: Morgan Guaranty Trust. *World Financial Markets,* Various issues
(a) Provisional estimates up to December 1978.

GLOSSARY OF FOREIGN EXCHANGE TERMS

Covered interest arbitrage. The process of borrowing a currency, converting it into another currency where it is invested, and selling this other currency for future delivery against the initial currency.

Exchange arbitrage. A simultaneous three-way transaction wherein exchange dealers gain a profit from a temporary difference between two currencies in terms of a third.

Forward exchange. Foreign exchange bought or sold for future delivery (hence the term 'futures' sometimes used in America) against payment in home currency on delivery.

Forward premium (or discount when negative). The difference between the forward and spot rates expressed as a percentage of the spot exchange rate. When forward exchanges are worth more than the corresponding spot exchanges they are at a premium; if they are worth less they are at a discount.

Hedging. An arrangement by means of forward exchange transactions to safeguard against an indefinite and indirect exchange risk arising from the existence of assets or liabilities, the value of which is subject to changes via spot rate movements.

Interest arbitrage. The international transfer of funds to a foreign centre, or the maintenance of funds in a foreign centre, instead of repatriating them, for the sake of benefiting from the higher yield on short-term investment in that centre.

Interest-rate differential (or sometimes 'interest-rate spread'). The difference between uncovered short-term interest rates prevailing in two money centres at a given moment.

Open position. The difference between the total of a foreign currency owned or receivable and the total of the same currency payable under definite contracts. If the amount held and receivable exceeds the amount payable, the difference represents a long position. If the amount held or receivable is less than the amount payable, it constitutes a short position.

Outright transaction A transaction in which the purchase or sale of forward exchange is not linked with a spot transaction.

Speculation. The deliberate assumption or retention of a net open (long or short) position in foreign exchange in consideration of the expected future spot rate (or sometimes expected forward rate).

Spot exchange. Foreign exchange bought and sold for delivery two days after conclusion of the exchange and paid for upon delivery.

Swap transaction. The purchase or sale of spot exchanges against the sale or purchase of forward exchange.

GLOSSARY OF EUROBOND TERMS

Reprinted from *The Banker 1978* with permission of the editor

Advisory funds. Funds left to a bank for investment on a customer's behalf, but only after consultation with the customer. Having such funds at its disposal helps a bank place new issues of Eurobonds (see also 'discretionary funds' and 'in-house funds').

AIBD. Association of International Bond Dealers, founded in 1969 for the establishment of uniform market practices. It now has over 350 member banks active in the issuing and secondary markets.

Allocation. Also referred to as 'allotment'. The amount of a new issue allotted to syndicate members by the managing bank, or banks.

Asked. Price demanded by seller in the secondary market.

Average life. Maturity of a total borrowing after taking into account purchases by the borrower's sinking fund.

Bid. Price offered by purchaser in the secondary market.

Bracket. Banks making a new issue are grouped into 'brackets' with the lead-manager on top, followed in order by the co-managers, special under-writers (if any), underwriters and other selling group members. Banks in each 'bracket' are listed alphabetically or according to their commitments.

Bullet. A straight-debt issue without a sinking fund.

CEDEL. One of the market's two clearing systems, owned by several European banks.

Co-managers. Banks ranking next after the lead-manager in the marketing of a new issue; they are chosen for their ability to place large amounts of new issues among customers and sometimes take up more of a new issue than the lead-manager, who may owe his position to the fact of bringing a customer to market as a borrower.

Continental depository receipt. A bearer document which is equivalent to and which may be held instead of or exchanged into multiples of an equity issued through the Euromarket.

Conversion premium. The premium over a common stock's market price at which holders of a fixed-interest security may convert it into common stock. The bait is that there will be a rise in the price of the common stock during the period of the convertible bond's life, or a rise in the currency in which the common stock is quoted, or both. Thus the lower the premium, the bigger the bait. The interest rate on such a convertible is correspondingly lower than that on a comparable straight-debt bond.

Convertible. Fixed-interest borrowing convertible into the borrower's common stock on stipulated conditions.

Coupon. The fixed interest rate attached to a Eurobond.

Discretionary funds. Funds placed with a bank by customers for investment on their behalf by the bank at the bank's own discretion. Such funds are held in particularly large amounts by Swiss banks, and their use for investment in Eurobonds enhances a bank's ability to place new issues. See also 'advisory funds'.

Eurobond. A security marketed internationally in an internationally acceptable currency, which need not be that of either the borrower or the investors. Eurobonds are issued in units of, or equivalent to, $1,000 each.

Euroclear. One of the market's two clearing systems, provided under contract by Morgan Guaranty for over 100 banks which own it.

Eurocurrencies. Bank deposits beneficially held outside a currency's country of orgin; ie, dollar deposits held in London. Likewise Euro-Deutschemark, Euro-French francs, and Euro-gulden (or florin).

Floating rate notes. Securities issued on the Euromarket with a floating rather than a fixed rate of interest; this has often been set, recently, at $\frac{1}{4}$-point above 6-months LIBOR (London interbank offered rate for Eurodollar deposits), to which it is adjusted at half-yearly intervals. Often such notes carry a minimum interest rate.

Foreign bond. A security issued by a borrower in the national capital market of another country (as distinct from a Eurobond, marketed internationally). Except in New York, the flow of new foreign issues on national markets is regulated, if permitted at all.

In-house funds. Advisory and discretionary funds, which banks invest for customers; command of such funds increases a bank's placing power in the Eurobond new issue market.

Issue price. The price at which bonds are sold on issue, normally expressed as a percentage of the bond's face value, which is usually $1,000 in the Eurobond market. Par is the equivalent of face value; a sale price of $99\frac{1}{2}$ means that the bond is sold at a discount for $995; quotations above 100 represent a premium over face value.

Lead manager. Bank responsible for bringing a new issue to market.

Listing. Quotation on a stock exchange, normally London or Luxembourg for Euro-dollar issues, Frankfurt for Euro-DM bonds. Luxembourg for Euro-French franc issues.

Market maker. Bank undertaking to make a secondary market for Eurobonds by taking bonds offered onto its own books or by finding takers for them among or through other banks active in the secondary market. Most market makers specialise in groups of stock or categories (like convertibles or floating rate notes).

Placing power. A bank's ability to sell newly issued securities to investors.

Protection. An undertaking given by a managing bank during the selling period to one or more favoured banks in the selling group that they will receive specified allotments of a new issue in full.

Secondary market. Market in which bonds are traded after issue, normally in minimum lots of $10,000 or 10 bonds dealt through banks acting as market makers. Also known as the 'after market'.

Selling group. All banks marketing a new Eurobond issue.

Selling period. A week or ten days during which managing banks canvass demand for a new issue among under-writers and other selling group banks on the basis of provisionally indicated coupon and issuing price. These terms are formally agreed at the end of the selling period on the basis of demand expressed.

Sinking fund. A fund provided by the borrower for the repurchase of securities during their life, the effect being to reduce the average maturity of the issue as a whole.

'Small investor'. Defined as individuals holding less than 10 or 15 Eurobonds, thus having less than $10,000 to $15,000 at stake. Sales to them are sometimes referred to as the retail market.

Special bracket. Advertisements of record for a recently sold issue group manager, co-managers, underwriters and other selling group banks into separate 'brackets'. The 'special bracket' is reserved for banks underwriting relatively large amounts of a new issue, often consisting of banks which narrowly missed inclusion in the co-managers' 'bracket'.

Spread. Difference between a seller's asked and a buyer's bid price in the secondary market, normally split between banks acting as market makers. 'Spread' is also used to describe the total of fees and commissions earned from the borrower by banks making a new issue.

Statistics. Regular data on the Eurobond and other international markets are now supplied by, among others, OECD, the Bank for International Settlements, the World Bank, Morgan Guaranty, Credit Suisse White Weld, and Kredietbank.

Straight debt. A security without rights of conversion into a borrower's common stock.

Tombstone. Advertisement placed by banks shortly after a new issue to record their part in its management and sale.

Underwriting group. Banks receiving a $\frac{3}{8}$ per cent fee for 'underwriting' a new Eurobond issue, although they are seldom required to fulfil the obligation for which they have been paid, and often not even asked to do so. The full amount of any new Eurobond issue is always underwritten by the manager, co-managers and underwriting banks; but since part is usually marketed by selling group banks who are not underwriters, the underwriters as a group need rarely take up their full commitiments.

Units of account. Multi-currency units used to denominate about 4 per cent of Eurobond issues made in the market's history. It is claimed that they provide equality of currency risk to investors and borrowers. In practice they are more useful in getting around new issue controls applying in all markets excepting New York. They include the EUA (European Unit of Account, originally based on the parities of the 17 members of the European Payments Union and now on those of the remaining members of the joint European float); the ECU (or European Currency Unit, based on the parities of the active participants of the joint European currency float); the EURCO (European Composite Unit, valued at daily market rates of a group of European currencies, rather than on the central rates or parities of those in the joint float, as are the EUA and ECU); and SDR units valued in terms of the IMF's Special Drawing Rights.

Yield. The return on a fixed-interest security based on coupon, price and its average remaining life. An 8 per cent bond sold at par yields that return; it yields less than 8 per cent if bought above par, and more than 8 per cent if bought below par.

Bibliography

The following list is of books and articles that have proved of some interest in the preparation of this present work. It is in no sense comprehensive. Two texts are worthy of special attention:—

Rodriguez, R.M. and Carter, E.E., *International Financial Management,* (Prentice-Hall, 1976.)

Eiteman, D.K. and Stonehill, A.I., *Multinational Business Finance*, (Addison-Wesley Publishing Company, 1978)

Chapter 1

Brooke, M.Z. and Remmers, H.L. *The Strategy of Multinational Enterprise: Organisation and Finance,* (Longman, 1970)

The Multinational Company in Europe, (Longman, 1972)

The International Firm (Pitman, 1977)

Buckley, P. and Casson, M. *The Future of the Multinational Enterprise,* (Macmillan, 1976)

Daniels, J.D., Ogram, E.W. and Radebaugh, L.H., *International Business: Environments and Operations,* (Addison-Wesley, 1976)

Dunning, J.H., *The Multinational Enterprise,* (Allen and Unwin, 1971)

International Business, (Penguin, 1972)

Economic Analysis and the Multinational Enterprise, (Allen and Unwin, 1974)

Dymsza, W.A. *Multinational Business Strategy,* (McGraw-Hill, 1972)

Franko, L.G. *The European Multinationals,* (Harper , Row, 1976)

Johnson, H.G. 'The Efficiency and Welfare Implications of the International Corporation', Chapter 2 in C.P. Kindleberger, ed. *The International Corporation: A Symposium.* (Cambridge, Mass, The MIT Press 1970)

Magee, S.P. 'Information and the Multinational Corporation; An Appropriability Theory of Direct Foreign Investment'. *Working Paper 77–11,* College of Business Administration, University of Texas at Austin, October 1976

Ragazzi, G. 'Theories of the Determinants of Direct Foreign Investment'. *IMF Staff Papers.* Vol. XX No. 2 July 1973

Robock, S.H., Simmonds, K. and Zwick, J. *International Business and Multinational Enterprises.* (Richard D. Irwin, 1977)

Stopford, J.M. The origins of British-based multinational manufacturing enterprises. *Business History Review* (Autumn 1974) 303-335

Stopford, J.M., and Wells, L.T. (Jnr). *Managing the Multinational Enterprise* (Longman, 1972)

Vernon, R. and Wells, L.T. (Jnr) *Manager in the International Economy* Prentice-Hall, 1976)

Economic Environment of International Business (Prentice-Hall, 1976)

Chapter 2

Aliber, R.Z. *The International Money Game* (New York: Basic Books 1976).

Caves, R.E. and Jones, R.W. *World Trade and Payments: An introduction,* (Little, Brown & Co, 1973)

Kemp, M. 'Balance of payments concepts: What do they really mean? *Federal Reserve Bank of St. Louis Review,* July 1975

Kindleberger, C.P. *International Economics* (Richard D. Irwin, 1973)

Heller, H.R. *International Monetary Economics,* (Prentice-Hall, 1974)
  International Trade: Theory and Empirical Evidence, (Prentice-Hall, 1973)

Riechel, K-W. *Economic Effects of Exchange Rate Changes.* (Lexington Books 1978)

Scammell, W.M. *International Trade and Payments,* (Macmillan, 1974)

Sodersten, B. *International Economics,* (Macmillan, 1974)

Tosini, P.A. 'Leaning against the wind: A standard for managed floating. *Princeton Essays in International Finance* No. 126, (December 1977)

Yeager, L.B. *International Monetary Relations: Theory, History and Policy,* (Harper , Row, 1976)

Chapter 3

Baschnagel, H. *'Fundamentals and techniques of foreign exchange dealings' Finanz und Wirtschaft,* September 1971 and January 1972

Cohen, B.J. *Balance of Payments Policy,* Ch. 2 (Penguin, 1973)

Coninx, R.G.F. *Foreign Exchange Today* (Woodhead-Faulkner, 1978)

Einzig, P. *A History of Foreign Exchange* (Macmillan, 1963)
  A Textbook of Foreign Exchange (Macmillan, 1973)

Evitt, H.E. *A Manual of Foreign Exchange* (Pitman, 1971)

Frenkel, J.A. and Levich, R.M. 'Covered interest arbitrage: Unexploited profits'. *Journal of Political Economy 83 No. 2* (April 1975)
  Transaction costs and interest arbitrage: tranquil versus turbulent periods'. *Journal of Political Economy 85 No. 6* (December 1976)

Grubel, M.G. *Forward Exchange, Speculation and the International Flow of Capital* (Palo Alto: Stanford University Press. 1966)

Herring, R.J. and Marston, R.C. *National Monetary Policies and International Financial Markets.* (Amsterdam North Holland 1976. Chapter 4)

Holgate, H.C.F. *Exchange Arithmetic* (Macmillan, 1973)

Holmes, A., and Scholt, F.H. *The New York Foreign Exchange Market* (New York Federal Reserve Bank, 1965)

Kubarych, R.M. *Foreign Exchange Markets in the United States* (Federal Reserve Bank of New York, 1978)

McKenzie, G. *The Monetary Theory of International Trade,* Chs. 8 and 9 (Macmillan, 1974)

Prissert, P. *Le Marché des changes* (Sirey, Paris, 1972)

Stein, J.L. *'The nature and efficiency of the foreign exchange market'* Essays in *International Finance,* No. 40 (Princeton, October 1962)

Weisweller, R. *Foreign Exchange* (George Allen and Unwin, 1972)

Chapter 4

Balassa, B. 'The purchasing power parity: a reappraisal.' *Journal of Political Economy*, December 1974

Bilson, J.F.O. 'The Monetary Approach to the Exchange Rate: Some Empirical Evidence'. *IMF Staff Papers*, March 1978.

Coninx, R.G.F. *Foreign Exchange Today* Chs. 5 and 6 (Woodhead-Faulkner, 1978)

Dufey, G., and Giddy, I.H. 'Forecasting Exchange Rates in a floating world, *Euromoney* Nov. 1975
'The random behaviour of flexible exchange rates: implications for forecasting'. *Journal of International Business,* Spring 1975

Einzig, P. *A Dynamic Theory of Forward Exchange,* (Macmillan, 1975)
Euromoney 'Mobbing up the treasurer' August 1978

Folks, W.R. (Jnr). and Stansell, S.R. 'The use of discriminant analysis in forecasting exchange rate movements'. *Journal of International Business Studies* 6 *No. 1* (Spring 1975)

Gailliot, H.J. Purchasing power parity as an explanation of long-term changes in exchange rates. *Journal of Money, Credit and Banking,* August 1970.

Gray, A.K. 'Foreign exchange forecasting —how far can the computer help?' *Euromoney* July 1974.

Jacque, L.L. *Management of Foreign Exchange Risk.* Lexington Books. 1978 (Chapter 3).

Johnson, H.G., and Frenkel, J.A.,*The Monetary Approach to the Balance of Payments* (Allen and Unwin, 1976)

Kohlhagen, S.W. 'The Performance of the Foreign Exchange Markets: 1971–1974', *Journal of International Business Studies 6, No. 2* (Fall 1975)

Kubarych, K.M., *Foreign Exchange Markets in the United States.* Ch. 3 (Federal Reserve bank of New York, 1978)

Laidler, D.E.W., *Essays on Money and Inflation* (Manchester University Press, 1977)

Levich, R.M. *The International Money Market: Tests of forecasting Models and Market Efficiency.* New York University 1978.

Murenbeeld, M. 'Economic factors for forecasting foreign exchange rate changes' *Columbia Journal of World Business* Summer 1975

Norris, J.F., and Evans, M.K. 'Beating the futures market in foreign exchange rates,' *Euromoney* February 1976

Officer, L.H. 'The Purchasing Power Party Theory of Exchange Rates: A review Article'. IMF Staff Papers 23 No. 1 (March 1976)

Parkin, M., and Zis, G. *Inflation in the World Economy* (Manchester University Press, 1977)

Poole, W. 'Speculative Prices as Random Walks: An Analysis of Ten Time Series of Flexible Exchange Rates'. *Southern Economic Journal 33 No. 4,* (April 1967).

Porter, R.R. 'Forecasting exchange rates' *Euromoney* September 1973

Riehl, H., and Rodriguez, R.M. *Foreign Exchange Markets: A Guide to Foreign Currency Operations* (McGraw-Hill, 1977)

Schulman, R.B., 'Are foreign risks measurable?'. *Columbia Journal of World Business,* May-June 1970

Westerfield, J.M. 'An examination of foreign exchange risk under fixed and floating rate regimes.' *Journal of International Economics* 7 (1977) 181–200.

Zenoff, D.B. and Zwick, J. *International Financial Management,* ch. 3 (Prentice-Hall, 1969)

Chapter 5

Aliber, R.Z. *National Monetary Policies and the International Financial System.* (University of Chicago Press, 1974.)

   The International Money Game (New York: Basic Books 1976).

Bank For International Settlements *Annual Reports.*

Black, S.W. *Floating Exchange Rates and National Economic Policy.* (Yale University Press 1977).

Burns, A.F. 'The need for order in international finance' *Federal Reserve Bank of Richmond Economic Review* July/August 1977.

Coombs, C. *The Arena of International Finance* (John Wiley, 1976)

Corden, M. *Inflation Exchange Rates and the World Economy* Particularly Chs. 7–11. (Clarendon Press, 1977)

Crockett, A. *International Money: Issues and Analysis.* (Thomas Nelson, 1977)

De Vries, T. 'Jamaica, or the non-reform of the international monetary system' *Foreign Affairs* March 1976.

Hirsch, F.*Money International* (Penguin, 1969)

Kettell, B. 'The measurement of exchange exposure risk. *International Currency Review,* Vol 10, No.1 (1978)

Solomon, R. *The International Monetary System 1945–1976. An Insiders View* (Harper and Row, 1976

Strange, S. *International Monetary Relations* (Oxford University Press, 1976)

Spero, J.E. *The Politics of International Economic Relations* (George Allen , Unwin, 1977)

Tew, B. *Evolution of the International Monetary System 1945–1977* (Hutchison, 1977)

Tosini, P.A. 'Leaning against the wind: A standard for managed floating'. *Princeton Essays in International Finance. No. 126* (December 1977).

Williamson, J. *The Failure of World Monetary Reform, 1971–1974* (Thomas Nelson, 1977)

Chapter 6

British Overseas Trade Board *Export Handbook: Services for British Exporters* (1975)

Harrington, J.A. *Specifics on Commercial Letters of Credit and Bankers Acceptances* (Scott Printing Corp, Jersey City N.J, 1974)

Hambros Bank 'The Importance of financial management' *International Trade,* September 1976

Kahler, R. and Kramer, R.L. *International Marketing.* Ch.15. (South Western Publishing Co, 1977)

Morgan Guaranty Trust Co., *The Financing of Exports and Imports* (New York, 1973)

Watson, A., Finance of International Trade. Institute of Bankers. London. 1976.

Weston, J.F. and Sorge, B.W., *International Managerial Finance.* Chapters 4, 8, 9. (Richard D. Irwin. 1972).

Whiting, D.P., *Finance of Foreign Trade.* (Macdonald and Evans. 1977).

Chapter 7

Aliber, R.Z. and Stickney, C.P. 'Accounting Measures of Foreign Exchange Exposure: The Long and Short of It'. *Accounting Review,* January 1975

Burns, J.M., *Accounting Standards and International Finance* (Washington D.C.: American Enterprise Institute for Public Policy Research 1976.

FASB Statement 8. *International Currency Review,* June 1977

FASB 8 'A spirited accounting controversy' *Morgan Guaranty Survey,* July 1976

Flower, J.F. 'Coping with currency fluctuations in company accounts' *Euromoney,* June 1974

Furlong, W.L. 'Minimising foreign exchange losses, 'Accounting Review. April 1976

Harrigan, P., 'The double sand-bag in foreign exchange accounting' *Euromoney,* June 1976

Hayes, D.J. 'Translating foreign currencies'. *Harvard Business Review 50 No. 1* (January/February 1972).

Hoyt, N.K. 'The management of currency exchange risk by the Singer Company' *Financial Management,* Spring 1972

Jacque, L.L. *Management of Foreign Exchange Risk.* Lexington Books 1978.

Katz, S.I. 'Exchange-Risk under Fixed and Flexible Exchange Rates,' *The Bulletin.* Institute of Finance, Graduate School of Business Administration, Nos. 83–84. New York University, June 1972.

Kunrath L.F. 'Foreign exchange versus purchasing power gains and losses' *Management Accounting,* May 1972

Liebermann, G., 'Two ways to measure foreign exchange risk' *Euromoney,* June 1976

Management of Foreign Exchange Risk. *Euromoney Publications* 1978.

Norr, D. 'Currency translation and the analyst' *Financial Analysts Journal,* July/August 1976

Ravenscroft, D.R. 'Translating Foreign Currency under U.S. Tax Laws'. *Financial Executive* (September 1974).

Rodriguez, R.M. 'FASB No.8. What has it done for us?' *Financial Analysts Journal,* March/April 1977

Shank, J.K.'FASB Statement 8 resolved foreign currency—Or did it?' *Financial Analysts Journal,* July/August 1976.

Snyder, L. 'Have the accountants really hurt the multinationals?' *Fortune,* February 1977

Teck, A. 'Control your exposure to foreign exchange' *Harvard Business Review,* January/February 1978

'International business under floating rates?' *Columbia Journal of World Business,* Fall 1976.

Wainman, D. *Currency Fluctuation: Accounting and Taxation Implications* Woodhead–Faulkner, Cambridge, 1976

Wheelwright, S.C. 'Applying decision theory to improve corporate management of currency-exchange risks' *California Management Review'*, Summer 1975

Zenoff, D. 'Applying management principles to foreign exchange exposure' *Euromoney,* September 1978

Chapters 8 and 9

Adams, R. and Perlman, R., 'Long term contracts in a floating world'. *Euromoney.* December 1973.

Aliber, R.Z., *Exchange Risk and Corporate International Finance.* (Macmillan 1978).

Archeim, J. and Park, Y.S. 'Artificial Currency Units: The Functional Currency Areas'. *Princeton Essays in International Finance.* No. 114. April 1976.

Aubey, R.T., and Cramer, R.H. 'The Use of International Currency Cocktails in the Reduction of Exchange Rate Risk'. *Journal of Economics and Business 29. No. 2* (Winter 1977).

Business International, *Hedging Foreign Exchange Risks.* Management Monograph 49 (New York: Business International Corporation, 1971).

Coussement, Dr. A.M. 'Maturity at 17 for the EUA' *Euromoney,* June 1978

Chown, J.F. *Taxation and Multinational Enterprise* (Longman, 1974)

Euromoney Publications *Management of Foreign Exchange Risk,* 1978

Finney, M. and Meade, N. 'Currency risk: a practical approach to corporate borrowing and exchange risk' *Euromoney,* October 1978

Goeltz, R.K. 'Managing liquid funds on an international scale' Presentation to the American Management Association Conference on International Cash Management, November, 1971.

Gull, D.S. 'Composite foreign exchange risk'. *Columbia Journal of World Business* (Fall 1975)

Hague, D.C., Oakeshott, W.E.F. and Strain, A.A. *Devaluation and Pricing Decisions* (London: George Allen and Unwin Ltd., 1974)

Jacque, L.L. *Management of Foreign Exchange Risk.* Lexington Books 1978

Kohlhagen, S.W. 'The Performance of the Foreign Exchange Markets: 1971–1974'. *Journal of International Business Studies 6, No. 2* (Fall 1975).

Lessard D.R. and Lorange, P. 'Currency changes and management control. Resolving the centralization/ decentralization dilemma through the use of internal forward exchange rates' M.I.T., Sloan School, *Working Paper 849–76,* April 1976.

Liebowicz, B. 'Hedging in foreign currency: Capital or Ordinary'. *The Tax Adviser* (August 1976)

Levich, R.M. *The International Money Market: Tests of Forecasting Models and Market Efficiency.* N.Y.U. 1978

Logue, D.E. and Oldfield, G.S. "Managing foreign exchange assets when foreign exchange markets are efficient". *Financial Management 6. No. 2* (Summer 1977)

Meister, J.W. 'Managing the International Financial Function' National Industrial Conference Board, Inc., New York, 1970

Norris, J.F. and Evans, M.K. 'Beating the futures market in foreign exchange rates'. *Euromoney* February 1976.

Prindl, A.R. 'Financial Management in the Multinationals' *Euromoney,* April 1975

Robbins, S.M. and Stobaugh, R.B. 'Financing foreign affiliates.' *Financial Mangement,* Winter 1972

Wooster, J.T. and Thoman, G.R. 'New financial priorities for MNCs.' *Harvard Business Review,* May-June 1974.

Zenoff, D.B. 'Remitting funds from foreign affiliates' *Financial Executive,* March 1968

Chapter 10

Bank for International Settlements *Annual Reports* (Basel)

Crockett, A.D. 'The euro-currency market: an attempt to clarify some basic issues' IMF Staff Papers, 1977

Einzig, P and Quinn, B.S. *The Euro-Dollar System, Practice and Theory of International Interest Rates* (Macmillan, 1977)

Financing Foreign Operations. *Business International* (Geneva and New): (regularly updated)

Herring, R.J. and Marston, R.C., *National Monetary Policies and International Financial Markets.* (Amsterdam. North Holland 1976. See Chapter 4)

Hewson, J and Sakakibara, E., 'The euro-currency markets and their implications.' Toronto, London 1975.

International Currency Review (Published six times per year)

Kern, D. 'Interest rates, and the currency structure of the Euro-markets' *Euromoney*, 1973.

Klopstock, F.H. 'The Euro-dollar market: some unresolved issues' Princeton Essays. No. 65. (March 1968)

Machlup, F. 'The magicians and their rabbits' *Morgan Guaranty Survey,* May 1971

Mayer, M.W. 'Multiplier effects and credit creation in the Euro-dollar market. *Banca Nazionale del Lavoro Quarterley Review*, 98 (September 1971)

McKenzie, G.W. *The Economics of the Euro-Currency System* (Macmillan, 1976)

McMahon, C.W. 'Controlling the Euro-markets' *Bank of England Quarterly Bulletin*, March 1976.

Morgan Guaranty Trust Co *World Financial Markets* (Published monthly)

Organisation for European co-operation and Development (OECD) *Financial Markets Trends* Published five times per year)

Quinn, B.S. *The New Euromarkets.* (Macmillan 1978)

Revell, J. *The British Financial System* Ch. 11 (Macmillan, 1973)

Chapter 11

Bank for International Settlements *Annual Reports* (Basel)

Craven, J.A. 'The supersonic rise of the floating rate note' *Euromoney*, October 1976

Dufey, G and Giddy, I.H. *The International Money Market* (Prentice-Hall, 1978) 'The linkages that tie together international interest rates.' *Euromoney*, November 1978.

Eurobond market issues '*Euromoney*', April 1978.

Einzig, P. *Parallel Money Markets, Volume One: The New Markets in London.* (Macmillan, 1974)

Parallel Money Markets, Volume Two: Overseas Markets (Macmillan, 1974)

Howlett, K. 'Tell the small investor the truth about financial cycles' *Euromoney*, July 1977

International Currency Review (Published six times per year)

Merrill Lynch International *Basics About Eurobonds* 1978

Morgan Guaranty Trust Co. *World Financial Markets* (Published Monthly)

OECD *Financial Market Trends* (Published five times per year)

Quinn, B.S. *The New Euromarkets* (Macmillan, 1978)

Index